9   £4

THE WORKS OF J. B. PRIESTLEY

ALSO BY
J. B. PRIESTLEY

Fiction

THE GOOD COMPANIONS
ANGEL PAVEMENT
WONDER HERO
FARAWAY
ADAM IN MOONSHINE
BENIGHTED
FARTHING HALL (*with Hugh Walpole*)
THE TOWN-MAJOR OF MIRAUCOURT

Essays, etc.

FOUR-IN-HAND
ENGLISH JOURNEY
SELF-SELECTED ESSAYS
BRIEF DIVERSIONS
PAPERS FROM LILLIPUT
I FOR ONE
TALKING
OPEN HOUSE
APES AND ANGELS
THE BALCONINNY

Criticism

FIGURES IN MODERN LITERATURE
THE ENGLISH COMIC CHARACTERS
MEREDITH (*English Men of Letters*)
PEACOCK (*English Men of Letters*)
THE ENGLISH NOVEL
ENGLISH HUMOUR (*English Heritage Series*)

Plays

CORNELIUS
EDEN END
DANGEROUS CORNER
LABURNUM GROVE
THE ROUNDABOUT

THE
WORKS OF
J. B. PRIESTLEY

THREE PLAYS
AND A PREFACE

LONDON
WILLIAM HEINEMANN LTD.

First published in One Volume 1935

*Printed in Great Britain
at the Windmill Press, Kingswood, Surrey*

CONTENTS

PREFACE
page vii

DANGEROUS CORNER
A PLAY IN THREE ACTS
page 1

EDEN END
A PLAY IN THREE ACTS
page 91

CORNELIUS
A BUSINESS AFFAIR IN THREE TRANSACTIONS
page 203

PREFACE

MORE than once when I have read volumes of plays I have been sorry that the authors of them have been so completely hidden, so silent in their own persons, and I have wished that the dramatists would take me behind the scenes for a few minutes. As I cannot believe that other readers of plays have not felt like this, I am coming forward in this Preface to talk a little about these three plays. Austere persons, who want the drama but not the author of it, are under no compulsion to read this Preface. There is nothing to prevent them going straight to the plays themselves, leaving the rest of us to gossip awhile in the green room.

Dangerous Corner, my first play proper, was written early in 1932. I had thought about it at odd times for some months, but it was actually written at a great speed. It seemed to me then—as it seems to me now—far more a technical exercise in dramatics than a genuine study of human nature. I wanted to write the kind of play that the experts always say that novelists, and newcomers cannot write: a very compact affair with one set, only a few characters, and continuous action. Although I still think the mechanics of the piece are ingenious, I see now that it actually has some technical deficiencies. Its mood is too monotonous; there is too much tension; and the audience is not allowed sufficient opportunity to relieve its feelings by laughter, with the result that, no matter how good the production is, there are always several "bad laughs." I have heard friendly critics condemning *Dangerous Corner* audiences because they indulged in these "bad laughs"; but actually the fault is mine. On the other hand, even with a faulty production, a hasty repertory job with bad casting, the play (as I know from personal experience) does succeed in creating its own atmosphere and imposing itself upon all manner of audiences. Even those playgoers who expect a much higher standard of morality from a dramatist's characters than they ever expect from their neighbours (a common weakness of English playgoers), are usually held by the play.

We were fortunate in our actual production but unlucky in everything else. Fortunate because we managed to snatch Flora Robson, as leading lady, and Tyrone Guthrie, as producer, from the Westminster Theatre. We were unlucky in taking a theatre much too big for us, the Lyric in Shaftesbury Avenue, and in opening during a muggy Whit Week, at the beginning of what proved to be one of the worst summer seasons the London Theatre has ever had. The first night went well, as it could hardly fail to do with such a brilliant cast, but the daily Press heartily disliked the piece and told me I did not know how to write a play and probably would never learn. Fortunately James Agate and one or two others were enthusiastic, and throughout the run there were little spurts of enthusiasm for it, chiefly from theatrical folk themselves. (Here let me say that such encouragement as I have received as a dramatist has chiefly come from fellow writers and intelligent actors and actresses. A few critics, notably James Agate and Ivor Brown, have always been helpful. And the least encouragement has come from managers and the fashionable West End theatrical public.) The play ran through to the autumn, and then went on tour, with a Number Two company following. It was produced in New York, and though not so happily cast as in London, it contrived to run quite a long time, even returning to New York after a good many weeks on the road. Various foreign versions were made and produced, and it has been turned into a film. But it has enjoyed its greatest success as a repertory piece, and is something of a favourite with the more ambitious amateur societies. Before leaving *Dangerous Corner*, I must add that it is not to be regarded as a "dream play", even though most of it is a What Might Have Been. Nor has it any profound mystical significance, although it has an idea or two in it and is not straightforward melodrama.

Eden End, my own favourite among the eight or nine plays I have written, was the fruit of odd moments of day-dreaming during several years, but was actually composed rather quickly during the early summer of 1934. It was written for the theatre, the Duchess, of which, after the long and successful run of *Laburnum Grove*, I was co-director with my friend, J. P. Mitchelhill. The auguries were very happy. Everybody concerned in the production was enthusiastic about the play. We had plenty of time. We had the perfect theatre for it, and had arranged that my wife should re-decorate the building inside, which she did very successfully indeed, just before we were ready to open. The producer, Irene Hentschel, had proved that she had a flair for this intimate type of play. We cast it carefully (with Ralph Richardson and Edward Irwin as inspired choices) and then rehearsed it for a much longer period than is customary in the West End Theatre. We had decided, perhaps unwisely, not to have the usual week's "try out", and so gave ourselves more time for rehearsal in London. The result was that the finest performance of the play—at least the one that easily moved me most—was at one of the dress rehearsals, with the further and inevitable result that the actual performance on the first night was rather flat and disappointing. The press notices were an astonishing mixture. Most of the dailies did not like the piece. The Sunday papers did, and were most warm in their welcome. The box office, which had been desolatingly quiet the first two days, was besieged on the Monday and Tuesday, and for the first few weeks the theatre took more money than it had ever done before. This seemed too good to be true, with a play that did not pretend to be conventional entertainment. It was, for gradually the rush subsided and there was no longer any talk of a "smash hit." But the people who liked it seemed to like it a great deal, and many of them, including not a few dramatists and leading players, came to see it more than once. It was pleasant to find certain American and Continental people of the Theatre saying complimentary things about the production.

One frequent criticism of the play was that "nothing happens in it." I was always amused by this, especially as my previous play at that theatre, *Laburnum Grove*, a light comedy in which very little *did* happen, had never, been criticised in this fashion. The fact is that a great deal happens in *Eden End*, but no attempt was made to magnify and thoroughly exploit, in the conventional "strong play" manner, every situation. Character came first. Moreover, everything was deliberately keyed down a little to suggest the distance of years between us and the period and people of the scene. This was helped too by Irene Hentschel's excellent device of fading in the beginning of Act One and fading out the end of Act Three. What some people thought were faults in the play and production were considered by others to be its chief virtues. Thus, there were complaints that the disagreement between the two sisters in Scene One, Act Three, was an anti-climax after the big quarrel between them in Act Two; but one famous novelist wrote to me saying that the relation between these two scenes, one like a dying echo of the other, was to him something quite new and fascinating. Again, the drunk scene at the beginning of Act Three is not a little comic relief, but was necessary to the action; and I tried to make it as funny and pathetic (for there is something pathetic in their egoism and their attempts to get more out of life than they can grasp), and true as I knew how; and I do not think I altogether failed. Nevertheless, one serious and intelligent critic, who seemed to have made up his mind to be stupid about the play, dismissed this scene contemptuously as "fun with the decanter." The phrase still leaves me in despair. By using the same method, I could guarantee to charge through the

dramatic masterpieces of the world, leaving them a
wreck behind me. The end of *Hamlet* would be dismissed as "business with foils." Which does not mean
that I consider *Eden End* a masterpiece. I do not. But
it is at least a serious piece of drama, not a concoction,
and so had a right to serious consideration on its
first entrance into the world. Some of its critics said
that it had only one stock theatrical character in it,
unworthy of the piece, and that was the old nurse. No
doubt they were right; but, oddly enough, the old nurse
was the only character in it I took directly from life.
Perhaps that is why she seemed out of key.

Cornelius, which followed *Eden End* at the Duchess,
took the shape it did, partly because I wanted to write
a play for my friend Ralph Richardson, and partly
because I wanted to write a play about an office and
about business during the depression. That meant
difficulties at once, because Ralph Richardson is not
a man one sees at once in an office, running a business
during the depression. As I first wrote it, *Cornelius*
was very much a play about one man, and it had a slow
and rather weak first act and two strong succeeding
acts. In actual production, somehow it became
altogether a play about an office, with the result that
people thought the first two acts very fine and the third
rather disappointing. This was inevitable, if you saw
it as a play about an office, because the office life
disintegrated about the middle of the third act and your
interest tended to vanish with it. You had to see it as
a play about Cornelius himself to find the interest
mounting towards the close. Before the play was
produced, I was told that the scene between Cornelius

and Biddle in Act Three, when they discuss suicide, was far too long and dull, but that the love scene between Cornelius and Judy afterwards was excellent. I was sorry about this, because I was far more interested in the suicide discussion than I was in the love scene. And so, to my secret joy, were all the people I knew who saw the play, though both scenes were equally well played. As a rule, offices on the stage are sketchy affairs. You cannot believe that any real business has ever been transacted in them. But Basil Dean's production made this office very real, down to the last detail, and his handling of the small part people was masterly and brilliant. Perhaps that is why the play almost changed its character. The office was too well done, and became the chief personage, dominating even Cornelius himself, though Ralph Richardson, never quite at ease with this City man, worked little miracles of technique in the part.

The production had a strange history. We tried it out in Birmingham, where indeed the action of the play might have been set, for that is the city of metal importers and brokers. If there was anything radically false about its atmosphere and action, Birmingham, I felt would soon discover it. However, Birmingham gave the play a splendid welcome. We descended upon London and our own theatre in the highest hopes. This time there was no disappointing performance on the first night. It was the best first night I had ever had. There followed the best press I had ever had. It is true that some papers told their readers that it was "no play for the tired business man", presumably because it was about business men. Nevertheless, it

xiii

was a fine press. The enthusiasm in the theatre, night after night, was such that Ralph Richardson was able to enjoy himself devising the most complicated speeches of thanks, knowing that he would be called upon to deliver them. The cast settled down for a comfortable long run. But there was not that sudden rush for seats there had been at the beginning of *Eden End*. Nor was there that steady growing interest at the box office which marks the commercial success. People came, remained at the end to clap and cheer, went away to tell their friends about it, but somehow those friends never came. The play was not a failure, but it definitely refused to be a success, at least at the box office. It is true that business generally in the theatre was bad. Lent had turned into a lenten pre-Jubilee period. I had to go abroad, and while I was away the Jubilee arrived and promptly emptied the theatres, with the exception of those housing musical successes. *Cornelius* sank and sank until we felt we could subsidise it no longer.

It was all rather bewildering. Blank failure is something that even the most conceited author can be made to understand. But here was a play that had opened with every promise of great success, with all the good fairies standing round its cradle, that was received with enormous enthusiasm at every performance, and yet it could not command the modest amount of attention from the public demanded by an intimate theatre. (Perhaps I ought to add that it was a fairly ambitious production for such a theatre, with a much larger cast than my two previous plays there.) I can only conclude that there was an impression abroad that it was a depressing piece, all about a dreary little office and a bankrupt business. As many playgoers have had enough of dreary little offices and declining businesses by the time evening comes, no doubt they preferred pieces that went further afield and contrived to pick up a little glamour on the way. Actually, I do not think many people found *Cornelius* depressing. It never seemed to me so, and though I do not think it is so successful in doing what it set out to do as *Eden End*, or think it has as much variety and depth of emotion in it, or believe with some of my friends that it is my best play to date, I do think that in some respects it comes nearer to what I would ultimately like to be able to do in the theatre than any other of my plays. It deals with tougher and more intractable material than *Eden End* or *Dangerous Corner*, does without all manner of customary stilts and springboards, and yet partly succeeds in creating solid human stuff, real drama. There are awkwardnesses, creakings and groanings, but it begins to pour out what seems to be the right mixture of ideas and personal relationships, and starting with an innocent "slice of life" look about it goes on to achieve pattern and rhythm. (Incidentally, it is the only play of my acquaintance that finishes each act with the same lines, used each time with a different significance. I do not think that one critic noticed this, though of course they may have thought it too unimportant to comment upon.) I hope that both producers and readers will see it as a finished play, something attempted and done. I hope they will see all three plays in this light. To me, however, all three seem experiments rather than achievements, shots at distant targets, voyages by dead reckoning, try outs. If the Theatre (a fantastic and not very healthy collaborator) and my impatience will let me, I can do better than these which only represent the more serious efforts of three years crowded with other kinds of work. If the Theatre itself were the magnificent institution it could be, and ought to be, in this country, if it were really the English People's source of intelligent recreation, I for one would be delighted to serve it day and night in any capacity it preferred to have me in; but that Theatre is still a dream, compared with which the reality is a very rickety affair; there are too many good people I know who remain outside; and so I do not feel that the time has come to call myself dramatist and nothing else. In any event it is possible that in these days, when a few ideas about the world and life in general ought to find their way into drama, a man may be a better writer of plays just because he has at least one foot outside the Stage Door.

J. B. PRIESTLEY.

DANGEROUS CORNER

A Play in Three Acts

CHARACTERS

Robert Caplan
Freda Caplan
Betty Whitehouse
Gordon Whitehouse
Olwen Peel
Charles Trevor Stanton
Maud Mockridge

———

Scene: *Drawing-room of the Caplan's house at Chantbury Close. After dinner.*

Acts II *and* III *same as* Act I.

Produced in May, 1932, at the Lyric Theatre, London, with the following cast:

ROBERT CAPLAN	RICHARD BIRD
FREDA CAPLAN	MARIE NEY
BETTY WHITEHOUSE	ISLA BEVAN
GORDON WHITEHOUSE	WILLIAM FOX
OLWEN PEEL	FLORA ROBSON
CHARLES TREVOR STANTON	FRANK ALLENBY
MAUD MOCKRIDGE	ESME CHURCH

Produced by TYRONE GUTHRIE.

ACT I

The curtain rises on a stage in darkness. There is a sound of a revolver shot, somewhat muffled, followed by a woman's scream, a moment's silence. After a small interval of silence, FREDA says, with a touch of irony, "There!" and switches on the lights at mantelpiece.

She is revealed as a handsome and vivacious woman of about thirty.

She remains standing by the mantelpiece for a second or two.

OLWEN, a dark, distinguished creature, FREDA's contemporary, is discovered sitting in a chair near the fireplace.

BETTY, a very pretty young thing, is lounging on a settee, and MISS MOCKRIDGE, who is your own idea of what a smart middle-aged woman novelist should be, is seated securely in the middle of the room.

They are all in evening dress, and have obviously been listening to the wireless—from the cabinet on the table and waiting for the men to join them. FREDA starts to move across to switch off the set when the wireless announcer, speaking in the accents of his kind, begins:

ANNOUNCER: You have just been listening to a play in eight scenes, specially written for Broadcasting, by Mr. Humphrey Stoat, called "The Sleeping Dog."

FREDA (*crossing slowly to radio*): And that's that. I hope it didn't bore you, Miss Mockridge?

MISS M.: Not in the least.

BETTY: I don't like the plays and the stuffy talks. I like the dance music and so does Gordon.

FREDA (*switching off the wireless*): You know, Miss Mockridge, every time my brother Gordon comes here he annoys us by fiddling about trying to get dance music.

BETTY: I *adore* switching off the solemn pompous lecturers—just extinguishing them.

MISS M.: What did they call that play?

OLWEN: "The Sleeping Dog."

MISS M.: Why the sleeping dog?

BETTY: Because you had to let him lie.

FREDA: Let who lie?

BETTY: Well, they were all telling lies, weren't they? Or they had been.

MISS M.: How many scenes did we miss?

OLWEN: Five, I think.

MISS M.: I suppose they must have been telling a lot of lies in those scenes. That's why that man was so angry—the husband, I mean.

BETTY: But which was the husband? Was it the one with the adenoidy voice?

MISS M. (*briskly*): Yes, the one with the adenoidy voice, and he went and shot himself. Very pathetic, I'm sure.

FREDA: Rather too many adenoids.

Miss M.: They're rather pathetic, too.

They laugh, and then there comes a subdued burst of laughter from the men in the dining-room.

Betty: Listen to the men.

Miss M.: They're probably laughing at something very improper.

Betty: No, just gossip. Men gossip like anything.

Freda: Of course they do.

Miss M.: Quite right. People who don't like gossip aren't interested in their fellow creatures. I insist upon my publishers gossiping.

Betty: Yes, but the men pretend it's business.

Freda: They've got a marvellous excuse now that they're all three directors of the firm.

Miss M.: Yes, of course. Miss Peel, I think you ought to marry Mr. Stanton.

Olwen: Oh, why should I?

Miss M.: To complete the pattern here. Then there'd be three pairs of adoring husbands and wives. I was thinking so all through dinner.

Freda: There you are, Olwen.

Miss M.: I'm almost prepared to marry Charles Stanton myself to be one of your charmed circle. What a snug little group you are.

Freda: Are we?

Miss M.: Well, aren't you?

Freda (*giving the tiniest laugh*): Snug little group. How awful.

Miss M.: Not awful at all. I think it's charming.

3

FREDA (*smiling*): It sounds disgusting.

BETTY: Yes. Like Dickens or a Christmas card.

MISS M.: And very nice things to be. In these days almost too good to be true.

FREDA (*apparently amused*): Oh, why should it be?

OLWEN: I didn't know you were such a pessimist, Miss Mockridge.

MISS M.: Didn't you? Then you don't read the reviews of my books—and you ought to, you know, being an employee of my publishers. I shall complain of that to my three directors when they come in. (*Gives a slight laugh.*) Certainly I'm a pessimist. But I didn't mean it that way, of course. I think it's wonderful.

FREDA: It *is* rather nice here. We've been lucky.

OLWEN: Enchanting. I hate to leave it. (*To* MISS M.) You know I'm in the town office now—not down here at the press—but I come back as often as I can.

MISS M.: I'm sure you do. It must be so comforting to be all so settled.

BETTY: Pretty good.

MISS M. (*to* FREDA): But I suppose you all miss your brother-in-law. He used to be down here with you too, didn't he?

FREDA (*who obviously does not like this*): You mean Robert's brother, Martin.

MISS M.: Yes, Martin Caplan. I was in America at the time and never quite understood what happened. Something rather dreadful, wasn't it. (*There is a pause and* BETTY *and* OLWEN *look at* FREDA. MISS M. *looks from one to the other*.) Oh, have I dropped a brick? I always am dropping bricks.

FREDA (*very quietly*): No, not at all. It was distressing for us at the time, but it's all right now. Martin shot himself. It happened nearly a year ago—last June, in fact—not here, but at Fallows End, about twenty miles away. He'd taken a cottage there.

MISS M.: Oh, yes—dreadful business, of course. I only met him twice, I think. I remember I thought him very amusing and charming. He was very handsome, wasn't he?

>   *Enter* STANBON *and* GORDON. STANTON *is a man about forty, with a rather studied and slightly sardonic manner.* GORDON *is in his earlier twenties, and an attractive if somewhat excitable youngster.*

OLWEN: Yes, very handsome.

STANTON (*with jovial condescension*): Who's very handsome?

FREDA: Not you, Charles.

STANTON: May we know or is it some grand secret between you?

GORDON (*taking* BETTY'S *hand*): They were talking about me. Betty, why do you allow them all to talk about your husband in this fulsome fashion. Have you no shame, girl?

BETTY (*holding his hand*): Darling, I'm sure you've had too much manly gossip and old brandy. You're beginning to look purple in the face and bloated—a typical financier.

>   *Enter* ROBERT. *He is in his early thirties and is a*

good specimen. You might not always respect his judgment, but you cannot help liking him.

ROBERT: Sorry to be so late, Freda—but it's that wretched puppy of yours.

FREDA: Oh, what's it been doing now?

ROBERT: It was eating the script of Sonia William's new novel, and I thought it might make him sick. You see, Miss Mockridge, how we talk of you novelists.

MISS M.: Yes, I heard you. I've just been saying what a charming cosy little group you've made here, all of you.

ROBERT: I'm glad you think so.

MISS M.: I think you've all been lucky.

ROBERT: I agree, we have.

STANTON: It's not all luck, Miss Mockridge. You see, we all happen to be nice easy-going people.

ROBERT (*playfully, perhaps too playfully*): Except Betty —she's terribly wild.

STANTON: That's only because Gordon doesn't beat her often enough—yet.

MISS M.: You see, Miss Peel, Mr. Stanton is still the cynical bachelor—I'm afraid he rather spoils the picture.

STANTON: Miss Peel can't afford to talk—she's transferred herself to the London office and deserted us.

OLWEN: I come back here as often as I'm asked.

GORDON: But whether it's to see me or Robert, we can't yet decide. Anyhow, our wives are getting jealous.

BETTY (*laughing*): Oh, frightfully.

6

GORDON (*beginning to fiddle about with wireless*): What's disturbing the ether to-night? Anybody know?

FREDA: Oh, Gordon, don't start it again. We've only just turned it off.

GORDON: What did you hear?

FREDA: The last half of a play.

OLWEN: It was called "The Sleeping Dog."

STANTON: Why?

MISS M.: We're not sure—something to do with lies, and a gentleman shooting himself.

STANTON: What fun they have at the B.B.C.

OLWEN (*who has been thinking*): You know I believe I understand that play now. The sleeping dog was the truth, do you see, and that man—the husband—insisted upon disturbing it.

ROBERT: He was quite right to disturb it.

STANTON: Was he? I wonder. I think it a very sound idea—the truth as a sleeping dog.

MISS M. (*who doesn't care*): Of course we do spend too much of our time telling lies and acting them.

BETTY (*in her best childish manner*): Oh, but one has to. I'm always fibbing. I do it all day long.

GORDON (*still fiddling with the wireless*): You do, darling, you do.

BETTY: It's the secret of my charm.

MISS M. (*rather grimly*): Very likely. But we meant something much more serious.

ROBERT: Serious or not, I'm all for it coming out. It's healthy.

7

STANTON: I think telling the truth is about as healthy as skidding round a corner at sixty.

FREDA (*who is being either malicious or enigmatic*): And life's got a lot of dangerous corners—hasn't it, Charles?

STANTON (*a match for her or anybody else present*): It can have—if you don't choose your route well. To lie or not to lie—what do you think, Olwen? You're looking terribly wise.

OLWEN (*very seriously*): I agree with you. I think telling everything is dangerous. The point is, I think—there's truth *and* truth.

GORDON: I always agree to that. Something *and* something.

STANTON: Shut up, Gordon. Go on, Olwen.

MISS M.: Yes—go on.

OLWEN (*thoughtfully*): Well—the real truth—that is, every single little thing, with nothing missing at all, wouldn't be dangerous. I suppose that's God's truth. But what most people mean by truth, what that man meant in the wireless play, is only half the real truth. It doesn't tell you all that went on inside everybody. It simply gives you a lot of facts that happened to have been hidden away and were perhaps a lot better hidden away. It's rather treacherous stuff.

GORDON: Yes, like the muck they drag out of everybody, in the law courts. Where were you on the night of the 27th of November last? Answer yes or no.

MISS M. (*who obviously likes a discussion*): I'm not convinced, Miss Peel. I'm ready to welcome what you call half the truth—the facts.

ROBERT: So am I. I'm all for it.

8

FREDA (*enigmatically*): You would be, Robert.

ROBERT: What do you mean by that, Freda?

FREDA (*nonchalantly*): Anything, nothing. Let's talk about something more amusing. Who wants a drink? Drinks, Robert. And cigarettes.

ROBERT (*examining cigarette box on table*): There aren't any here.

FREDA: There are some in this one. (*Taking up musical cigarette box from table.*) Miss Mockridge, Olwen —a cigarette? (*Offering the box.*)

OLWEN (*looking at the box*): Oh, I remember that box. It plays a tune at you, doesn't it? I remember the tune. Yes, it's the Wedding March, isn't it? (*She opens the box, taking a cigarette, and the box plays its own charming tinkly version of the Wedding March.*)

ROBERT: Good, isn't it?

FREDA (*shutting the box*): It can't have been this box you remember. This is the first time I've had it out. It belonged to—someone else.

OLWEN: It belonged to Martin, didn't it? He showed it to me.

> *There is a tiny silence. The two women look at one another steadily.*

FREDA: He couldn't have shown it to you, Olwen. He hadn't got it when you saw him last.

STANTON: How do you know he hadn't got it, Freda?

FREDA: That doesn't matter. I do know. Martin couldn't have shown you this box, Olwen.

OLWEN: Couldn't he? (*Looks at* FREDA *significantly for a*

second, then makes a quick change of manner.) No, perhaps he couldn't. I suppose I got mixed up. I must have seen a box like this somewhere else, and then pushed it on to poor Martin because he was always so fond of things like this.

FREDA *moves away.*

ROBERT: Olwen, I'm going to be rather rude, but I know you won't mind. You know *you* suddenly stopped telling the truth *then*, didn't you? You're absolutely positive that this is the box Martin showed you, just as Freda is equally positive it isn't.

OLWEN: Well, does that matter?

GORDON (*fiddling with wireless*): Not a hoot. I'm trying to find some dance music, but this thing has suddenly decided not to function.

ROBERT (*with irritation*): Then don't fiddle about with it.

BETTY: Don't bully Gordon.

ROBERT: Well, you stop him. No, I don't suppose it does matter, Olwen, but after what we'd been saying, I couldn't help thinking that it was rather an odd provoking situation.

MISS M. (*anxious to be entertained*): Just what I was thinking. It's all terribly provoking. More about the cigarette box, please.

FREDA: It's all perfectly simple——

OLWEN: Wait a minute, please, Freda. I don't think it is all perfectly simple, but I can't see that it matters now.

FREDA: I don't understand you.

10

ROBERT: Neither do I. First you say that it can't have been the same box and now you say it's not all perfectly simple and begin to hint at grand mysteries. I believe you're hiding something, Olwen, and that isn't like you. Either that box you saw was Martin's or it wasn't——

STANTON (*with his own blend of good humour and brutality*): Oh, damn the box.

BETTY: ⎰Oh, but Charles—we'd like to hear——
MISS M.: ⎱But Mr. Stanton——

STANTON: Sorry—but I hate a box that plays tunes at you like that anyway. Let's forget it.

GORDON (*with a sudden touch of bitterness*): Yes, and Martin too. He's not here—and we are, all warm and cosy—such a charming group.

ROBERT: Shut up, Gordon.

GORDON: Don't let's mention Martin or think about him. Bad form. He's dead.

FREDA: Well, there's no need to be hysterical about it, Gordon. One would think you owned Martin, to hear you talk.

BETTY: Instead of which, nobody owned Martin. He belonged to himself. He'd some sense.

ROBERT (*who is rapidly getting out of his depth*): What does all that mean, Betty?

BETTY (*with a laugh*): It means that I'm being rather stupid and that you're all talking a lot of rot and I think I'm going to have a headache any minute.

ROBERT: Is that all?

BETTY· Isn't that quite enough? (*She smiles at him.*)

11

ROBERT: Go on, Freda.

FREDA: I wish you wouldn't be so absurdly persistent, Robert. But it's quite simple about the cigarette box. It came to us with some other of Martin's things from the cottage. I put it away and this is the first time it's been out here. Now the last time Olwen was at the Fallows End cottage, was that Saturday when we all went over—you remember, at the very beginning of June.

GORDON (*with an undercurrent of real emotion*): Gosh—yes. What a day that was. And a marvellous night, wasn't it? That was the time when we all sat out in the garden for hours and Martin told us all about those ridiculous people he'd stayed with in Cornwall—the handwoven people——

BETTY: Yes—and the long, long, thin woman who always said, "Do you belong?"

GORDON (*who means it*): I don't think I ever had had a better day. We'll never have another like that.

ROBERT: Yes, it was a good day. Though I'd no idea you'd been so excited about it, Gordon.

FREDA: Neither had anybody else. Gordon seems to have decided that he ought to be hysterical every time Martin is mentioned.

BETTY: I suspect it's Robert's old brandy. And those enormous glasses. They go to his head.

GORDON: Well, where do you want them to go to?

ROBERT (*to* FREDA): The point is, then, that that first Saturday in June was the last time Olwen was at Martin's cottage.

12

FREDA: Yes, and I know that he hadn't got this cigarette box then.

ROBERT: No, he'd have shown it to us if he'd had it then. As a matter of fact, I never remember seeing the thing at the cottage. So there you are, Olwen.

OLWEN (*with an uncertain smile*): There I am.

ROBERT: Yes, but—hang it all—where are you?

OLWEN (*smiling at him affectionately*): You *are* a baby, Robert. I don't know where I am. Out of the dock or the witness box I hope.

MISS M.: Oh no, please. That would be too disappointing.

BETTY (*who has been thinking*): You know, that *wasn't* the last time you were at the cottage, Olwen. Don't you remember, you and I ran over the next Sunday afternoon, to see Martin about those little etchings?

OLWEN: Yes.

ROBERT: Yes, that's true.

BETTY: But I don't remember him showing us this cigarette box. In fact, I've never seen it before.

STANTON: I've never seen it before, and I don't think I ever want to see it again. I never heard such a lot of fuss about nothing.

FREDA: I wouldn't be too sure about that, Charles. But I may as well tell you—if only to have done with it—that Martin couldn't have shown you the box that Sunday anyhow, because he hadn't got it then.

STANTON (*not without malice*): You seem to know a lot about that box, Freda.

GORDON: That's just what I was going to say. Why are you so grand and knowing about it?

BETTY (*pointing triumphantly*): I know why. You gave it to him.

They all look at FREDA.

ROBERT: Did you, Freda?

FREDA (*calmly*): Yes, I gave it to him.

ROBERT: That's queer. I don't mean it's queer your giving him the cigarette box—why shouldn't you? But it's queer your never mentioning it. When did you give it to him? Where did you pick it up?

FREDA (*still mistress of the situation*): That's all quite simple too. You remember the day before that awful Saturday. You were staying up in town, and I came up for the day. Well, I happened to see the cigarette box at Calthrop's. It was amusing and rather cheap, so I bought it for Martin.

ROBERT: And Calthrop's sent it to Martin, down at Fallows End, so that he never got it until that last Saturday?

FREDA: Yes.

ROBERT: Well, that's that.

GORDON: I'm sorry, Freda, but it's not quite so simple as all that. You mustn't forget that I was with Martin at the cottage that very Saturday morning.

ROBERT: Well, what about it?

GORDON: Well, I was there when the parcel post came, with the letters in the morning. I remember Martin had a parcel of books from Jack Brookfield—I don't forget anything about that morning, and neither would you if you'd been dragged into that hellish

14

inquest as I was. But he didn't have that cigarette box.

FREDA: I suppose it must have arrived by the afternoon post then. What does it matter?

GORDON: It doesn't matter at all, Freda darling, except that at Fallows End, parcels are never delivered by the afternoon post.

FREDA: Yes they are.

GORDON: No.

FREDA (*sharply*): How do you know?

GORDON: Because Martin used to grumble about it and say that he always got books and manuscripts a day late. That cigarette box didn't arrive in the morning, because I saw the post opened, and it couldn't have been delivered in the afternoon. Freda, I don't believe those shop people in town ever *sent* the box. You *took* it to Martin yourself. You did, didn't you?

FREDA (*with a sudden rush of temper*): You are a fool, Gordon.

GORDON: Possibly. But remember I didn't start all this. You did take it to Martin, didn't you?

ROBERT: Did you?

FREDA (*hastily composing herself*): Well, if you must know—I did.

ROBERT: Freda.

GORDON: I thought so.

ROBERT (*amazed*): But, Freda, if you went to the cottage to give Martin the box after Gordon had left, you must have seen Martin later than anybody, only a few hours before he—before he shot himself.

FREDA: I did. I saw him between tea and dinner.

ROBERT: But why have you never said anything about it? Why didn't you come forward at the inquest? You could have given evidence.

FREDA: I could, but why should I? What good would it have done? It was bad enough Gordon having to do it——

GORDON: It was hell.

FREDA: If it could have helped Martin, I'd have gone. But it couldn't have helped anybody.

STANTON: That's true. You were quite right.

ROBERT: Yes, I can understand that. But why didn't you tell *me*? Why did you keep it to yourself, why have you kept it to yourself all this time? You were the very last person to talk to Martin.

FREDA: Was I the last person?

ROBERT: You must have been.

FREDA: Then what about Olwen?

ROBERT: Olwen—Oh—the cigarette box.

FREDA: Yes, of course—the cigarette box. Martin didn't get that box until after tea on that Saturday afternoon, and Olwen admitted that he showed it to her.

BETTY (*who obviously doesn't like all this*): No, she didn't. She said it was some other box, and I vote we believe her and have done with it.

MISS M.: No. No, Mrs. Whitehouse——

BETTY: Yes, I do. It's all wrong going on and on like this.

STANTON: And I second that.

ROBERT: And I don't.

16

BETTY: Oh, but Robert——

ROBERT: I'm sorry, Betty—though after all you don't come into this and it can't hurt you. But Martin was my brother and I don't like all these mysteries and I've a right to know.

OLWEN: All right, Robert. But must you know now?

FREDA (*coldly*): I don't see the necessity. But then I didn't see the necessity why I should have been cross-examined, with the entire approval of the company apparently. But now that it's your turn, Olwen, I've no doubt that Robert will relent.

ROBERT: I don't see why you should say that, Freda.

OLWEN: I'm sure you don't, Robert.

FREDA (*her turn now*): You might as well admit it, Olwen. Martin showed you that box, didn't he? So you must have seen him, you must have been to the cottage that Saturday night.

OLWEN: Yes, he did show me the box. That was after dinner—about nine o'clock—on that Saturday night.

ROBERT (*completely astounded*): You were there too? But this is crazy. First Freda—then you. And neither of you has said a word about it.

OLWEN: I'm sorry, Robert. I just couldn't.

ROBERT: But what were you doing there?

OLWEN: I'd been worried about—something— something that I'd heard—it had been worrying me for days, and at last I couldn't stand it any longer. I felt I had to see Martin to ask him about it. So I ran over to

Fallows End. I had some dinner on the way, and got to the cottage just before nine. Nobody saw me go and nobody saw me leave—you know how quiet it was there. Like Freda, I thought it wouldn't serve any good purpose to come forward at the inquest—so I didn't. That's all.

ROBERT: But you can't dismiss it like that. You must have been the very last person to talk to Martin. You must know something about it.

OLWEN (*wearily*): It's all over and done with. Let's leave it alone. Please, Robert. (*With change of manner.*) Besides, I'm sure we must be boring Miss Mockridge with all this stuff.

MISS M. (*briskly*): Oh no, I'm enjoying it—very much.

OLWEN: We don't mean to discuss it, do we, Freda? There's nothing to discuss. All over.

ROBERT (*who has been brooding. Emphatically*): But look here, Olwen, you must tell me this. Had your visit to Martin that night anything to do with the firm? You say you'd been worried about something.

FREDA: Oh, Robert, please.

ROBERT: I'm sorry, but I must know this. Was that *something* to do with that missing five hundred pounds?

GORDON (*excitedly*): Oh—for God's sake—don't drag that money into it. We don't want all that all over again. Martin's gone. Leave him alone, can't you, and shut up about the rotten money.

FREDA: Gordon, be quiet. You're behaving like an hysterical child to-night. (*To* MISS M.) I'm so sorry.

18

GORDON (*mumbling*): Oh, so am I. I beg your pardon, Miss Mockridge.

MISS M. (*rising*): Not at all. But I think—if you don't mind—it must be getting late.

FREDA: Oh, no.

ROBERT: It's early yet.

MISS M.: The Pattersons said they'd send their car over for me to take me back. Has it arrived yet, do you know?

ROBERT (*going to the door*): Yes, I heard it arrive when we left the dining-room and I told the man to wait in the kitchen. I'll get hold of him for you.

FREDA (*aware of the irony of this*): Oh, must you really go?

MISS M.: Yes, I really think I ought. It's at least half an hour's run to the Patterson's, and I don't suppose they like their car and chauffeur to be kept out too late. (*Shaking hands with* FREDA.) Thank you so much. (*Shakes hands with* OLWEN.) It's been so delightful seeing you all again—such a charming group you make here. (*Shakes hands with* BETTY.) Good-bye, Mrs. Whitehouse, good-bye. (*Shaking hands with* STANTON.)

FREDA (*going to door*): I think you left your wrap in my room. I'll get it for you.

MISS M. (*at the door*): Good-bye.

ALL: Good-bye.

FREDA (*going out*): I hear that you had a very good time in America. . . .

> Both women go out and door is shut. OLWEN looks at the books on shelves. BETTY moves up to the bay of

piano and takes a cigarette. STANTON, *after a sigh of relief, pours out a drink.*

GORDON: For this relief, much thanks.

BETTY: Good Lord—yes. I'm sorry, but I can't bear that woman. She reminds me too much of a geometry mistress we used to have at Lorsdale.

STANTON: I've always suspected your geometry, Betty. Drink, Gordon?

GORDON: No thanks.

STANTON: It's very rum—but nevertheless she's not at all a bad novelist. I don't mean she's just a good seller, but she's a goodish novelist too. Why is it there seems to be always something rather unpleasant about good novelists?

GORDON: I give it up. But I don't call Maud Mockridge a good novelist, Stanton.

BETTY: I bet she's a gossiper.

STANTON: She is. She's notorious for it. That's why they ought to have shut up. She'll embroider that cigarette box story and have it all round London within a week. The Pattersons will have it to-night, to begin with. It must have been agony for her to go away and not hear any more.

GORDON: She wouldn't have gone if she'd thought she'd have heard any more. But she's got something to be going on with. (*With a chuckle.*) She'll probably start a new novel in the morning and we'll all be in it.

BETTY (*bravely*): Well, she'll have to use her imagination a bit about me.

STANTON: And me. Perhaps she'll invent the most frightful vices for us, Betty.

20

BETTY (*with a laugh*): She can't really do much with what she's just heard, you know. After all, why shouldn't Freda have taken Martin a cigarette box, and why shouldn't Olwen have gone to see him?

OLWEN (*looking at book, idly*): Yes, why not?

BETTY: Oh—I'd forgotten you were there, Olwen. Can I ask you something? After all I don't think I've asked anybody anything, so far, have I?

OLWEN: You can ask. I don't promise to answer.

BETTY: I'll risk it then. Were you in love with Martin, Olwen?

OLWEN (*steadily*): Not in the least.

BETTY: I thought you weren't.

OLWEN: As a matter of fact, to be absolutely candid, I rather disliked him.

BETTY: Yes, I thought so.

GORDON: Oh—rot. I'll never believe that, Olwen. You *couldn't* dislike Martin. Nobody could. I don't mean he hadn't any faults or anything, but with him they just didn't matter. He was one of those people. You had to like him. He was Martin.

BETTY: In other words—your god. You know, Gordon literally adored him. Didn't you darling?

STANTON: Well, he could be fascinating. And he was certainly very clever. I must admit the firm's never been the same without him.

GORDON: I should think not.

BETTY (*mockingly*): How could it be?

OLWEN *puts book back. Enter* ROBERT *who goes to*

table, pours out drink, followed by FREDA *who takes a cigarette.*

ROBERT: Now we can thrash this out.

OLWEN: Oh no, please Robert.

ROBERT: I'm sorry, Olwen. But I want to know the truth now. There's something very queer about all this. First Freda going to see Martin, and never saying a word about it. And then you going to see him too, Olwen, and never saying a word about it either. It's not good enough. You've both been hiding this all along. You may be hiding other things too. It seems to me it's about time some of us began telling the truth —for a change.

FREDA: Do you always tell the truth, Robert?

ROBERT: I try to.

STANTON (*with irony*): Noble fellow. But don't expect too much of us ordinary mortals. Spare our weaknesses.

FREDA (*suddenly mischievous*): What weaknesses?

STANTON (*shrugging his shoulders*): Anything you like, my dear Freda. Buying musical cigarette boxes, for instance. I'm sure that's a weakness.

FREDA (*significantly*): Or making rather too much use of one's little country cottage. I think that, too, in certain circumstances might be described as a weakness.

STANTON: Do you mean Martin's cottage? I hardly ever went there.

FREDA: No, I wasn't thinking of Martin's. I must have been thinking of another one—perhaps your own.

STANTON (*looking at her steadily*): I'm afraid I don't understand.

22

ROBERT (*exasperated*): Look here, what's all this about. Are *you* starting now, Stanton?

STANTON: Certainly not. (*Laughs.*)

ROBERT: Well, I want to get to the bottom of this Martin business. And I want to do it now.

GORDON: Oh Lord, is this going to be another inquest?

ROBERT: Well, it wouldn't be necessary if we'd heard more of the truth perhaps when there was an inquest. And it's up to you, Olwen. You were the last to see Martin. Why did you go to see him like that? Was it about the missing money?

OLWEN: Yes, it was.

ROBERT: Did you know then that Martin had taken it?

OLWEN: No.

ROBERT: But you thought he had?

OLWEN: I thought there was a possibility he had.

GORDON (*bitterly*): You were all damned ready to think that.

BETTY (*urgently*): Gordon, I want to go home now.

ROBERT: So soon, Betty?

BETTY: I'm going to have an awful headache if I stay any longer. I'm going home—to bed.

GORDON: All right. Just a minute.

STANTON: I'll take you along, Betty, if Gordon wants to stay on.

BETTY (*going to* GORDON): No, I want Gordon to come along too.

23

GORDON: All right. (*Rising.*) I'll come along. But hang on a minute.

BETTY (*with sudden hysterical scream*): I tell you I want to go now. Take me home.

ROBERT: Why, what's the matter, Betty?

BETTY: I don't know. I'm stupid I suppose.

GORDON: All right. We'll go. (*Follows her.* FREDA *rises.*)

STANTON: I'll come along too.

ROBERT: But, Betty, I'm awfully sorry if all this stuff has upset you. I know it's nothing to do with you, anyhow——

BETTY (*pushing him aside and running to the door*): Oh, don't go on and on about it. Why can't you leave things alone?

> *She rushes out and slams the door.*

GORDON (*at the door*): Well, good night everybody.

STANTON (*going to door*): I'll see these infants home and then turn in myself.

OLWEN (*with irony*): Very good of you.

STANTON (*smiling grimly*): Good night.

> *After he goes out, the three who are left drift nearer the fire and one another, and the room has a nice intimate atmosphere.*

ROBERT: And now, Olwen, you can tell me exactly why you rushed to see Martin like that about the missing money.

OLWEN: We're all being truthful now, are we?

ROBERT: I want to be.

OLWEN: What about you, Freda?

FREDA (*rather wearily*): Yes, yes, yes, I don't care. What does it matter?

ROBERT (*puzzled again*): Queer way of putting it.

FREDA: Is it? Well sometimes, Robert, I'm rather a queer woman. You'd hardly know me.

OLWEN: You started all this, you know, Robert. Now it's your turn. Will you be truthful with me?

ROBERT: Good God. Yes—of course I will. I loathe all these silly mysteries. But it's not my turn. I asked you a question that you haven't answered yet.

OLWEN: I know you have. But I'm going to ask you one before I do answer yours. I've been wanting to do it for some time but I've never had the chance or never dared. Now, I don't care. It might as well come out. Robert—did you take that money?

ROBERT (*amazed*): Did I take the money?

OLWEN: Yes.

ROBERT: Of course not. You must be crazy, Olwen. (OLWEN *gives a laugh of great relief.*) Do you think, even if I had taken it, I'd have let poor Martin shoulder the blame like that? But Martin took it, of course. We all know that.

OLWEN: Oh, what a fool I've been.

ROBERT: I don't understand. Surely you must have known that Martin took it. You can't have been thinking all this time that I did.

OLWEN: Yes, I have. And I've not been thinking it— I've been torturing myself with it.

ROBERT: But why, why? Damn it all—it doesn't make sense. I might have taken the money—I suppose

25

we're all capable of that, under certain circumstances—but never on earth could I have let somebody else—and especially Martin, take the blame for it. How could you think me capable of such a thing. I thought you were a friend of mine, Olwen—one of my best and oldest friends.

FREDA (*calmly and boldly*): You might as well know, Robert——

OLWEN (*greatly agitated*): Oh no, Freda. Please. Please.

FREDA (*calmly and taking* OLWEN'S *arm*): Why not? What does it matter? You might as well know, Robert—and how you can be so dense baffles me—that Olwen is not a friend of yours.

ROBERT: Of course she is.

FREDA: She's not. She's a woman who's in love with you—a very different thing. She's been in love with you for ages.

OLWEN (*in great distress*): Freda, that's damnably unfair. It's cruel, cruel.

FREDA: It's not going to hurt you. And he wanted the truth. Let him have it.

ROBERT: I'm terribly sorry, Olwen. I suppose I've been stupid. We've always been very good friends and I've always been very fond of you.

OLWEN: Stop, stop. Oh, Freda, that was unforgivable. You'd no right to say that.

FREDA: But it's true, isn't it? You wanted the truth, Robert, and here it is—some of it. Olwen's been in love with you for ages. I don't know exactly how long,

26

but I've been aware of it for the last eighteen months. Wives always are aware of these things, you know. And not only that, I'll tell you now what I've longed to tell you for some time—that I think you're a fool for not being aware of it yourself, for not having responded to it, for not having done something drastic about it long before this. If somebody loves you like that, for God's sake enjoy it, make the most of it, hold on to it, before it's too late.

OLWEN (*staring at her*): Freda, I understand now.

FREDA: Understand what?

OLWEN: About you. I ought to have understood before.

ROBERT: If you mean by that, that you understand now that Freda doesn't care for me very much—you're right. We've not been very happy together. Somehow our marriage hasn't worked. Nobody knows——

FREDA: Of course they know.

ROBERT: Do you mean you've told them?

FREDA: No, of course I haven't told them. If you mean by *they*—the people we know intimately—our own group here—they didn't need to be told.

ROBERT: But Olwen here has just said she understood about it for the first time.

OLWEN (*gently*): No, I knew about that before, Robert. It was something else I've just——

ROBERT: Well, what is it?

OLWEN: I'd rather not explain. (*Looking away.*)

FREDA: Being noble now, Olwen? You needn't, you know. We're past that.

27

D

OLWEN (*in distress*): No, it's not that. It's—it's because I couldn't talk about it. There's something horrible to me about it. And I can't tell you why.

FREDA (*staring at her*): Something horrible?

OLWEN: Yes, something really horrible. Don't let's talk about that side of it.

FREDA: But, Olwen——

OLWEN: I'm sorry I said I understood. It slipped out. Please——

FREDA: Very well. But you've got to talk about that money now. You said you believed all along that Robert had taken it?

OLWEN: It looked to me as if he must have done.

ROBERT: But if you believed that, why didn't you say something?

FREDA: Oh, Robert—can't you see why she couldn't?

ROBERT: You mean—she was shielding me?

FREDA: Yes, of course.

ROBERT: Olwen—I'm terribly sorry. I'd no idea. Though it's fantastic, I must say, that you could think I was that kind of man and yet go on caring enough not to say anything.

FREDA   But it's not fantastic at all.

       (*together*): That's why I said I'd been tortur-

OLWEN   ing myself with it.

FREDA (*emphatically*): If you're in love with somebody, you're in love with them, and they can do all sorts of things, be as mean as hell, and you'll forgive them or just not bother about it. At least, some women will.

28

ROBERT: I don't see you doing it, Freda.

FREDA (*recovering her normal self*): Don't you? But there are a lot of things about me you don't see. But this is what I wanted to say, Olwen. If you thought that Robert had taken that money, then you knew that Martin hadn't?

OLWEN: Yes, I was sure—after I had talked to him that last night—that Martin hadn't taken it.

FREDA (*bitterly*): But you let us all think he had.

OLWEN: I know. I know. But it didn't seem to matter then. It couldn't hurt Martin any more. He wasn't there to be hurt. And I felt I had to keep quiet.

ROBERT: Because of me?

OLWEN: Yes, because of you, Robert.

ROBERT: But Martin *must* have taken it.

OLWEN: No.

ROBERT: That's why he did what he did. He thought he'd be found out. He was terribly nervy—always was, poor chap. And he simply couldn't face it.

OLWEN: No, it wasn't that at all. You *must* believe me. I'm positive that Martin never *touched* that money.

FREDA (*eagerly*): I've always thought it queer that he should. It wasn't Martin's style at all that—doing some sneaky work with a cheque. I know he could be wild—and rather cruel sometimes. But he couldn't be a cautious cunning little sneak-thief. It wasn't his style at all. And he didn't care enough about money.

ROBERT: He spent enough of it. He was badly in debt you know.

FREDA: Yes, but that's just the point. He didn't mind

29

being in debt. He could have cheerfully gone on being in debt. Money simply didn't matter. Now you loathe being in debt. You're entirely different.

OLWEN: Yes, that was one of the reasons, I thought that you——

ROBERT: Yes, I see that. Though I think those fellows who don't care about money, who don't mind being in debt, are just the sort of fellows who help themselves to other people's.

FREDA: Yes, but not in a cautious sneaky way. That wasn't like Martin at all.

ROBERT (*pausing and thinking*): I wonder—Olwen, where did you get the idea that I'd taken it?

OLWEN: Why, because Martin himself was sure that you had taken it. He told me so.

ROBERT (*amazed*): Martin told you so?

OLWEN: Yes. That was the first thing we talked about.

ROBERT: Martin thought I had taken it. But he knew me better than that. Why should he have thought that?

FREDA: You thought he'd been the thief. You didn't know him any better, it seems.

ROBERT: Yes, but that's different. There were special circumstances. And I'd been told something. Besides, I wasn't at all sure. It wasn't until after he shot himself that I felt certain.

OLWEN (*with growing excitement*): You say you'd been told something? But then Martin had been told something too. He'd practically been told that you'd taken that cheque.

30

ROBERT (*staring at her*): My God.

OLWEN: And do you know who told him that you'd taken the cheque?

ROBERT: I can guess now.

FREDA: Who?

ROBERT (*fiercely*): Stanton, wasn't it?

OLWEN: Yes, Stanton.

ROBERT: But Stanton told me that Martin had taken that cheque.

FREDA
OLWEN (*together*): { Oh, but he——
                      { My God he——

ROBERT: He practically proved it to me. He said he didn't want Martin given away—said we'd all stand in together, all that sort of thing.

OLWEN: But don't you see—he told Martin all that too. And Martin would never have told me if he hadn't known—well, that I would never give you away.

ROBERT (*brooding*): Stanton.

FREDA (*with decision*): Then it was Stanton himself who got that money?

OLWEN: It looks like it.

FREDA (*now counsel for the prosecution*): I'm sure it was. And he's capable of it. You see, he played Martin and Robert off against one another. Could you have anything more vile?

ROBERT (*thoughtfully*): You know, it doesn't follow that Stanton himself was the thief.

FREDA: Of course he was.

31

ROBERT: Wait. Let's get this clear. Old Slater wanted some money and Mr. Whitehouse signed a bearer cheque for five hundred. Slater always insisted on bearer cheques—though God knows why. The cheque was on Mr. Whitehouse's desk. Slater didn't turn up the next morning, as he said he would, and when he did turn up, three days afterwards, the cheque wasn't there. Meanwhile it had been taken to the bank and cashed. And the bank wasn't the firm's usual place, because the cheque was on Mr. Whitehouse's private account. Only Stanton, Martin or I could have got at the cheque—except dear old Watson, who certainly didn't take it. And—this is the point—none of us was known at this branch at all, but they said the fellow who cashed the cheque was about Martin's age or mine. They were rather vague, I gathered, but what they did remember of him certainly ruled out Stanton himself.

OLWEN: Mr. Whitehouse wouldn't have you identified at the bank I remember.

FREDA: No, he was too fond of them all, and too hurt. He wasn't well at the time either.

ROBERT: I understood that he simply wanted the one who had taken the money to confess and then go.

OLWEN: He told me that too.

FREDA: Me too. Father was like that, of course. But what made you believe Martin had taken the cheque?

ROBERT: The evidence pointed to Martin and me, and I knew I hadn't taken it.

FREDA (*slowly*): And Stanton told you——?

ROBERT: Stanton told me he'd seen Martin coming out of your father's room.

32

OLWEN: Stanton told Martin he'd seen *you* coming out of that room.

FREDA (*very emphatically*): Stanton took that money himself.

ROBERT (*fiercely*): Whether he took the money or not, Stanton's got to explain this. (*Moves to door, opens it and snatches up the telephone receiver.*) No wonder he didn't approve of this business and was glad to get out of it. He's got too much to hide.

OLWEN (*sadly*): We'd all got too much to hide.

ROBERT: Then we'll let some daylight into it for once, if it kills us. Stanton's got to explain this. (*Telephoning.*) *Chantbury one two.*

FREDA: When?

ROBERT: To-night.

FREDA: Are you going to get them all back, Robert?

ROBERT: Yes. (*Telephoning.*) Hello, is that you, Gordon? . . . He is, is he? Well, I want you both to come back here. . . . Yes, more and more of it. . . . It's *damned* important. . . . Yes, we're all in it. Oh, no, of course not. We can keep Betty out of it. (FREDA *and* OLWEN *exchange glances.*) All right then. Be as quick as you can. (*Puts back receiver on table in hall, closes the door, switches on the light at doorway and says:* "They're coming back," *as the curtain begins to fall.*)

END OF ACT ONE

33

ACT II

ROBERT, FREDA and OLWEN are discovered in exactly the same positions as they were at the end of ACT I.

ROBERT: They're coming back.

FREDA: All of them?

ROBERT: No, not Betty. She's going to bed.

OLWEN (*with a touch of bitterness*): Wise little Betty.

ROBERT: I don't see why you should use that tone of voice, Olwen—as if Betty was cleverly dodging something. You know very well she's not mixed up in this business.

OLWEN: Do I?

ROBERT (*alarmed*): Well, don't you?

FREDA (*grimly amused*): Poor Robert, look at him now. This is *really* serious he's saying to himself. How we give ourselves away. It's a wonder we have any secrets at all.

ROBERT: No, but—hang it all, Olwen—you've no right to sneer at Betty like that. You know very well it's better to keep her out of all this.

OLWEN: No, we mustn't soil her pure young mind.

ROBERT: Well, after all, she's younger than we are— and she's terribly sensitive. You saw what happened to her just before they went. She couldn't stand the atmosphere of all this.

34

OLWEN: But that wasn't——

ROBERT: Obviously you dislike her, Olwen. I can't imagine why. She's always had a great admiration for you.

OLWEN (*frankly, not maliciously*): Well, I'm sorry, Robert, but I can't return her admiration—except for her looks. I don't dislike her. But—well, I can't be as sorry for her as I'd like to be or ought to be.

ROBERT (*annoyed by this*): You can't be sorry for her. Is it necessary for you or anybody else to be sorry for her? You're talking wildly now, Olwen.

FREDA (*in her best form*): I suspect not, Robert. And anyhow it seems to be our evening for talking wildly. Also, I'm now facing a most urgent problem, the sort of problem that only women have to face. If a man has been dragged back to your house to be told he's a liar and a cad and a sneak and a possible thief, oughtn't you to make a few sandwiches for him?

ROBERT (*heavily*): He'll get no sandwiches from me.

FREDA (*mocking him*): No sincerity, no sandwiches— that's your motto, is it? No? Oh dear—how heavy we are without Martin. And how he would have adored all this. He'd have invented the most extravagant and incredible sins to confess to. Oh, don't look so dreadfully solemn, you two. You might be a bit brighter— just for a minute.

ROBERT (*heavily*): I'm afraid we haven't got your light touch, my dear Freda.

FREDA: I suppose I feel like this because, in spite of everything, I feel like a hostess expecting company, and

35

I can't help thinking about bright remarks and sand-wiches.

A bell rings out in the hall.

FREDA: And there they are. You'll have to let them in yourself, Robert.

> ROBERT *goes out. As soon as the two women are left together the atmosphere changes. They speak in quick whispers.*

OLWEN: Have you really known a long time?

FREDA: Yes. More than a year. I've often wanted to say something to you about it.

OLWEN: What would you have said?

FREDA: I don't quite know. Something idiotic. But friendly, very friendly. (*Taking both her hands.*)

OLWEN: And I only guessed about you to-night, Freda. And now it all seems so obvious. I can't think why I never guessed before.

FREDA: Neither can I.

OLWEN: This is quite mad, isn't it?

FREDA: Quite mad. And rapidly getting madder. I don't care. Do you? It's rather a relief.

OLWEN: Yes it is—in a way. But it's rather frighten-ing too. Like being in a car when the brakes are gone.

FREDA: And there are cross roads and corners ahead.

> *Noise of men outside.* STANTON *enters first.*

STANTON (*as he enters*): I can't see why. I'm sorry about this, Freda, but it's Robert's doing. He insisted on our coming back.

36

FREDA (*coldly*): Well, I think Robert was right.

GORDON (*who has gone straight to settee and sprawled on it*): That's a change, anyhow. Well, what's it all about?

ROBERT: Chiefly about that money.

GORDON (*disgusted*): Oh—hell—I thought as much. Why can't you leave poor Martin alone?

ROBERT: Wait a minute, Gordon. Martin didn't take that cheque.

GORDON (*leaping to his feet*): What. Is that true? Are you sure?

FREDA: Yes.

GORDON: You know, I never could understand that. It wasn't *like* Martin.

STANTON (*to* FREDA *and* ROBERT): Do you really believe that Martin didn't get that money? If he didn't, who did? And if he didn't, why did he shoot himself?

ROBERT (*very deliberately*): Stanton, we don't know. But we're hoping that you'll tell us.

STANTON (*with raised eyebrows*): Being funny, Robert?

ROBERT: Not a bit. I wouldn't have dragged you back here to be funny. You told me—didn't you—that you were practically certain that Martin took that cheque?

STANTON: Certainly I did. And I told you why I thought so. All the evidence pointed that way. And what happened afterwards proved that I was right.

ROBERT: Did it?

STANTON: Well, didn't it?

FREDA (*in a sudden flare of passion*): If it did, then why

37

did you tell Martin that you thought Robert had done it?

STANTON (*uneasy*): Don't be ridiculous, Freda. Why should I tell Martin that I thought Robert had done it?

FREDA: Yes, why should you? That's what we want to know.

STANTON: But of course I didn't.

OLWEN (*quietly*): Yes, you did.

STANTON (*turning to her, despairingly*): Olwen. Are you in this too?

OLWEN: Yes, I'm in it too. Because you lied like that to Martin, telling him you were sure Robert took the cheque, you've given me hours and hours and hours of misery.

STANTON: But I never meant to, Olwen. How could I know that you would go and see Martin and that he would tell you?

OLWEN: It doesn't matter whether you knew or not. It was a mean vile lie. After this I feel that I never want to speak to you again.

STANTON: I'm sorry, Olwen. I'd rather anything had have happened than that. You do believe that, don't you? (*Looks at her appealingly but gets no response.*)

FREDA (*coldly, cuttingly*): Apparently the rest of us don't matter very much. But you owe us a few explanations.

ROBERT: You'd better stop lying now, Stanton. You've done enough. Why did you play off Martin and me against each other like that?

FREDA: There can only be one explanation. Because he took that cheque himself.

GORDON (*fiercely*): My God—you didn't, did you, Stanton?

STANTON: Yes, I did.

GORDON (*excitedly, and rushing over to* STANTON *with threatening gestures*): Then you're a rotten swine, Stanton. I don't care about the money. But you let Martin take the blame. You let everybody think he was a thief.

STANTON: Don't be such a hysterical young fool. (*Pushing* GORDON *away.*)

ROBERT: Shut up, Gordon.

STANTON: Keep quiet and stop waving your hands at me. We don't want this to develop into a free fight.

GORDON: But you let——

STANTON: I didn't let Martin take the blame, as you call it. He wasn't the sort to take the blame, and you ought to know that. It happened that in the middle of all the fuss about this money, he went and shot himself. You all jumped to the conclusion that it was because he had taken the money and was afraid of being found out. I let you go on thinking it, that's all. You might as well think he shot himself for that as for anything else. And anyhow he was done with it, out of it. Besides—where he's gone to, it doesn't matter a damn whether people here think you've stolen five hundred pounds or not.

ROBERT: But you deliberately tried to fasten the blame on to Martin or me.

FREDA: Of course he did. That's what makes it so foul.

STANTON: Not really. I'd not the least intention of letting anybody else be punished for what I'd done. I

39

was only playing for time. I took that cheque because I'd got to have some money quickly and I didn't know where to turn. I knew I could square it up in a week, and I knew too that if necessary I could make it all right with old Slater, who's a sportsman. But when it all came out, I'd got to play for time, and that seemed to me the easiest way of doing it.

ROBERT: But you couldn't have cashed the cheque at the bank yourself?

STANTON: No, I got somebody else to do that—a fellow who could keep his mouth shut. It was pure coincidence that he was a fellow about the same age and build as you and Martin. Don't go thinking there was any deep laid plot. There wasn't. There never is in real life. It was all improvised and haphazard and damned stupid.

ROBERT: Why didn't you confess to this before?

STANTON (*turning to him*): Why the devil should I?

FREDA: If you can't understand why, it's hopeless for us to try and show you. But there's such a thing as common honesty and decency.

STANTON (*himself again now*): Is there? I wonder. Don't forget—before you become too self-righteous—that you happen to be taking the lid off me. It might be somebody else's turn before we've finished.

ROBERT: Possibly. But that doesn't explain why you've kept so quiet about all this.

STANTON: I should have thought it did. Martin's suicide put *paid* to the whole thing. Nobody wanted to talk about it after that. Dear Martin must have done it, so we won't mention it. That was the line. It wasn't the

40

five hundred. I'd have been glad to replace that. But I knew damned well that if I confessed the old man would have had me out of the firm in two minutes. I wasn't one of his pets like you and Martin. I'd had to work myself up from nothing in the firm. I hadn't been brought in because I had the right university and social backgrounds. If the old man had thought for a minute that I'd done it, there'd have been none of this hush-hush business. He'd have felt like calling in the police. Don't forget, I'd been a junior clerk in the office. You fellows hadn't. It makes a difference, I can tell you.

FREDA: But my father's been retired from the firm for six months.

STANTON: Well, what if he has? The whole thing was over and done with. Why open it up again? It might never have been mentioned if you hadn't started on this damn fool inquisition to-night. Robert, Gordon and I were all working well together in the firm. What would have happened if I'd confessed? Where are we? Who's better off because of this?

FREDA: You're not, it's true. But Martin is. And the people who cared about Martin.

STANTON: Are they?

FREDA: Of course they are.

STANTON: Don't be too sure.

FREDA: At least we know now that he wasn't a mean thief.

STANTON: And that's all you do know. But for all that he went and shot himself. And you don't suppose he did it for fun, do you?

FREDA (*terribly hurt*): Oh—you—you—— (*Turns away.*)

GORDON (*furious, rising and taking a step forward*): You are a rotter, Stanton.

ROBERT: Drop that sort of talk, Stanton.

These last three lines are spoken together.

STANTON (*turning on them*): Why should I? You wanted the truth, and now you're getting it. I didn't want to come back here and be put in the witness box. It's your own doing. I'll say what I damn well like. Martin shot himself, and he did it knowing that he'd never touched the money. So it must have been something else. Well, what was it? You see what you've started now.

FREDA (*coldly*): Well, what have we started? You're talking now as if you knew a lot more about Martin than we did.

STANTON: What I *do* know is that he must have had some reason for doing what he did, and that if it wasn't the money, it must have been something else. You're probably a lot better off for not knowing what that something is, just as you'd have been a lot better off if you'd never started poking about and prying into all this business.

ROBERT (*thoughtfully*): Perhaps he did it because he thought I'd taken the money.

STANTON (*sardonically*): And then again—perhaps not. If you think that Martin would have shot himself because he thought you'd taken some money—then you didn't know your own brother. Why he laughed when

42

I told him. It amused him. A lot of things amused that young man.

OLWEN (*wearily*): That's true, I know. He didn't care. He didn't care at all.

ROBERT: Look here—do you know why Martin did shoot himself?

STANTON: No. How should I?

FREDA (*with rising temper*): You talk as if you do.

STANTON: I can imagine reasons.

FREDA (*very sharply*): What do you mean by that?

STANTON: I mean he was that sort of chap. He'd got his life into a mess.

ROBERT: Well, I don't think it's——

STANTON: I don't blame him.

FREDA (*furious*): You don't blame him. Who are you to blame him or not to blame him? You're not fit to mention his name. You hung your mean little piece of thieving round his neck, tried to poison our memory of him, and now when you're found out and Martin's name is clear of it, you want to begin all over again and start hinting that he was a criminal or a lunatic or something.

ROBERT: That's true. The less you say now, the better.

STANTON (*harshly*): The less we all say, the better. You should have thought of that before. I told you as much before you began dragging all this stuff out. Like a fool, you wouldn't leave well alone.

ROBERT: Anyway, I've cleared Martin's name.

STANTON: You've cleared nothing yet, and if you'd a

43

E

glimmer of sense you'd see it. But now I don't give a damn. You're going to get all you ask for.

FREDA (*still furious*): One of the things we shall ask for is to be rid of you.

GORDON: Do you think you'll stay on with the firm after this?

STANTON: I don't know and I don't care.

FREDA: You did a year ago.

STANTON: Yes, but now I don't. I can get along better now without the firm than they can without me.

GORDON: Well, after this, at least it will be a pleasure to try. You always hated Martin, and I knew it.

STANTON: I had my reasons. Unlike the White-house family—father, daughter and son—who all fell in love with him.

ROBERT (*slowly*): Does that mean anything, Stanton? If it doesn't, just take it back—now. If it does, you'll kindly explain yourself.

STANTON: I'll take nothing back.

OLWEN (*coming between them*): Stanton—please. Don't let's have any more of this. We've all said too much already.

STANTON (*turning to her*): I'm sorry, Olwen. But you can't blame me.

ROBERT (*with cold deliberation*): I'm waiting for your explanation.

FREDA: Don't you see, it's me he's getting at.

ROBERT: Is that true, Stanton?

STANTON: I'm certainly not leaving her out.

ROBERT: Be careful.

STANTON: It's too late to be careful. Why do you think Freda's been so angry with me? There's only one reason, and I've known it for a long time. She was in love with Martin.

> FREDA *gives a cry.* ROBERT *stares at* FREDA, *then at* STANTON, *then at her again.*

ROBERT (*going to* FREDA *and standing behind her*): Is that true, Freda? I must know, because if it isn't I'm going to kick Stanton out of this house.

STANTON: Don't talk like a man in a melodrama, Caplan. I wouldn't have said it if I hadn't known it was true. Whether she admits it or not is another matter. But even if she doesn't admit it, you're not going to kick me out of the house. I'll go in the ordinary way, thank you.

ROBERT: Freda, is it true?

FREDA (*her last defence gone*): Yes.

ROBERT (*who speaks as if they were alone*): Has that been the trouble all along?

FREDA: Yes. All along.

ROBERT: When did it begin?

FREDA: A long time ago. Or it seems a long time ago. Ages.

ROBERT: Before we were married?

FREDA: Yes. I thought I could—break it—then. I did for a little time. But it came back, worse than ever.

ROBERT: I wish you'd told me. Why didn't you tell me?

FREDA: I wanted to. Hundreds of times I seem to

45

have tried to. I've said the opening words to myself—
you know—and sometimes I've hardly known whether
I didn't actually say them out loud to you.

ROBERT: I wish you had, I wish you had. But why
didn't I see it for myself? It seems plain enough now.
I must have been a fool. I know now when it began. It
was when we were all down at Tintagel that summer.

FREDA: Yes, it began then. Tintagel, that lovely,
lovely summer. Nothing's ever been quite real since
then.

ROBERT: Martin went away walking, and you said
you'd stay a few days with the Hutchinsons. Was
that——?

FREDA (very quietly): Yes, Martin and I spent that
little time together, of course. It was the only time we
did really spend together. It didn't mean much to
him—a sort of experiment, that's all.

ROBERT: But didn't Martin care?

FREDA (in great distress): No, not really. If he had
have done, it would have been all so simple. That's
why I never told you. And I thought when we were
married, it would be—different. It wasn't fair to you, I
know, but I thought it would be all right. And so did
Martin. But it wasn't. You know that too. It was
hopeless. But you don't know how hopeless it was—
for me.

ROBERT: But why didn't Martin himself tell me? He
knew how unhappy I was.

FREDA: He couldn't. He was rather afraid of you.

ROBERT: Martin afraid of me!

GORDON: Yes, he was.

ROBERT: Nonsense. He wasn't afraid of anybody—and certainly not of me.

FREDA: Yes, he was, in some queer way.

OLWEN (*very gently*): That's true, Robert. He was. I knew that.

GORDON: So did I. He told me that when you're really angry, you'll stop at nothing.

ROBERT (*brooding*): Queer. I never knew Martin felt like that. And it was he who—I wonder why? What was it? (*To* FREDA.) It couldn't have been—this——

FREDA: No, no. He didn't care. (*Breaks down completely.*) Oh, Martin, Martin——

OLWEN (*going to* FREDA *and putting her arms round her*): Freda, Freda—don't.

STANTON (*while* OLWEN *is still comforting* FREDA): That's how it goes on, you see, Caplan. A good evening's work this.

ROBERT: I'm not regretting it. I'm glad all this has come out. I wish to God I'd known earlier, that's all.

STANTON: What difference would it have made? You couldn't have done anything.

ROBERT: To begin with, I'd have known the truth. And then something might have been done about it. I wouldn't have stood in their way.

STANTON (*sardonically*): You didn't stand in their way.

GORDON (*on whom all this is having a very bad effect*): No, it was Martin himself, you see. He didn't care, as Freda says. I knew. He told me about it. (*At* FREDA.)

47

ROBERT (*turning, and incredulously*): He told you?

GORDON: Yes.

ROBERT: Freda's brother?

FREDA (*pushing* OLWEN *aside and looking up*): Gordon, I don't believe you.

GORDON (*hotly*): Why should I lie about it? Martin told me. He used to tell me everything.

FREDA: Rubbish. He thought you were a little nuisance—always hanging about him.

GORDON: That's not true.

FREDA: It is. He told me so that—that very last Saturday, when I took him the cigarette box. He told me then, you'd stayed the night before at the cottage and that he'd had to do everything he could to get rid of you.

GORDON (*plunging now into a quarrel*): Freda—you're making this up, every word about me, I know you are. Martin would never have said that about me. He knew how fond I was of him, and he was fond of me too, in his own way.

FREDA: He wasn't.

GORDON: You're just saying this because you're jealous.

FREDA: I'm not.

GORDON: You've always been jealous of Martin's interest in me.

FREDA (*hotly*): Gordon, that's simply a disgusting lie.

GORDON: It isn't.

FREDA: It is. He told me himself how tired he was of

48

your hanging about him and suddenly becoming hysterical. I see what he meant now. Every time he's been mentioned to-night, you've been hysterical. What are you trying to persuade me into believing you are? (*Putting her hands to her head and turning away.*)

ROBERT (*sharply*): Freda, you're mad.

GORDON (*shrilly, in a rage and turning to* ROBERT): It's all jealousy, jealousy. If he'd thought I was a nuisance, Martin wouldn't have kept asking me down to the cottage. (*Turning to* FREDA.) But he was tired of *you*, pestering him and worrying him all the time. He didn't care for women. He was sick of them. He told me so. He wanted me to tell you, so that you'd leave him alone.

FREDA (*wildly*): You're making me feel sick.

GORDON: Well, you just leave me——

OLWEN (*distressed and pushing* GORDON *away*): Stop it. Stop it, both of you.

STANTON (*grimly*): Let them have it out. They might as well, now they've started.

GORDON (*to* FREDA): And I was going to tell you too. Only then—he killed himself.

FREDA: I don't believe it. I don't believe it. Martin couldn't have been so cruel.

GORDON (*close to her*): Couldn't he? What did he say to you that afternoon when you took him the cigarette box?

FREDA: What does it matter what he said? You're just making up these abominable lies——

ROBERT (*roughly*): Look here, I'm not having any

49

more of this. You're like a pair of lunatics—screaming at each other like that over a dead man. I understand about you, Freda, and I'm sorry—but for God's sake keep quiet about it now. I can't stand any more. As for you, Gordon—you must be tight or something——

GORDON (*sulking*): I'm not. I'm as sober as you are.

ROBERT: Well, behave as if you were. You're not a child. I know Martin was a friend of yours——

GORDON (*turning on* ROBERT *hotly and scornfully*): Friend of mine. He wasn't a friend of mine. You talk like a fish. Martin was the only person on earth I really cared about. I couldn't help it. There it was. I'd have done anything for him. Five hundred pounds. My God, I'd have stolen five thousand pounds from the firm if Martin had asked me to. He was the most marvellous person I'd ever known. Sometimes I tried to hate him. Sometimes he gave me a hell of a time. But it didn't really matter. He was Martin, and I'd rather be with him, even if he was just jeering at me all the time, than be with anybody else I've ever known. I'm like Freda—since he died, I haven't really cared a damn, I've just been passing the time. He didn't really care for women at all. He tried to amuse himself with them, but he really distrusted them, disliked them. He told me so, many a time. Martin told me everything. And that was the finest thing that ever happened to me. And now you can call me any name you like, I don't care.

There is a silence, and he looks at them all defiantly.

ROBERT: But what about Betty?

GORDON (*sullenly*): You can leave her out of this.

ROBERT: I want to. But I can't help thinking about her.

GORDON: Well, you needn't. She can look after herself.

ROBERT: That's just what she can't do and she oughtn't to have to do. You ought to see that.

GORDON: Well, I don't see it. And I know Betty better than you do.

FREDA (*bitterly*): You know everybody better than anybody else does, don't you?

GORDON: You would say that, wouldn't you? I can't help it if Martin liked me better than he liked you.

FREDA: How do you know that he——

OLWEN: Oh, stop that. Stop it both of you. Can't you see that Martin was making mischief, just to amuse himself?

GORDON (*sulkily*): No, I can't. He wasn't like that.

STANTON (*with irony*): Oh no. Not at all like that. You couldn't ask for a quiet, simpler, more sincere fellow.

FREDA (*hotly*): Nobody's going to pretend he was that. But at least he didn't steal money and then try to put the blame on other people.

STANTON: We could all start talking like that, you know, Freda. Just throwing things at each other's heads. But I suggest we don't.

OLWEN: I agree. But I do want Freda and Gordon to understand that it's simply madness quarrelling over anything Martin ever said to them. He was a born mischief-maker and as cruel as a cat. That's one of the reasons why I disliked him so much.

ROBERT: Disliked him?

OLWEN: Yes, I'm sorry, Robert, but I didn't like Martin. I detested him. You ought to have seen that.

STANTON: I saw it. And you were quite right. I'm afraid you always are, Olwen.

OLWEN: No, I'm not.

STANTON: I'd trust your judgment.

ROBERT: So would I, for that matter.

OLWEN: No. No.

STANTON: And you're the only one of us who will come out of this as sound as you went in.

OLWEN (*embarrassed and a little alarmed*): No, that's not true.

GORDON: No—it was Olwen and that damned cigarette box that began the whole business.

STANTON: Oh, that was nothing. I knew about that all along.

OLWEN: You knew about what?

STANTON: I knew you'd been to see Martin Caplan that Saturday night.

OLWEN (*alarmed*): You knew?

STANTON: Yes.

OLWEN: But how could you? I don't understand.

STANTON: I was spending that week-end at my own cottage. You remember that garage, where the road forks? You stopped there that night for some petrol.

OLWEN (*remembering*): Yes, I believe I did.

STANTON: They told me, and said you'd taken the Fallows End road, and so I knew you must have been going to see Martin. You couldn't have been going anywhere else could you? Quite simple.

OLWEN (*staring at him*): And you've known all this time?

STANTON: Yes. All this time.

ROBERT (*rather bitterly*): I suppose, Stanton, it's no use asking *you* why you've never said a word about it?

STANTON (*coolly*): I'm afraid not. I think I've done my share in the confession box to-night.

GORDON: Well, I wish I'd known a bit more, that's all. There was I dragged into that foul inquest. Did I know this? Did I know that? My God—and all the time I wasn't the last person he'd talked to at all. Freda had been there some time in the afternoon. And Olwen was there that very night, at the very moment— for all we know.

STANTON: Don't talk rubbish.

GORDON: Well, is it rubbish? (*Indicating* OLWEN, *who turns away and moves up to the window.*) After all, what do we know? What was Olwen doing there?

ROBERT: She's told us that. She was there to talk to Martin about the money.

GORDON: And how far does that take us?

STANTON: What do you mean by that?

FREDA: He means—I imagine—that Olwen hasn't told us very much so far. We know she went to Martin to talk to him about the missing money. And we know that Martin thought Robert had taken it and that she thought so too. And that's all we do know.

GORDON: Yes, we don't know how long she was there or what Martin said to her, or anything. It's a good job *she* wasn't pushed in front of that coroner or they'd have had it out of her in no time. (*Turning round to* OLWEN.) I think it's up to *her* to tell us a little more.

STANTON: Well, there's no need to sound so damned vindictive about it.

> OLWEN, *who has just looked out through the window, pulling the curtain back a little, suddenly starts back and gives a little scream.*

ROBERT } (*together*): Hello, what's the matter.
STANTON }

> ROBERT *goes up to window, looks out, and* FREDA *rises and turns to window.*

ROBERT (*still looking out*): There's nobody there now.

OLWEN: No, they darted away. But I'll swear there was somebody. They'd been listening.

STANTON (*who has remained seated. Grimly*): Well, they couldn't have chosen a better night for it.

ROBERT: It's impossible, Olwen. And there isn't a sign of anybody.

GORDON: Thank the Lord for that.

> *They all start to move forward and as they move, there are several short rings of a door bell heard from off. They all stop and look at one another in surprise and consternation.*

ROBERT: Who on earth can this be?

FREDA: Don't ask me. I haven't the least idea. Go and see.

ROBERT: Yes, I know. But we don't want anybody interrupting us now.

FREDA: Well, don't let them interrupt us, whoever they are. But you'll have to see who it is.

The bell rings again and ROBERT *goes out. While he is away, nobody speaks and they all look somewhat constrained.*

Then the voices of ROBERT *and* BETTY *can be heard.*

ROBERT (*heard outside*): But we haven't I tell you. You've never been mentioned.

BETTY (*outside*): I know you have. I can feel it. That's why I had to come back.

ROBERT (*outside*): I tell you we haven't.

ROBERT *opens the door and* BETTY *is seen in front of him.*

GORDON: I thought you'd gone to bed, Betty. What's the matter?

BETTY (*just inside the door*): You're talking about me, all of you. (*Looking round at them all.*) I know you are. I wanted to go to bed. I started to go. And then I couldn't. I knew you were all talking about me. I couldn't stand it. I had to come back.

FREDA (*coldly*): Well, you were wrong. As a matter of fact, you're the one person we *haven't* been talking about.

BETTY (*looking at* GORDON, STANTON *and then* ROBERT): Is that true?

ROBERT: Yes, of course.

OLWEN: You were outside just now, weren't you? Outside the window, listening.

BETTY (*confused*): No, I wasn't listening. I was trying to peep in, to see exactly who was here and what you all looked like. You see, I was sure you were all saying things about me. And I meant to go to bed and I was tired but I felt too excited inside to sleep and so I took three of those tablets I have to make me sleep and now I feel absolutely dopey. God knows what I shall be saying in a minute. You mustn't mind me. (*Sinks into the chair.*)

ROBERT (*leaning over her*): I'm so sorry Betty. Can I get you anything? (*As she shakes her head.*) Sure? (*She shakes her head again.*) And not a word's been said about you. In fact, we all wanted to keep you out of this. It's all rather unpleasant.

FREDA (*with irony*): But seeing that Betty has married into one of the families concerned, I think she ought not to be too carefully protected from the sordid truth.

ROBERT (*losing his temper*): Oh shut up, Freda.

FREDA: I won't. Why should I? I thought we should see a different Robert now.

ROBERT: After what you've said to-night, I can't see that it matters much to you how different I may be.

FREDA: Perhaps not, but I still like reasonably decent manners.

ROBERT: Then set us an example.

GORDON: Oh, shut up, both of you.

BETTY: But what have you been talking about then?

GORDON: It began about the money.

BETTY: You mean that Martin took?

GORDON: Martin didn't take it. We know that now. Stanton took that money. He's admitted it.

BETTY *gives a short cry.*

BETTY: Admitted it. Stanton? Oh surely—it's impossible.

STANTON (*sardonically*): It sounds impossible, doesn't it, Betty, but it isn't. I'm sorry to go down with such a bump in your estimation, my dear Betty, but this is our night for telling the truth, and I've had to admit that I took that money. Terrible isn't it?

STANTON *looks at* BETTY *and she avoids his glance, uncomfortably.* ROBERT *looks from one to the other of them.*

ROBERT: What did you mean by that, Stanton?

STANTON: I meant what I said. I nearly always do.

ROBERT: Why did you use that tone of voice to Betty?

STANTON: Perhaps—because I think that Betty has not a very high opinion of me—and so need not have sounded so surprised and shocked.

ROBERT (*slowly*): I don't quite understand that.

FREDA (*sarcastically*): I'm sure you don't, Robert.

ROBERT (*turning on her sharply*): Do you?

FREDA (*sweetly*): Yes, I think so.

BETTY: But if Martin didn't take the money—then why—why—did he shoot himself?

GORDON: That's what we want to know. Olwen saw him last of all, that very evening, and she knew he hadn't taken the money, but that's all she's told us.

OLWEN: I've told you that he thought Robert had taken the money.

ROBERT: And that was enough—in the state he was in then—to throw him clean off his balance. All that stuff about his merely being amused is nonsense. That was just his bluff. Martin hated anybody to think he was really moved or alarmed by anything.

GORDON: That's true.

ROBERT (*with growing excitement*): And he depended on me. He used to laugh a lot at me, but that was nothing. He depended on me. You've told me your-selves—that he was secretly rather frightened of me. It was because Martin had a respect for me. He thought I was the solid steady one. I was one of the very few people he had a respect for. I tell you, it must have been a hell of a shock to poor Martin.

OLWEN: I don't think it was, Robert.

STANTON: Neither do I.

ROBERT: But neither of you knew him as I did. What's the good of talking. He was in a wretched state, all run down and neurotic, and when he heard that I'd taken the cheque he must have felt that there was nobody left he could depend on, that I'd let him down. He'd probably been brooding over it day and night— he was that sort. He wouldn't let you see it, Olwen. But it would be there all the time, giving him hell. Oh, what a fool I was.

GORDON: You!

ROBERT: Yes, of course. I ought to have gone straight to Martin and told him what Stanton had told me.

GORDON: If this is true, then the person really responsible is Stanton.

58

FREDA: Yes.

STANTON: Rubbish.

FREDA: It isn't. Don't you see what you did?

STANTON: No, because I don't believe it.

GORDON: No, because you don't choose to, that's all.

STANTON: Oh, talk sense. Can't you see Martin had his own reasons?

ROBERT: No. What drove Martin to suicide was my stupidity and your damned lying, Stanton.

BETTY (*bursting into tears*): Oh!

ROBERT: Oh, sorry, Betty—but this has got to be settled, once and for all.

STANTON (*grimly*): You're none of you in a state to settle anything.

ROBERT: Listen to me, Stanton——

STANTON: Oh, drop it, man.

GORDON: You've got to answer.

ROBERT: I'll never forgive you for telling Martin what you did—by God, I won't!

STANTON: You've got it all wrong.

GORDON: They haven't, you rotten liar. (*Moves as if to strike him.*)

STANTON (*pushing him aside*): Oh, get out.

GORDON (*shouting and about to go for him again*): You made Martin shoot himself.

OLWEN: Wait a minute, Gordon. (*Everybody turns and looks at her.*) Martin didn't shoot himself.

END OF ACT TWO

59

F

ACT III

All are discovered in exactly the same positions as they were in at the end of ACT II.

OLWEN: Martin didn't shoot himself.

FREDA: Martin didn't——

OLWEN: Of course he didn't. I shot him.

    BETTY *gives a little scream, the others gasp and stare.*

ROBERT: That's ridiculous, Olwen. You couldn't have done.

GORDON: Is this your idea of a joke?

OLWEN: I wish it was. (*Suddenly sits down and buries her face in her hands. She does not make any sound, however.*)

GORDON: Olwen.

ROBERT (*with lowered voice*): She must be hysterical or something. I believe people often confess to all sorts of mad things in that state, things they could not possibly have done.

STANTON (*shaking his head*): Olwen's not hysterical. She means it.

BETTY (*in a whisper*): But she can't mean—she *murdered* him. Can she?

STANTON (*gently*): You might as well tell us exactly what happened now, Olwen, if you can stand it. And

60

I might as well tell you—before you begin—that I'm not at all surprised. I suspected it was you at the first.

OLWEN (*staring at him*): You suspected I'd done it? But why?

STANTON: For three reasons. The first was that I couldn't understand why Martin should shoot himself. You see, I knew he hadn't taken the money, and though he was in every kind of mess, he didn't seem to me the sort of chap who'd get out of it that way. Then I knew you'd been with him quite late, because—as I said before—I'd been told you'd gone that way. And the third reason—well, that'll keep. You'd better tell us what happened now. It was an accident, wasn't it?

OLWEN (*in a low, strained voice*): Yes, it was really an accident. I'll tell you what happened, but I can't go into details. It's all too muddled and horrible. But I'll tell you the complete truth. I won't hide anything more, I promise you. I think we'd all better tell everything we know now, really speak our minds.

ROBERT (*also in a low voice*): I agree.

STANTON: Wait a minute, Olwen. Will you have a drink before you begin?

OLWEN: I'll just have a little soda water, if you don't mind.

He pours out drink and gives it to her.

ROBERT: Sit here.

OLWEN (*to* STANTON): Thank you. (*Sips drink.*) (*To* ROBERT) No, I'll sit by the fire.

OLWEN: I went to see Martin that Saturday night, as you know, to talk to him about the missing money.

61

Mr. Whitehouse had told me about it. He thought that either Martin or Robert must have taken it. I gathered it was more likely Robert. So I went to see Martin. I didn't like Martin and he knew it, but he knew, too, what I felt about Robert, and after all, he was Robert's brother. He believed that Robert had taken the money, and he wasn't a bit worried about it. I'm sorry, Robert, but he wasn't. I hated him for that, too. He was rather maliciously amused. The good brother fallen at last— that sort of thing.

FREDA (*in a low, bitter voice*): I can believe that. I hate to, but I know he could be like that sometimes. He was that day.

OLWEN (*gently*): You found that, too, that day?

FREDA: Yes, he was in one of his worst moods. He could be cruel—torturing—sometimes.

OLWEN: I've never seen him as bad as he was that night. He wasn't really sane.

ROBERT (*shocked*): Olwen.

OLWEN (*very gently*): I'm sorry, Robert. I didn't want you to know all this, but there's no help for it now. You see, Martin had been taking some sort of drug——

ROBERT: Drug. Do you mean dope stuff?

OLWEN: Yes. He'd had a lot of it.

ROBERT: Are you sure? I can't believe it.

STANTON: It's true, Caplan. I knew it.

GORDON: So did I. He made me try some once, but I didn't like it. It just made me feel rather sick

ROBERT: When was this?

62

GORDON: You remember when he went to Berlin and how nervy he was just then?

STANTON: Yes, I remember.

GORDON: Well, a fellow he met there put him on to it—some new drug that a lot of the literary and theatrical set were doping themselves with——

FREDA: But did Martin——

GORDON: Yes. He liked it and took more and more of it.

ROBERT: But where did he get it?

GORDON: Through some German he knew in town. When he couldn't get it, he was pretty rotten. Not so bad as those dope fiends one reads about, you know, but nevertheless pretty rotten.

STANTON: But didn't you try to stop him?

GORDON: Of course—but he only laughed. I don't blame him really. None of you can understand what life was like to Martin—he was so sensitive and nervy. He was one of those people who are meant to be happy.

STANTON (*grimly*): We're all those people who are meant to be happy. Martin's no exception.

ROBERT: Yes, that's true. But I know what Gordon means.

FREDA: You couldn't help knowing what he means, if you knew Martin. There was no sort of middle state, no easy jog-trot with him. Either he had to be gay—and when he was gay, he was gayer than anybody else in the world—or he was intensely miserable.

BETTY (*impulsively*): I'm like that. Everybody is—aren't they?—except old and stuffy people.

ROBERT: But what about this drug, Olwen?

OLWEN: He took some—-it was in little white tablets —while I was there, and it had a horrible effect on him. It gave him a sort of devilish gaiety. I can see him now. His eyes were queer. Oh—he really wasn't sane. (*Stops.*)

ROBERT: What happened?

OLWEN (*quiet, but very agitated*): It's horrible to talk about. I've tried not to think about it. He knew I disliked him, but he couldn't believe I *really* disliked him. He was frightfully conceited about himself. He seemed to think that everybody young, male or female, ought to be falling in love with him. He saw himself as a sort of Pan, you know.

FREDA (*in a low voice*): Yes, he did. And he'd every reason to.

OLWEN: He began taunting me. He thought of me— or pretended to—as a priggish spinster, full of re- pressions, who'd never really lived. All rubbish, because I'm really not that type at all. But he pretended to think I was, and kept telling me that my dislike of him showed that I was trying to repress a great fascina- tion he had for me. And of course that all these repressions were bad for me. I'd never lived, never would live, and all the rest of it. He talked a lot about that. I ought to have run out and left him, but I felt I couldn't while he was in that state. In a way I was sorry for him, because really he was ill, sick in mind and body, and I thought perhaps I could calm him down. I might dislike him, but after all he wasn't a stranger. He was one of our own set, mixed up with

64

most of the people I liked best in the world. I tried hard to stop him. But everything I said seemed to make him worse. I suppose it would when he was in that excited, abnormal state. Well, he talked about my repressions, and when I pretended to laugh at him, he got more and more excited. And then he tried to show me some beastly foul drawings he had—horrible, obscene things by some mad Belgian artist——

FREDA (*swaying*): Oh—my God! (*Sobs.*)

OLWEN (*going to her*): Oh, Freda, I'm so sorry. Please forgive me. I know how this must be hurting you.

FREDA (*distraught*): Martin. Martin.

OLWEN: Don't listen to any more. I'll stop if you like. Or go and lie down.

FREDA: I couldn't. Oh—he wasn't like that really. If you'd known him as I'd known him—before.

OLWEN: I know that. We all do. He was different. He was ill.

FREDA (*in a muffled tone*): Go on, Olwen.

ROBERT: Yes, Olwen. You can't stop now.

OLWEN: There isn't a lot to tell now. When I pushed his beastly drawings away and was rather indignant about them, he got still more excited, completely unbalanced, and shouted out things about my repressions. And then I found he was telling me to take my clothes off. I told him not to be a fool and that I was going. But then he stood between me and the door. And he had a revolver in his hand and was shouting something about danger and terror and love. He wasn't threatening me with it or himself. He was just waving it about—

being dramatic. I didn't even believe it was loaded. But by this time I'd had more than enough of him—I couldn't be sorry for him any more—and I told him to get out of the way. When he wouldn't, I tried to push him out of the way. And then we had a struggle. (*She is distressed now and a trifle incoherent.*) He tried to tear my clothes. We really fought one another. It was horrible. He wasn't any stronger than I was. (*Illustrating this by grabbing her own wrist and slowly turning it.*) I'd grabbed the hand with the revolver in it. I'd turned the revolver towards him. His finger must have been on the trigger. I must have given it a jerk. (*Covers her face with her hands.*) The revolver went off. Oh— horrible—horrible. I've tried and tried to forget that. If he'd just been wounded, I'm sure I would have stopped with him—even though I was in such a panic. But he wasn't. He was dead.

ROBERT: Yes, we understand that. You needn't tell us.

OLWEN: When I realised what had happened I rushed out in a dreadful panic and sat in my car outside for I don't know how long. I couldn't move a finger. There was nobody about. It was fairly late and you know how lonely that cottage was. I just sat on and on in the car, shivering, and it was so quiet in the cottage, so horribly quiet. I've gone through that over and over again. (*Buries her face in her hands and sobs soundlessly.*)

BETTY (*in a whisper and turning her head away*): God!

ROBERT: You can't be blamed, Olwen.

STANTON (*decisively, and rising*): Of course she can't be

66

blamed. And there must never be a word spoken about this—not to anybody. We must all promise that.

They all nod or murmur their assent.

GORDON (*bitterly*): It's a pity we can't all be as cool and business-like about this as you are, Stanton.

STANTON: I don't feel very cool and business-like about it. But you see, it's not as big a surprise to me as it is to you people. I guessed long ago that something like this had happened.

ROBERT: But it looked so much like suicide that no-body bothered to suggest it wasn't. It never seemed to me to be anything else. All the evidence pointed that way. I can't think how you could have guessed even though you knew Olwen had been there.

STANTON: I told you I had a third reason. I was over fairly early next morning—the postmistress at Fallows End rang me up—and I was there before anybody but the village constable and the doctor. And I spotted something on the floor that the village bobby had missed, and I picked it up when he wasn't looking. I've kept it in my pocket-book ever since. (*Brings out pocket-book and produces from it a small square of patterned silk.*) I'm rather observant about such things.

OLWEN: Let me see. (*Examines it.*) Yes, that's a piece of the dress I was wearing. It was torn in the struggle we had. So that's how you knew?

STANTON (*dropping piece of silk in the fireplace*): That's how I knew.

OLWEN: But why didn't you say anything?

GORDON (*bitterly*): I can tell you that. He didn't say anything because he wanted everybody to think that

67

Martin had shot himself. You see, that meant that Martin must have taken the money.

ROBERT (*wearily*): That's about it, I suppose. It falls into line with everything we've heard from him to-night.

STANTON: No, there happened to be another reason, much more important. I knew that if Olwen had had a hand in Martin's death, then something like that must have happened, and so Olwen couldn't be blamed. I knew her better than any of you—or I felt I did. And I trusted her. She's about the only person I would trust. She knows all about that. I've told her often enough. She's not interested, but there it is.

OLWEN (*wonderingly*): And you never even hinted to me that you knew.

STANTON: Surprising, isn't it? What a chance I missed to capture your interest for a few minutes. But I couldn't take that line with you. I suppose even nowadays, when we're all so damned tough, there has got to be one person that you behave to always as if you were Sir Roger de Coverly, and with me you've been that person for a long time now. And I knew all along that you were saying nothing because you thought Robert here had taken the money and that he was safe after everybody put it down to Martin. And that didn't always make it any easier for me.

BETTY (*with shrill irony*): No? What a shame! But what a fine romantic character you are, aren't you?

ROBERT (*gently*): Steady, Betty. You don't understand.

FREDA (*bitterly*): How could she?

68

BETTY (*indignantly, and turning to* FREDA): Why do you say that—in that tone of voice?

FREDA (*wearily*): Why does one say anything—in any tone of voice?

OLWEN (*to* STANTON): You know, I nearly did take you into my confidence. And that might have made a difference. But I chose a bad moment.

STANTON (*eagerly*): Why? When was this? Tell me.

OLWEN: I told you I sat in my car that night for some time not able to do anything. But then, when I felt a little better, I felt I had to tell somebody, and you were the nearest person——

STANTON (*alarmed*): But you didn't go there—that night?

OLWEN (*quietly*): Yes, I did. I drove over to your cottage at Church Marley that very Saturday night. I got there about eleven o'clock or just afterwards. I left my car at the bottom of that tiny narrow lane and walked up to your cottage. And then—I walked back again.

STANTON: You walked up to the cottage?

OLWEN: Yes, yes—don't be stupid about it, please, Stanton. I walked right up to your cottage and saw enough to set me walking straight back again.

STANTON: So that's when you came. After that, it was hopeless, I suppose.

OLWEN: Quite hopeless. I think that added the last touch to that night. I don't think I've ever felt the same about people—not just here, but everybody, even the people who walk into the office or sit opposite one in buses and trains—since that night. I know that's stupid, but I couldn't help it. And (*forcing a smile*) you must all have noticed that I've been completely off country cottages.

FREDA (*maliciously*): Yes, even Betty's noticed that.

BETTY *bursts into tears and hangs her head.*

ROBERT: Why, what's the matter, Betty?

GORDON: What a little liar you are, Betty.

BETTY (*in muffled voice*): Haven't we all been liars.

ROBERT (*puzzled*): But you haven't, Betty.

GORDON: Oh, don't be a fool, Robert. Of course she has. She's lied like fury.

ROBERT: What about?

FREDA: Why don't you ask her?

OLWEN (*wearily*): Oh, what does it matter. Leave the child alone.

BETTY: I'm not a child. That's the mistake you've all made.

ROBERT (*who has been thinking*): Not you—and Stanton? (*A pause. She does not reply.*) Is that what they mean? (BETTY *just keeps still and looks defiant.*) Why don't you tell them it's ridiculous?

FREDA (*contemptuously*): How can she? Don't be absurd.

OLWEN (*gently*): You see, Robert, I saw them both in Stanton's cottage that night.

ROBERT: I'm sorry, Olwen, but I won't take even your word for this. Besides, there are other possible explanations.

STANTON: Oh, drop this, Caplan. We've had too much of it already. I'm going.

ROBERT (*ferociously turning on him*): You're not going.

STANTON: Don't be a fool. It's no business of yours.

FREDA (*maliciously*): That's where you're wrong, Stanton. This is where Robert's business really begins.

ROBERT: I'm waiting for an answer, Betty.

BETTY (*frightened*): What do you want me to say?

ROBERT: Were you with Stanton at his cottage?

BETTY (*whispers*): Yes.

ROBERT: Were you his mistress?

BETTY: Yes. (*Turns away and drops her head.*)

ROBERT (*quietly but with great passion. Turning to* STANTON.) My God, I could—— (*A pause, then turns to* BETTY, *in extreme agitation.*) But why—why—in God's name—why? How could you ? How could you?

BETTY (*suddenly stung into life*): How could I? Because I'm not a child and I'm not a little stuffed doll, that's why. You would drag all this out and now you can damned well have it. Yes, I stayed with Stanton that night, and I've stayed with him other nights. And he's not in love with me and I know it, and I'm not in love with him. I wouldn't marry him if I could. But I'd got to make something happen. Gordon was driving me mad. If you want to call someone a child, then call him one, for that's all he is. This damned marriage of ours that you all got so sentimental about is the biggest sham there's ever been. It isn't a marriage at all. It's just nothing—pretence, pretence, pretence. Betty darling and Gordon darling, when all the time he's mooning over his Martin and the very sight of him makes me want to scream. (*Her voice now had become a shriek.*)

FREDA: Betty, you mustn't go——

BETTY: It's not my fault. I was in love with him when we were married, and I thought everything was going to be marvellous. I wouldn't have looked at anybody else if he'd been—real. But he just isn't, there. He can't even *talk* to me.

GORDON: For God's sake, shut up, Betty.

BETTY (*with shrill emphasis*): I won't shut up. They want to know the truth, and they can have it. I don't care. I've had nothing, nothing out of my marriage but shame and misery.

OLWEN: Betty, that's simply nonsense.

BETTY: If I were the nice little doll you all thought me, perhaps it wouldn't have mattered. But I'm not. I'm not a child either. I'm a woman. And Stanton was the one person who guessed what was happening and treated me like a woman.

GORDON (*scornfully*): I wouldn't have blamed you if you'd gone and fallen in love properly with someone, but this was just a low sordid intrigue, a dirty little affair, not worth all your silly lies. I suppose Stanton was the rich uncle in America who kept giving you all those fine presents?

BETTY: Yes, he was. You couldn't even be generous though you'd have given your precious Martin everything we'd got. I knew Stanton didn't really care for me, so I got what I could out of him. (STANTON *turns*

72

to her and gives an amused grin mixed with surprise.)
It served you right. Men who say they're in love with
one woman and keep spending their week-ends with
another deserve all they get.

FREDA (*to* STANTON): Is that why you suddenly found
yourself so short of money that you had to have that
five hundred pounds?

STANTON: Yes. Queer how it works out, isn't it?

GORDON: Then Betty is responsible for everything,
for all this misery, for Martin.

BETTY (*turning round to them*): You see? Always
Martin. If I was responsible for all that, then it's your
fault really, Gordon. Because you're responsible for
everything that happened to me. You ought never to
have married me.

GORDON: I didn't know. It was a mistake.

FREDA (*bitterly*): We seem to make that kind of
mistake in our family.

BETTY (*moving down to end of piano*): I ought to have
left you long before this. That was *my* mistake—staying
on—trying to make the best of it—pretending to
be married to somebody who wasn't there, simply
dead.

GORDON: Yes, I think I am dead. I think I died last
summer. Olwen shot me.

OLWEN: Gordon, I think that's unfair and also rather
stupid and affected.

GORDON (*quietly*): It may have sounded like that, but
it wasn't. I meant it, Olwen.

ROBERT (*who has just had half a glass of neat whisky*):

73

I began this, didn't I? Well, I'll finish it. I'll say something now. Betty, I worshipped you, I suppose you knew that?

FREDA: If she didn't, she must have been very dense.

ROBERT (*turning on* FREDA. *He is not drunk but speaks in a thick voice and is a trifle wild in manner*): I'm talking to Betty now. You might leave us alone for a minute. (*Turning to* BETTY.) Did you realise that I felt like that, Betty?

BETTY: Yes. But I didn't care very much.

ROBERT (*bitterly*): No, why should you?

BETTY: No, it isn't that. But I knew you weren't in love with me. You didn't know me. You were only worshipping somebody you'd invented, who looked like me. And that's not the same thing at all.

ROBERT: I didn't do much about it. I couldn't, you see. I thought that you and Gordon were reasonably happy together——

BETTY: Yes, we put up a good show, didn't we?

ROBERT: You did. (*Goes for another drink.*)

GORDON: Yes, we did. What would have happened if we'd gone on pretending like hell to be happy together?

BETTY: Nothing.

GORDON (*thinking it out*): No. If we'd gone on pretending long enough, I believe we might have *been* happy together, sometimes. It often works out like that.

BETTY: Never.

OLWEN: Yes, it does. That's why all this is so wrong

74

really. The *real* truth is something so deep you can't get at it this way, and all this half truth does is to blow everything up. It isn't *civilised*.

STANTON: I agree.

ROBERT (*after another drink, cynically*): *You* agree!

STANTON: You'll get no sympathy from me, Caplan.

ROBERT: Sympathy from you! I never want to set eyes on you again, Stanton. You're a thief, a cheat, a liar, and a dirty cheap seducer.

STANTON: And you're a fool, Caplan. You look solid, but you're not. You've a good deal in common with that cracked brother of yours. You won't face up to real things. You've been living in a fool's paradise, and now, having got yourself out of it by to-night's efforts—all your doing—you're busy building yourself a fool's hell to live in.

ROBERT (*picking up the glass that* STANTON *had left*): I think this was your glass, Stanton. (*Moves up to window and throws it out.*) And now take yourself after it. Get out. (*Pours out another drink for himself.*)

STANTON: Good-night, Olwen. I'm sorry about all this.

OLWEN: So am I. (*Offers him her hand. He takes it.*) Good-night.

STANTON: Good-night, Freda.

FREDA: Good-night.

STANTON (*turning at door. To* BETTY *and* GORDON): I suppose you're coming along?

GORDON: Not with you, I'm afraid. And don't

75

G

forget, Stanton, you owe the firm five hundred pounds —and a resignation.

STANTON: Oh, you're going to take it that way, are you?

GORDON: Yes, I'm going to take it that way.

STANTON: You'll regret it. Good-night. (*With ironical politeness.*) No, don't trouble. I can find my way out. (*He goes out.*)

OLWEN: Don't be too hasty, Gordon. Whatever his faults Stanton's a first-class man at his job. If he goes, the firm will suffer.

GORDON: I can't help it. I couldn't work with him after this. The firm will have to suffer, that's all.

ROBERT: Don't worry. It's not a case of the firm suffering. The firm's smashed to hell *now*.

FREDA: Nonsense.

ROBERT: Is it? I don't think so.

GORDON (*bitterly*): Well, Betty darling, I think we'd better return to our happy little home, our dear little nest——

BETTY: Oh, don't, Gordon.

FREDA (*going out with* GORDON): I'll let you out.

ROBERT (*as* BETTY *turns to move off*): Good-bye. (*Staring at her.*)

BETTY: Why do you look like that?

ROBERT: I'm not saying good-bye to *you*. I don't know you. I never did, it seems. I'm saying good-bye to this. (*Indicates her face and body.*) That's all. (*Turns away abruptly, and goes up for another drink.*)

BETTY *stares for a second and then goes quickly out.*

OLWEN (*distressed*): Robert, please don't drink any more to-night. I know how you feel, but it'll only make you worse—really it will.

ROBERT: What does it matter? I'm through, anyway.

OLWEN: Robert, I can't bear seeing you like this. You don't know how it hurts me.

ROBERT: I'm sorry, Olwen, I really am sorry. You're the only one who's really come out of this. I know that. Strange, isn't it—that you should have been feeling like that about me all the time?

OLWEN: Yes, all the time.

ROBERT: I'm sorry.

OLWEN: I'm not. I mean about myself. I suppose I ought to be, but I'm not. It's hurt like anything sometimes, but it's kept me going too.

ROBERT: I know. And you see, now I've stopped going. Something's broken—inside.

OLWEN: It won't seem bad to-morrow. It never does.

ROBERT: All this isn't going to seem any better to-morrow, Olwen.

OLWEN: Freda will help too. After all, Robert, she's fond of you.

ROBERT: No, not really. It isn't that she dislikes me steadily, but every now and then she hates me—and now I see why, of course. She hates me because I'm Robert Caplan and not Martin, because he's dead and I'm alive.

OLWEN: She may feel differently—after to-night.

ROBERT: She may. I doubt it. She doesn't change easily—that's the trouble. And then again, you see, I

77

don't care any more. That's the point. Whether she changes or doesn't change I don't care now.

OLWEN (*with deep feeling*): And you know there's nothing I wouldn't do, Robert. I'll—— (*She gives a little laugh.*) I'll run away this very minute with you if you like.

ROBERT (*simply*): I'm terribly grateful, Olwen. But nothing happens here—inside. That's the damned awful cruel thing. Nothing happens. All hollow, empty.

FREDA *enters and shuts the door.*

FREDA: I'm sure it's not at all the proper thing to say at such a moment, but the fact remains that I feel rather hungry. What about you, Olwen? You, Robert? Or have you been drinking too much?

ROBERT: Yes, I've been drinking too much.

FREDA: Well, it's very silly of you.

ROBERT (*wearily*): Yes. (*Buries his face in his hands.*)

FREDA: And you did ask for all this.

ROBERT (*half looking up*): I asked for it. And I got it.

FREDA: Though I doubt if you minded very much until it came to Betty.

ROBERT: That's not true. But I can understand you're thinking so. You see, as more and more of this rotten stuff came out, so more and more I came to depend on my secret thoughts of Betty—as someone who seemed to me to represent some lovely quality of life.

FREDA: I've known some time, of course, that you were getting very sentimental and noble about her. And I've known some time, too, all about Betty, and I've often thought of telling you.

78

ROBERT: I'm not sorry you didn't.

FREDA: You ought to be.

ROBERT: Why?

FREDA: That kind of self-deception's rather stupid.

ROBERT: What about you and Martin?

FREDA: I didn't deceive myself. I knew everything—or nearly everything—about him. I wasn't in love with somebody who really wasn't there, somebody I'd made up.

ROBERT: I think you were. Probably we always are.

OLWEN: Then it's not so bad then. You can always build up another image for yourself to fall in love with.

ROBERT: No, you can't. That's the trouble. You lose the capacity for building. You run short of the stuff that creates beautiful illusions, just as if a gland had stopped working.

OLWEN: Then you have to learn to live without illusions.

ROBERT: Can't be done. Not for us. We started life too early for that. Possibly they're breeding people now who can live without illusions. I hope so. But I can't do it. I've lived among illusions——

FREDA (*grimly*): You have.

ROBERT (*with growing excitement*): Well, what if I have? They've given me hope and courage. They've helped me to live. I suppose we ought to get all that from faith in life. But I haven't got any. No religion or anything. Just this damned farmyard to live in. That's all. And just a few bloody glands and secretions and nerves

79

to do it with. But it didn't look too bad. I'd my little illusions, you see.

FREDA (*bitterly*): Then why didn't you leave them alone, instead of clamouring for the truth all night like a fool?

ROBERT (*terribly excited now*): Because I *am* a fool. Stanton was right. That's the only answer. I had to meddle, like a child with a fire. I began this evening with something to keep me going. I'd good memories of Martin. I'd a wife who didn't love me, but at least seemed too good for me. I'd two partners I liked and respected. There was a girl I could idealise. And now——

OLWEN (*distressed*): No, Robert—please. We know.

ROBERT (*in a frenzy*): But you don't know, you *can't* know—not as I know—or you wouldn't stand there like that, as if we'd only just had some damned silly little squabble about a hand at bridge.

OLWEN: Freda, can't you——

ROBERT: Don't you see, we're not living in the same *world* now. Everything's gone. My brother was an obscene lunatic——

FREDA (*very sharply*): Stop that.

ROBERT: And my wife doted on him and pestered him. One of my partners is a liar and a cheat and a thief. The other—God knows what he is—some sort of hysterical young pervert—— (*Both women try to check and calm him.*) And the girl's a greedy little cat on the tiles——

OLWEN (*half screaming*): No, Robert, no. This is

horrible, mad. Please, please don't go on. (*Quieter.*)
It won't seem like this to-morrow.

ROBERT (*crazy now*): To-morrow. *To-morrow.* I tell
you, I'm through. I'm through. There can't be a
to-morrow. (*He goes swaying to the door.*)

FREDA (*screaming and moves to* OLWEN *and grips her
arm*): He's got a revolver in his bedroom.

OLWEN (*screaming and running to the door*): Stop,
Robert. Stop. Stop.

> *For the last few seconds the light has been fading,
> now it is completely dark. There is a revolver shot, a
> woman's scream, a moment's silence, then the sound
> of a woman sobbing, exactly as at the beginning of*
> ACT I.

OLWEN (*in the darkness, with great emphasis but with
a certain hysterious quality*): It can't happen. It *shan't*
happen.

> *And now* MISS MOCKRIDGE'S *voice can be heard
> faintly, and the lights come up slowly, showing the four
> women in just the same places as they were at the
> beginning of* ACT I.

MISS MOCKRIDGE: How many scenes did we miss?

OLWEN: Five, I think.

> FREDA *goes to wireless and switches it off.*

MISS M.: I suppose they must have been telling a lot
of lies in those scenes. That's why that man was so
angry—the husband, I mean.

> *There is a subdued burst of laughter from the men
> in the dining-room.*

BETTY: Listen to the men.

81

Miss M.: They're probably laughing at something very improper.

Betty: No, just gossip. Men gossip like anything.

Freda: Of course they do. And they've got a marvellous excuse now that they're all three directors of the firm.

Miss M.: What a snug little group you are.

Freda (*making a face*): Snug little group. It sounds disgusting.

Olwen: Enchanting. I hate to leave it.

Miss M.: I should think you do. It must be so comforting to be all so settled.

Betty: Pretty good.

Miss M. (*to* Freda): But I suppose you all miss your brother-in-law. He used to be down here with you too, didn't he?

Freda: You mean Robert's brother, Martin.

> Olwen, Betty *and* Freda *exchange glances, and there is a pause.*

Miss M.: I say, have I dropped a brick? I always am dropping bricks.

Freda (*very quietly*): No, not at all. It was very distressing at the time, but it's all right now. Martin shot himself.

Miss M.: Oh, yes—dreadful business, of course. He was very handsome, wasn't he?

> *Enter* Stanton, *followed by* Gordon, *who goes to front of settee and takes* Betty's *hand.*

Olwen: Yes, very handsome.

STANTON (*with jovial condescension*): Who's very handsome? May we know?

BETTY: Not you, Charles.

GORDON: They were talking about me. Betty, why do you allow them to talk about your husband in this fulsome fashion. Have you no shame, girl?

BETTY (*taking his hand*): Darling, I'm sure you've had too much manly gossip and old brandy.

ROBERT *enters*.

ROBERT: Sorry to be so late, Freda—but it's that wretched puppy of yours.

FREDA: Oh, what's he been doing now?

ROBERT: He was trying to eat the script of Sonia William's new novel. I was afraid it might make him sick. You see, Miss Mockridge, how we talk of you novelists.

MISS M.: Yes, I hear you. I've just been saying what a charming, cosy little group you've made here. I think you've been lucky.

STANTON: It's not all luck, Miss Mockridge. You see, we all happen to be nice easy-going people.

ROBERT: Except Betty, she's terribly wild.

STANTON: That's only because Gordon doesn't beat her often enough—yet.

MISS M.: You see, Miss Peel, Mr. Stanton is still the cynical bachelor, I'm afraid he rather spoils the picture.

GORDON: What's disturbing the ether to-night. Anybody know? (*Beginning to fiddle with the wireless set.*)

FREDA: Oh, Gordon, don't start it again. We've only just turned it off.

83

GORDON: What did you hear?

FREDA: The last half of a play.

OLWEN: It was called "The Sleeping Dog."

STANTON: Why?

MISS M.: We're not sure, but it ends with a gentleman shooting himself.

STANTON: What fun they have at B.B.C.

FREDA: Yes. Shots and things.

OLWEN: I think I understand that play now. The sleeping dog was the truth, do you see, and that man, the husband, insisted upon disturbing it.

ROBERT: He was quite right to disturb it.

STANTON: Was he, I wonder? I think telling the truth is about as healthy as skidding at sixty round a corner.

FREDA: And life's got lots of dangerous corners, hasn't it, Charles?

STANTON: It can have if you don't choose your route well.

FREDA (*nonchalantly*): Let's talk about something else. Who wants a drink? Drinks, Robert, and cigarettes.

ROBERT (*examining box on table*): There aren't any here.

FREDA: There are some in this one. (*Coming forward with musical cigarette box.*) Miss Mockridge, Olwen, a cigarette. (*Offers box to them.*)

OLWEN (*looking at the box*): Oh, I remember that box. It plays a tune at you, doesn't it? I remember the tune. Yes, it's the Wedding March. (*Opens box, and it plays.*)

84

GORDON (*who has been fiddling with the wireless*): Wait a minute. Listen to this.

"Can't we talk it over" gradually fades in on the wireless set.

BETTY (*rising*): Oh, I adore that tune.

STANTON: What is it?

BETTY: "Can't we talk it over."

MISS M.: What?

GORDON: "Can't we talk it over."

On this ROBERT *pulls back the chair that* MISS M. *has been sitting in.* FREDA *moves the table back to window.*

STANTON *asks* MISS M. *to dance. She declines.*

OLWEN *crosses to* ROBERT *and they dance.*

They are all very gay and the music gets louder and louder as the curtain falls.

END OF ACT THREE.

EDEN END

A Play in Three Acts

CHARACTERS
(in order of appearance)

WILFRED KIRBY

SARAH

LILIAN KIRBY

DR. KIRBY

STELLA KIRBY

GEOFFREY FARRANT

CHARLES APPLEBY

ACT   I.   Tuesday Afternoon

ACT   II.   Friday Afternoon

ACT III.   Scene I.   Saturday Night
             Scene II.   Sunday Afternoon

The action takes place in the sitting-room of Dr. Kirby's house at Eden End in the North of England, the last week in October, 1912.

First produced at the Duchess Theatre, London, on September 13th, 1934, with the following cast:

WILFRED KIRBY	JOHN TEED
SARAH	NELLIE BOWMAN
LILIAN KIRBY	ALISON LEGGATT
DR. KIRBY	EDWARD IRWIN
STELLA KIRBY	BEATRIX LEHMANN
GEOFFREY FARRANT	FRANKLYN BELLAMY
CHARLES APPLEBY	RALPH RICHARDSON

Play produced by IRENE HENTSCHEL

ACT I

*Sitting-room of Dr. Kirby's house, Eden End.   An afternoon
of early autumn in the year* 1912.   *A comfortable, well-
worn room furnished in the taste of an earlier period.
A door at the back, preferably up a few steps, leading
from the rest of the house.   A door on the right leading
to a small room, originally the nursery, now used by*
SARAH *to sit in and to do small jobs.   Unless otherwise
stated, all characters enter and leave by the main door
on the left.   A window at left looking out upon a distant
grey-green hill of the North-country type.   A bookshelf
on right wall.   A telephone prominently placed in corner
near door on left.   Upstage on left a cottage piano and
old piano stool.   WILFRED is discovered at this piano,
carefully picking out with one finger, and sometimes vamp-
ing an accompaniment in left hand, a waltz refrain from
"Gipsy Love."   He is wearing a tweed suit but a linen
collar and dark tie.   He is about* 24, *and though sun-
burned and in possession of a small moustache, he looks
young, unsophisticated, rather weak.   After a few
moments, during which he can improve a little and even
attempt to sing the tune,* SARAH *enters through door on
right, carrying some things she has presumably been
ironing in her little room.* SARAH *is an old North-
Country nurse, now about* 70, *a queer old creature, at
once simple and shrewd, and very earthy.   She still slaves*

91

*for all the family, but her tone towards them is still
indulgent, as if they were children.*

WILFRED: I'm getting it, Sarah.   I'm getting it.

SARAH: You've been at it long enough.

WILFRED: Now just listen.   (*He plays again and she
stops in the middle, halfway between doors to listen.*)

WILFRED (*wheeling round*): What do you think of
that?

SARAH: It sounds like proper playing—a'most.

WILFRED: Not so much of the *almost*.   What more
do you want?

SARAH: Well, I'm not saying you're not doing very
well with it.   But you'll never shape at it like Miss
Stella, never in all your born days you won't.

WILFRED: Do you know how many times you've
said that?

SARAH: For playing and singing and suchlike——

WILFRED: She was wonderful.   I know.   Well I'm
wonderful too.

SARAH: You're a right untidy lad.

WILFRED: I'm not a lad.

SARAH: Bother I've had wi' your clothes.

WILFRED: Did you do anything to my blue shirt?

SARAH: Ay, that's mended.   And two more beside.
And two of the doctor's.

WILFRED: When I'm in Africa, Sarah, black women
wash my clothes.

SARAH: I remember seeing four black women once at Martinbro Fair. Black as your boots they were. And fuzzy hair.

WILFRED: Where I work, when I go away, there are thousands and thousands of people like that. And I'm the boss. And then when I come home on leave, you call me a lad.

SARAH: These women kept rubbing their teeth with bits of stick, I remember. And I fancy it was the same year you went and fell into that duck pond just outside Martinbro. You wor only a little lad and you had your best sailor suit on. (*Goes to door on left.*)

WILFRED: What would you do if you saw a hippo-potamus?

SARAH: I don't know what they are. I've no time to be bothering wi' them things now.

WILFRED: Good old Sarah!

SARAH: You get on wi' your piano playing, and frame a bit better. (*Goes out.*)

(WILFRED *begins playing again, then leaves off, as if in disgust with himself. But hearing somebody coming through the door on left, he hastily plunges into a very noisy, inaccurate rendering of the waltz.* LILIAN *enters. She is a year or two older than her brother; neither pretty nor ugly; neatly but not well dressed in indoor clothes. She has more sweetness of character than would superficially appear from what she says and does. When she is not taking refuge in sarcasm, she is quick and eager. She goes over to the bookcase and takes a book that is lying open on the top.*)

93

LILIAN: What's that awful row?

WILFRED: That's the waltz from "Gipsy Love."

LILIAN: It sounds a mess.

WILFRED: That's because I can't play it properly.

LILIAN: That's obvious.

WILFRED: You ought to hear it as they do it. Gertie Millar and Robert Michaelis.

LILIAN (*ironically*): Wonderful!

WILFRED (*ignoring this, eagerly*): You know—somehow—it completely carried me away. It's rot, I suppose——

LILIAN (*now trying to read*): Of course it's rot.

WILFRED: Yes, but just think. (*Breaks off.*) You *might* listen, Lilian. Hang it all, I'm not always here to tell you things. And I listen to you.

LILIAN (*looking up from book*): Go on then.

WILFRED (*warming as he goes on*): Just think of it. Back from Africa. London. First night on leave. A jolly good dinner with two other chaps from the Company. Then Daly's. Lights, and everybody in the stalls dressed, stunning girls, the band playing—and then Gertie Millar—and—oh—everything. Do you know, Lilian, I felt quite queer. I nearly cried.

LILIAN: Did you?

WILFRED: I didn't really cry, you know. But I nearly did. Felt like it.

LILIAN: That's the only bit you haven't told me twenty times already.

WILFRED (*hotly*): That's not true.

LILIAN: Sorry, but it is. I can tell you the names of the chaps—as you call them—who went with you that night. One was called Patterson, and he comes from Cumberland and he's a good footballer. The other's called Bell—Bell—Bellingham——

WILFRED (*gloomily*): Bellington.

LILIAN: That's it. Not much difference. He's called Bellington and he comes from Devonshire, and he's got a sister who's married to a Captain in the Navy. There!

WILFRED (*getting up, huffily*): Sorry. Didn't know I'd been boring you.

LILIAN (*beginning to read*): You haven't. Don't apologise. (*She looks at him as he stands looking out of the window.*) By the way, you wouldn't like to walk into the village to give an order to Gregson's, would you?

WILFRED: No thanks.

LILIAN: Then I suppose I'll have to go. Soon. (*Begins reading again.*)

WILFRED (*turning to look at her*): Don't you ever get tired of reading?

LILIAN (*without looking up*): Yes.

WILFRED: You're always reading.

LILIAN (*without looking up*): I'm not. I spend most of the day looking after this house, and Dad, and you when you're at home.

WILFRED: Yes, but the minute you've done you begin reading. What's that?

95

LILIAN: Wells's new book. *Marriage*. (*Goes on reading.*)

WILFRED: You never seem to stop reading H. G. Wells. I don't know how you can stick him. I can't. He always makes me feel so uncomfortable. Doesn't seem to *like* anything. What's the point of reading if it makes you feel uncomfortable? It's bad enough in real life.

LILIAN (*still reading*): That's stupid.

WILFRED: Why is it stupid? (*She gives no reply but goes on reading.*) Geoffrey Farrant was saying just the same thing the other day. (*She looks up. He guffaws.*) I knew that would make you look up.

LILIAN (*crossly*): Don't be absurd. (*Hesitates.*) Did Geoffrey really say that?

WILFRED (*teasing*): Wouldn't you like to know?

LILIAN: It doesn't matter in the least.

WILFRED: Is Geoffrey coming round to-night?

LILIAN: I don't know. He might.

WILFRED (*wandering about, after lighting a cigarette*): Good old Geoffrey! By jove, when I was a kid, about fourteen, I used to think he was marvellous. That was when he was mad on Stella. He was my hero all right; regular soldier, captain, wounded in the Boer War——I used to follow him round like a little dog. I must have been a nuisance when he wanted to be alone with Stella. She used to tease him and say he came round just to be a hero to me. That's a long time ago. Nearly ten years. I say.

LILIAN (*rather wearily*): Well?

96

WILFRED: You see a lot of Geoffrey these days. Does he ever talk about Stella?

LILIAN (*shortly*): No, why should he? Give me a cigarette.

WILFRED: What for? You don't smoke.

LILIAN: I do if I want to. Give me one, please. (*Holds out hand.*)

WILFRED: Oh, all right, Christabel Pankhurst. (*Giving her one.*) But mind you don't make yourself sick.

LILIAN: Why should I? I'm better at not being sick than you are. You admit yourself you're always sea-sick.

WILFRED: That's different. Besides, just you try going through the Bay of Biscay in winter—as I've done, three times now.

LILIAN: And then there was the time when we both went on the swings at Martinbro Fair, and you were horribly sick and I wasn't. (*She awkwardly lights cigarette, and then, when it gets going, takes too deep a breath and coughs.*)

WILFRED: You see. Take it easy. What if Dad marches in?

LILIAN: He won't mind. Mother would have minded, but Dad won't. (*She does not make a success of her smoking.*)

WILFRED: One of our chaps in Nigeria told me his father wouldn't let him do *anything*. Terribly strict. That's why he cleared out.

LILIAN: Lucky chap.

WILFRED (*wandering over to the telephone*): You know, when I came home and saw the telephone, brand new, I thought I'd be able to have a lot of fun with it, but I haven't. There's nobody to ring up here in Eden End.

LILIAN: Who were you ringing up yesterday?

WILFRED (*indignantly*): You were listening!

LILIAN: I wasn't. I happened to hear your voice when I was in the hall, putting some things away. Who was it?

WILFRED: Oh—just somebody I know.

LILIAN: A girl, obviously. You're keeping her very dark, aren't you?

WILFRED: I don't know her very well, and, anyhow, she lives miles away, the other side of Martinbro. Never mind about her.

LILIAN : I'm not minding. But I suspect she's a barmaid and that's why you can get her on the telephone.

WILFRED: You know, Lilian, one thing puzzles me.

LILIAN: And if she's a barmaid, on the telephone, and the other side of Martinbro, she's probably at that big pub at the crossroads near Denly Dene—the "White Hart."

WILFRED (*angrily*): Will you listen?

LILIAN: Do you really like her, Wilfred? Or do you just think that being sweet on a barmaid is very manly and West African?

98

WILFRED: I'm trying to say something important.

LILIAN: Well, what is it?

WILFRED: You don't really want to know. You'll only laugh.

LILIAN: You've got to risk that. I mightn't. Tell me.

WILFRED (*hesitating*): It's difficult to explain. But I feel as if I'm being done in the eye.

LILIAN: You probably are.

WILFRED: You see, when I'm out there, in Africa, I think of Eden End here—home and you and Dad, and everything, and I long for leave, and when at last it comes—well, of course, it's ripping. But then when I've been here a week or two——

LILIAN: It all begins to look dull. Doesn't it?

WILFRED: Well, not quite as bad as that.

LILIAN: Yes it is. Don't sound so apologetic. I don't blame you.

WILFRED: Anyhow it isn't what I expected. And then I begin to think about Nigeria, and I begin to feel it won't be bad getting back there. But now I know that once I *am* back there I'll be longing to be on leave again, and this place will seem all different. I've got into a sort of life where I'm never in the right place at the right time.

LILIAN: Poor Wilfred. You were just like that when you were at school.

WILFRED: I know. And I thought it would be different when I left school and grew up. Perhaps it will, later on.

LILIAN: Perhaps it will. You've plenty of time.

WILFRED: Things can't stay like this. When I've more money I shall have more fun on leave. And it'll be more amusing out there when I'm promoted. It's Nineteen Twelve now. In three or four years time— say in Nineteen Sixteen, I may have a district of my own.

LILIAN: Could I come out and see you then?

WILFRED: You might. Depends where I'm sent.

LILIAN: You may be married before then.

WILFRED: I don't suppose so. Three or four years isn't really a long time. Hurry up, Nineteen Sixteen. Sounds a nice ripe sort of year, doesn't it?—Nineteen Sixteen.

> *From the door on left come three deliberate knocks. The two look at it sharply, rather startled—though they must avoid any nervous jump.* WILFRED *goes to the door and opens it.* SARAH *enters, carrying a large basket heaped with old clothes.*

SARAH (*breathlessly*): I didn't want to put this down to open the door because I'm not so good at stooping as I was—gives me palpitations—and I've been stooping enough.

LILIAN: What have you been doing?

SARAH: I've been up in the back garret, samming up these old clothes for the doctor. He wants to give 'em away. (*She comes forward as she says this and rests the basket on the table.*) Eh, and look what I found. (*Holds out an old fancy costume.*)

LILIAN: What is it?

SARAH: Don't you remember? It's very same dress Miss Stella wore that time she acted in the Town Hall at Martinbro, and they all clapped her so long, and she came back and told her poor mother she was going on the stage for a living, and we had such a do—all shouting and bawling and crying. Don't you remember it?

WILFRED: I do.

LILIAN: Yes, I do now.

SARAH: And I should think so. I helped her to make it, and right bonny she looked in it. But she never took it with her when she went, and it's been behind some boxes in the back garret. I fancy your mother threw it there. Moths has been at it a bit, but I'm thinking it'ud clean and mend.

LILIAN: What for? It's quite useless.

SARAH: How do you know? We might send it to her and she might be glad of it for her acting.

WILFRED (*laughing*): You're cracked, Sarah.

SARAH (*indignant*): What's there to laugh at, I'd like to know?

LILIAN: Nothing. Only, you see, we couldn't send it to Stella—even if it would be useful—because we don't know where she is.

SARAH: Isn't she out—you know—where's it? That big place?

WILFRED: Timbuctoo.

SARAH: Not Timbuctoo neither, you daft lad. It's where she said there was all eucalyptus.

LILIAN: It was Australia. But that was three years ago, and we haven't heard anything from her since.

SARAH: Is it three year since we heard last?

LILIAN: Yes. And she's been away more than eight years.

SARAH (*her face working as she fingers the costume*): I didn't think it was so long. I'm getting old and I forget. I'm dreaming half my time.

LILIAN (*looking at the costume*): I remember. It was pretty. I believe I was jealous because I hadn't one like it.

SARAH: Yes, you wor. You wor a jealous little madam in them days, let me tell you. See. I sewed them on myself for her. It was all a secret. She used to sneak in there (*pointing to door on right*) to try it on. It only seems yesterday. I mun sort these out.

WILFRED: Here, I'll take them.

> *Picks up basket, etc., and takes them into room on right.* SARAH *moves towards door, after him, carrying the costume.*

SARAH (*turning*): Your father's in. He called at Gregson's. (*The telephone bell rings. She looks at it mistrustfully.*) That wants answering now. Daft thing. Got to wait on a machine, that's what we're coming to. It'll never get me waiting on it, and it can ring its head off.

> *She goes into room on right.* LILIAN *goes to the telephone, but* DR. KIRBY *enters quickly and forestalls her. He is a pleasant homely man about sixty, wearing an old house coat over a dark professional suit. He attends to the telephone rather pompously and proudly.*

DR. KIRBY (*at telephone*): Hello, yes. Yes, Dr. Kirby here. Oh—is that you, William? . . . She's what? . . . Oh I see . . . Well, what do you expect? . . . No pains? . . . I see . . . Yes, keep her warm. And don't worry. Nothing new. It's all happened before. . . . That's right, let me know. And, William, just keep out of the Eden Moor Hotel for a night or two, will you? . . . That's it. You're not in the right state of mind to do yourself any good in the bar of the Eden Moor . . . (*chuckles*). All right. Don't worry. (*Puts down receiver and begins lighting his pipe.*) William Sugden worrying about his wife. She'll be all right. Stronger than he is. Now it just shows you, Lilian, how useful a telephone is here. That little chat across the wires has saved William or me a useless journey. Pity we hadn't it here years ago. We're too old-fashioned round here. Out of date.

LILIAN: You don't think you're out of date, do you?

DR. KIRBY: Me? Years out of date. I've just been trying to understand what some of these young fellows are writing now in the medical journals. Too clever for me. Too Nineteen Twelve altogether. But I could probably give 'em points when it comes to dealing with William Sugden and his wife. (*As* WILFRED *enters from room on right.*) Hello, Wilfred, what have you been doing in there?

WILFRED: Helping Sarah to sort out some old clothes for you.

DR. KIRBY: Good. They can do with some of them down in the village. Lloyd George is going to give 'em ninepence for fourpence soon, with me thrown in, but in the meantime we'll give them some old clothes to be going on with.

WILFRED: Would you like to hear my gramophone, Dad?

DR. KIRBY: No, thank you. I've got to get back to the surgery. But if I was staying I'd just as soon not hear your gramophone. I've got to listen to too many patients to want to hear mechanical music—if it is music. By the way, old Burton tells me they had a fire in the post office at Martinbro late last night. He said they think it's suffragettes. Lot of nonsense. They've got suffragettes on the brain, some of 'em. (*Goes to door on left*.)

WILFRED: Well, it might be, Dad.

DR. KIRBY (*turning at door*): What, at Martinbro! What would they be doing there? Looking for Mr. Asquith! All nonsense. And talking about nonsense, I forgot to tell you I've just been invited to dine at Grosvenor House with the Duke of Westminster.

LILIAN and WILFRED (*together*): Dad, you haven't?

DR. KIRBY: I have. And so has everybody else. The only condition is that we each pay a thousand pounds to Chamberlain's birthday fund for Tariff Reform. I'm not accepting. (*He goes out and* LILIAN *settles down to read again*.)

WILFRED (*restlessly*): We ought to have a billiard table here. If I got more chance to play, I believe I should be good at billiards. I made a break of twenty-seven when I played at the club at Akassa.

LILIAN (*staring at him, quietly*): Isn't it ridiculous that you should go to all these places while I have to stay here?

WILFRED: No, I don't see that.

LILIAN: But I used to be much more adventurous than you, and much keener on exploring and wild places. I'll bet I've read far more about Africa than you have.

WILFRED: What's that? Reading about it! I've been.

LILIAN: I believe I'd rather have gone with Captain Scott to the South Pole than done anything in the world. And if he lectures about it when he comes back I shall go, I don't care where it is.

WILFRED: Well, you can't be so jolly adventurous— as you call it—else you'd have cleared out. After all, Stella did.

LILIAN (*rather bitterly*): Yes, Stella did. And what happened then? Mother died. Father was left, miserable, with nobody to look after him. As soon as I'd done with school I'd obviously got to come back here and look after things. It's easy enough to do what Stella did—just to clear out and do what you want to do.

WILFRED: Yes, but she knew what she wanted to do.

LILIAN: Perhaps I did, too.

WILFRED: You know, that night I went to Daly's, I thought how queer it would be if I suddenly saw Stella come on the stage.

LILIAN (*with slight sardonic emphasis*): Very queer.

WILFRED: I always look at advertisements and programmes and bills to see if she's on. It's silly having a sister on the stage if you've never *seen* her on the stage. Wouldn't it be grand if she became a star—like Gertie Millar or Phyllis Dare?

LILIAN (*sardonically*): Yes. And if the British West African Company suddenly appointed you managing director. And if the king fell ill and they all said, " Send for Dr. Kirby of Eden End." And if Pierpoint Morgan or Rockefeller said " I must give Lilian Kirby a million pounds, she's been such a good girl."

WILFRED (*guffawing*): And if old Sarah won a prize for doing the Turkey Trot. And if Geoffrey Farrant— what do we do for Geoffrey?

LILIAN: Something with horses or dogs in it.

WILFRED: We'll let him win next year's Derby then. You're not very keen on horses and dogs, are you?

LILIAN (*coldly*): What's that got to do with it?

WILFRED (*grinning*): Nothing.

LILIAN: Don't be an oaf.

WILFRED: One of our chaps in Benin used to own two racehorses when he was in England. Awful nut. What about a good old row on the gramophone?

LILIAN: Must you?

WILFRED (*going over to gramophone*): Yes, I must. I shall take this back with me. (*Putting on record.*) You know, these things are getting awfully good.

Plays a tune. If lighting is changed, this is the time to change it. While the record is being played, WILFRED. *can light one lamp and* LILIAN *another. Before record is*

quite finished LILIAN, *who is nearer door on left, must
listen and hold up her hand.* WILFRED *takes off the
record. They hear a voice coming through the door. The
voice,* STELLA'S, *must be audible everywhere, but it does
not matter if actual words are not caught. Actually she
is saying "Yes, put it down there, please. What do I
pay you? There you are. Thank you."* STELLA *is
five or six years older than* LILIAN, *and looks her age,
but is extremely attractive. She is dressed as an actress,
hoping to be smart, would be dressed at that time, but
her clothes must not be really good or very new, so that it
is obvious to an acute feminine spectator that she is not
really flourishing. She plays at once in a higher key than
the rest of the family, and is obviously an actress as well
as a prodigal daughter. All her emotions are quite
sincere, but she cannot help being a little larger than life.
This gradually wears off during her stay until the scene
of her departure when there are glimpses of the actress
again.*

WILFRED: Stella!

STELLA: Oh it's Wilfred. All grown up. And a
moustache. (*Embraces and kisses him. Then looks at*
LILIAN.) And Lilian. All grown up, too. Here, let
me take this damned hat off. (*Hastily takes it off and
flings it aside, then rushes over to* LILIAN *and embraces and
kisses her.*) Lilian darling, you're not at all what I
expected you to look like, and yet you're completely
Lilian and just right. Isn't it odd? (*Looking round.*)
And everything just the same. Only smaller.

> SARAH *comes in and stands just inside, from door on
> right, staring at* STELLA *with puckered face.*

STELLA (*seeing her, and rushing over*): Why, Sarah. My precious, precious lovely old Sarah. (*Kisses her.*)

SARAH (*in tears*): Nay—I can't talk.

STELLA (*laughing and crying*): And I can't.

SARAH (*making an effort*): Eh—you haven't altered a bit, love.

STELLA: Oh, but I have. I'm old, Sarah—yes, old. I'll never see thirty again. My hair's turning grey.

SARAH: It isn't.

STELLA: Some of it is. I pulled three grey hairs out yesterday. Where's Dad? Is he—all right?

LILIAN: Yes. He's in the surgery.

WILFRED: Shall I tell him?

STELLA: No, don't disturb him. We'll give him a surprise. Is he just the same?

WILFRED: Of course.

STELLA: *Of course?* There isn't any *of course* about it. Oh Wilfred—that just shows how young you are, in spite of that moustache. People change. Everything changes. Does he still watch birds and collect eighteenth century engravings?

LILIAN: Yes. Dad hasn't changed at all.

STELLA: Thank God!

LILIAN: But why didn't you tell us you were coming?

STELLA: Oh—my dear—I couldn't. I didn't know. And I couldn't just write. I think I was afraid to. Either I had to stay away or come just like this, with a rush. Don't you understand?

LILIAN: Yes. You'd been away so long.

STELLA: So long. And to so many places.

WILFRED: Where have you been, Stella?

STELLA: Where haven't I been? All over England. Then out East. Then Australia—I wrote to you from there—

SARAH: Yes, you did, love.

STELLA: I was nearly dying of homesickness when I wrote that letter. You can't imagine what it's like.

WILFRED (*proudly*): I can. I'm in Nigeria now. Got a job with the British West African Development Company. I'm on leave.

STELLA (*smiling at him*): Africa and on leave. Wilfred, it's incredible. It seems only yesterday since you were a fat little schoolboy. I'm sorry but it does. I didn't really believe in that moustache. Somehow I thought of you just sticking it on for fun.

WILFRED: I'm twenty-four. I've been four years with the British West African.

STELLA: Isn't that wonderful? And then after Australia, I went to America. We travelled thousands of miles. I seem to have lived in railway trains—with cinders in my eye and a headache—for centuries. None of it real. Like a long stupid dream. And now I'm home. You don't know what it means.

SARAH: Aren't you famished, love? Can't I get you something?

STELLA: No, thank you. Not just now, Sarah. (*She looks about her.*) It's just as I remembered it, only so much smaller. All the time I've been away, it's been shrinking and shrinking. Like life. Oh—(*darting over*) there's the china castle. Still there. Not broken. All sorts of things can get broken—people can be broken— and yet a thing like this can go on and on. (*Holding it, looking at it.*) I remember how I used to wonder what was happening inside it. Tiny people all made of china.

WILFRED: You used to tell me stories about that castle.

STELLA: And look—the boy's still riding on his goat. What did we used to call him?

LILIAN: Llewellyn. Because he came from Wales.

STELLA: Yes. Dear, dear Llewellyn. His nice silly face has come popping up in dreams. I saw him distinctly once—oh, when was it?—on some long, awful train journey, hot and dusty. And there was Llewellyn riding his goat. (*Goes round touching things.*) And here's Coblentz. (*Looking at old colour print.*) The three soldiers talking. The man carrying the load. The woman with the red petticoat. And the two holding hands. Do you remember how we used to look at it for hours and wonder what was happening round the corner? But where's the other one, you know, Frankfort, with the river and the barges and the little fat woman?

WILFRED: Yes, where is Frankfort? I hadn't noticed it was gone.

SARAH: That's the picture that fell down, isn't it?

LILIAN: Yes, it was broken. About a year ago.

STELLA: Tell me about people. The Mowbrays and the Oldroyds and the Burtons—and everybody. Oh—

and my old admirer, Geoffrey Farrant. What's happened to him?

LILIAN: He's still here. His father died.

STELLA: Is he married? Do you ever see him?

LILIAN: He's not married.

WILFRED: And we often see him. He's a great pal of Lilian's now.

LILIAN: Where are your things?

STELLA: My trunk? It's in the hall. I got a trap from the station, but I didn't know the man who brought me. I didn't recognise anybody at the station either. But Eden Moor and Eden End looked just the same. And, coming up, there was a lovely deep rich autumn smell—smoke and dead leaves and the moors all mixed up—and I was absolutely drowned in it and I didn't seem to have been away at all. Millions of smells, mostly beastly, that I've smelt these last eight or nine years were completely washed out. Nothing had really happened. I might have only been in to Martinbro for the day. You were still at school, Wilfred. You'd only just left, Lilian, and you'd still two long plaits. And Dad and Mother—— (*she breaks off, hesitates, then in a low voice*) Was it awful, Lilian—about Mother?

LILIAN (*quietly*): Yes, for a time. But it's six years ago, you know. She wasn't ill very long, but she'd a lot of pain. It was Dad I was sorry for. (STELLA *begins to cry quietly*.)

SARAH (*going to her*): Miss Stella—love.

STELLA (*through her tears*): Such a silly thing happened in the train. A man sitting opposite me—he looked

like WINSTON CHURCHILL, only fatter—carefully unpacked
a lot of sandwiches on the seat, stood up for something,
and then suddenly sat down on the sandwiches.   There
was another woman in the carriage, and we suddenly
laughed and laughed, and then the man laughed too.
They were very eggy sandwiches.   Why are some things
so silly?

WILFRED: Do you remember the time when a little
man with a very funny face—what was his name?—
Flockton—he'd known Dad at college—and we started
giggling and then had to go outside in turns to laugh?

STELLA: Yes, Mr. Flockton.   And it was much worse
for me because I was so much older and I had to be
polite.   And then the time when poor Aunt Mary
brought that new bun flour?

WILFRED: Yes, and the time when the young man
called Egg-something came to see you and dropped the
tea tray?

LILIAN: And the time when we all went to the
Mowbrays for a party on the wrong day?

STELLA: And the snow was so thick we had to stay
and they were so cross, and we were so cross, and all
the chimneys smoked.   (*Laughs.*)

WILFRED (*laughing*): And I broke a huge ornament
and put the pieces in the coal scuttle.

STELLA: I was thinking about all those things coming
up in the train.   And I've got millions of questions to
ask.

WILFRED: So have we, haven't we, Lilian?

LILIAN: I suppose you'd like your old room,
wouldn't you?

STELLA: I'd love it if it's free.

LILIAN: It's full of odds and ends at the moment——

SARAH (*eagerly*): I'll get it ready, Miss Lilian.

LILIAN: No, I'll do it. Wilfred can give me a hand. There may be some furniture to move.

WILFRED: Rather.

STELLA: Can't I do anything?

LILIAN: No. You're tired. Besides you don't know where things are now. And Dad will be in in a minute. You wait here. (*She goes out.*)

WILFRED: You know, Stella, when you were home I was only a kid and didn't bother about the theatre, but now I'm very keen. I saw "Gipsy Love" at Daly's a few weeks ago—and you've got to tell me all about it.

STELLA: All right. I'll tell you miles and miles of it.

> SARAH *goes into room on right.*

WILFRED: Good. I expect you've done jolly well, haven't you? I was telling Lilian only this afternoon how I always looked out for your name, but never saw it.

STELLA: I've been out of England so much, you see.

WILFRED: Yes, that accounts for it. Well, you're looking an awful swell.

STELLA: I should have thought I was looking like nothing on earth.

WILFRED: I expect you've had a marvellous time, haven't you?

STELLA: Well—mixed, you know.

WILFRED: You'll find it pretty dull here.

STELLA: I shan't. (*Draws a long breath.*) It's heavenly. Even though you have been in Africa and come on leave you can't imagine what it means to me to be back again—home. It's real. Everything's real again.

> SARAH *re-enters, carrying dress behind her back.*

WILFRED: I'm going to give Lilian a hand with your room. Then I'll come down and ask you thousands of questions. (*Hesitates.*) I say, you don't think this moustache looks silly, do you?

STELLA: Wilfred, it's a *grand* moustache, and you look a real African adventurer with it. It's tremendously exciting to be a sister to such a moustache. In a year or two it's going to be a terrific heart-breaker.

WILFRED (*smiling*): You're pulling my leg. You always did, you know.

STELLA: Well, isn't it nice that I'm starting all over again?

WILFRED (*shyly*): Yes. (*Smiles.*) Good old Stella! (*Goes out.*)

> STELLA *looks after him and smiles. Then she turns and sees* SARAH.

STELLA: I think Wilfred's grown up to be a very nice young man. Don't you?

SARAH: Oh—Master Wilfred's all right. But he's only a bit of a lad, for all his big talk. Miss Lilian's different. She's properly grown up. Always was a bit old-fashioned. Never gave herself away. And there's

times now when—dang me!—you'd think she wor
fifty—to hear her talk. Not that she talks much.

STELLA: I don't suppose poor Lilian's had a very
easy life all these years I've been away. She's a bit—
queer. Sort of sunk into herself. On her guard, somehow. Almost as if I were a stranger. Perhaps I am a
stranger, Sarah. But I don't seem like one to myself—
only Stella Kirby, back home again in Eden End.

SARAH: And look what I found—not an hour since
—it might ha' been waiting for you to come home.
Look. (*Holds out fancy costume.*)

STELLA: Why it's the one I wore, ages ago, in that
show at the Town Hall at Martinbro. The one you and
I made, Sarah.

SARAH: I know it is. I was going to clean and mend
it. Moths has been at it.

STELLA: The moths have been at us all, Sarah
darling. But I never thought I'd see this costume
again. The excitement there was here about it! Do
you remember?

SARAH: I should think I do.

STELLA: I thought I was a real actress the night I
put this on.

SARAH: Well they clapped you enough.

STELLA: More than some people have clapped me
since. That was the night. Look at it. Pathetic!

SARAH: Why, I see nowt wrong wi' it, except where
moths has been. It's a right bonny dress. I thowt so
then and I think so now.

STELLA: So do I. It's a lovely dress. I must put it on. Oh, I've torn it! The belle and leading juvenile of the Martinbro Amateur Dramatic Society. And fat old Mr. Burton gave me a box of chocolates, do you remember?

SARAH: Ay, and he'd have given a lot more besides chocolates if you'd let him, that chap would. I've heard tales of him since.

STELLA *poses and curtsies before* SARAH.

SARAH: Eh, I'm thankful to have seen this day, love. I've prayed to be spared to see you come home.

STELLA: I'm sorry I have been so long.

SARAH: You didn't forget me?

STELLA: Never, never, never. All over the world, in the oddest places, I've thought about you, longed to see you again. You needn't pray any more. I've come home. (*Kisses her.*)

SARAH (*looking hard at her*): You've always been a bonny piece. You wor a grand baby, and a fine little lass, and a bonny young woman when you grew up.

STELLA: Bless you for those kind words.

SARAH: But there's lines in that face that weren't there when I last saw it.

STELLA: I'm getting on. And all those years I was away haven't been easy.

SARAH: No, that's it. I can see as much. You've had your troubles, haven't you? (*When* STELLA *does not reply.*) Nay, you can tell me even if you never tell another soul. I'll say nowt.

STELLA: Yes. I've had my troubles.

116

SARAH: Disappointments?

STELLA: Yes. A fair share.

SARAH (*gently*): Didn't they treat you well on the stage, love?

STELLA: Nearly as well as I deserved, I suppose. But —and this is our secret, Sarah—I wasn't the great actress I thought I was going to be. I wasn't bad. I'm not bad. But somehow I've never been able to do what I thought I could do. Something gets in the way. I feel it all inside, but it doesn't come out right. I've disappointed myself. I think even mother would have been sorry for me if she'd known. I don't say I've had wonderful chances, but I have had chances. And somehow I've missed them. Perhaps I came nearer to being a really good actress the night I wore this pathetic thing than I've ever done since. It's all gone wrong, Sarah, my dear. My work, my life. Oh—(*tears off the dress*)—I'm a dismal failure. (*Breaking down.*)

SARAH: Don't worry, love, don't worry. There's plenty of time. You're young.

STELLA: No, I'm not.

SARAH: I think I hear the doctor.

STELLA (*springing up, alarmed*): Dad mustn't see me like this. (*Begins doing her face.*) And he mustn't know.

SARAH (*fussing over her*): He won't from me. Nobody will. I'll see if he's there.

> *She goes to door on left.* STELLA *hastily concludes her powdering and begins to look brighter.* SARAH *goes out, leaving the door open, and* DR. KIRBY *comes to the doorway and stands amazed.*

DR. KIRBY: Is it Stella?

STELLA: Yes, Father. (*Then, with a little cry, she runs over to him, and he meets her at the bottom of the steps and they kiss and hug one another.*)

STELLA: You're just the same, Dad. Only a little greyer, that's all.

DR. KIRBY: No, I'm a lot older. And you're older too, you know. I'm not going to flatter you even if you are a famous actress. You look a bit tired. But then I expect you are after your journey. Where did you come from?

STELLA: London. I caught the eleven o'clock to Martinbro.

DR. KIRBY: Ah, yes—the good old eleven o'clock. Why didn't you let us know? We'd have had the fatted calf ready for you.

STELLA: I couldn't. I came—oh—it was a sudden impulse. I'm still impulsive, you know.

DR. KIRBY: We thought you'd forgotten us.

STELLA: I've never forgotten you for a single moment. How could I? But I've been out of England for years—touring, working hard. My plans always seemed so confused. It was difficult to write.

DR. KIRBY: Yes, I can understand that, though in a quiet corner like this, we're apt to forget what the hustling and bustling world—*your* world—is like. You know, Stella, I've been thinking a lot just lately—(*his voice trails away*).

STELLA (*after a pause*): Yes, Father?

DR. KIRBY: Something happened that made me start thinking. You might call it taking stock. Thinking about life—my life—your life. You know, I've come to the conclusion that you were right, and your mother and I were wrong.

STELLA (*hastily, painfully*): No, no——

DR. KIRBY: That's all right. It's all old history now. We can talk frankly and freely now. And you're a grown-up woman, not a bit of a girl. You were right to do what you did. I'm not saying that you didn't cause any pain——

STELLA: I did, I know.

DR KIRBY: But that wasn't your fault. That's life. Life can't move on without inflicting pain. We can't come into this world without somebody being hurt. As well I know. I shall be lucky if I don't see a bit more of it late to-night. The great cosmic processes have a habit of reaching a climax round here just when I've got comfortably off to sleep.

STELLA: Poor Dad. Who is it this time?

DR. KIRBY: A Mrs. Sugden. I think she's since your time. Well, I think I've done my duty by her and her like in this neighbourhood for nearly forty years.

STELLA: I know you have. And I'm sure they still worship you.

DR. KIRBY: Not they. I only wish they'd pay a bit more attention and then pay a few more bills. But I'm not complaining. I've had a good life here. Your mother and I were happy. We'd all the friends we wanted. This has been a real home. Even to you, it was once.

119

STELLA (*softly*): Do you think I could forget it.

DR. KIRBY: And then, besides my work and my family, I'd my little hobbies—my birds. (*With sudden animation.*) And by the way, don't let anybody tell you that you can't see a needle-tailed swift in this country, because I saw one myself, only this last summer. A needle-tailed swift. No mistake about it.

STELLA (*affectionately, laughing*): Oh—Dad—I won't let anybody tell me. I'll put them in their place at once.

DR. KIRBY: That's right. There's as much clap-trap talked about birds now as there is about anything else. Why, only the other day——

STELLA (*laughing*): But Dad, you can't go on about birds now. You were just going to tell me something important, something serious.

DR. KIRBY (*with a twinkle*): Well this is important.

STELLA: Yes, and I'd love to hear it, but that will do any time. Perhaps this other thing won't.

DR. KIRBY (*seriously*): That's true. This is something I wouldn't say to the younger children. What I was going to say was this. Looking back on my life, it's been a reasonably good one——

STELLA: And you wouldn't change it.

DR. KIRBY: That's where you're wrong. I would.

STELLA (*surprised*): Dad!

DR. KIRBY: There was a time when I had to make a choice.

STELLA: Between this—and another kind of life?

DR. KIRBY: Yes. I wasn't always a plodding old G.P., you know, years behind the times. Once, I was thought to be a very clever young man. I had a brilliant career as a student. Then I had to make a choice, between settling down here, quietly and comfortably, or taking a risk in London. I might have failed there. On the other hand, I might have been successful. Men who walked the hospitals when I did, men who hadn't the reputation I had, have been very successful. Some of them—I could give you their names—have been knighted and so forth, are now rich and famous.

STELLA: Pooh!—what's that!

DR. KIRBY: Mere vulgar rewards, if you like.

STELLA: In Harley Street you'd never have seen a bird—except a dirty London sparrow.

DR. KIRBY: I'm not envying them, Stella. Nevertheless, they've had brilliant careers, done original work, met all the great personalities of their time, missed none of the prizes of life.

STELLA: How do you know? They've missed the larks on Eden Moor.

DR. KIRBY: The larks and the moors are there if they want them, and they've probably more leisure now to enjoy such things than I have. And in addition, they've had all the rest. They've lived as I haven't lived, and as you—I'm glad to say—*are* living. You were right, Stella, to cut and run when you did. And now, looking back when it's all nearly ended——

STELLA (*sharply*): Don't talk like that, Father. You're not old yet.

DR. KIRBY (*firmly*): I say, looking back when it's all nearly ended, I wish now that I'd had the same sort of courage.

STELLA: It's not courage.

DR. KIRBY: I won't envy my—er—distinguished colleagues. But I can envy you, my dear. And I do. You made a bolt for the main road. You're doing what you always wanted to do, and you've made a success of it, gone all over the world, been applauded and admired everywhere, given pleasure to thousands and thousands——

STELLA (*jumping up, in distress*): Oh—Dad—please, please stop.

DR. KIRBY (*astonished*): What's the matter? I never knew actresses suffered from such modesty.

STELLA (*trying to take hold of herself*): It isn't that.

DR. KIRBY: What is it then?

STELLA: Oh—I don't know. Perhaps it's hearing *you* say these things.

DR. KIRBY: Don't try to be kind to me. It's the truth, and you know it.

STELLA (*bursting out*): It's—— (*Checks herself.*) Well, I suppose it's embarrassing.

DR. KIRBY: I can talk to you properly. I see you now as a grown-up person.

STELLA (*with irony*): Thank you, Dad.

DR. KIRBY: Ah well—it's not easy for a parent. I suppose I ought to see Lilian and Wilfred as grown-up people now, too, but I can't. Not only because they're younger than you, but because there hasn't been the same break. I ought to be frank with them, but it's difficult.

STELLA (*gravely*): You can be frank with me, then?

DR. KIRBY: Yes. I find it quite easy.

STELLA (*after an effort*): Then—then why did you talk about "looking back when it's all nearly ended"? You're not really old, you know.

DR. KIRBY: I'm not young.

STELLA (*relieved*): Oh—is that all?

DR. KIRBY: No, I'm afraid it isn't. There's something I can tell you that I can't tell the other two. You can stand it. They can't. You're older. You have your profession. You're enjoying life. You've really done with us. So you can stand it.

      STELLA *laughs bitterly*.

DR. KIRBY: What does that mean?

STELLA: Nothing. Go on. I can stand it. (*Suddenly alert, alarmed.*)   Dad—does this mean that there's something wrong with you—that you're ill?

DR. KIRBY: Take it easy, Stella. I'm afraid it does. (*Smiling.*) One advantage of being in my profession is that you get to know what's happening inside you. I've got a bad heart. I had a very nasty bout of influenza a few years ago, and I did a very silly thing, the sort of thing I've warned hundreds of people against doing. I got up and started work again far too early. So I landed myself with a bad heart.

STELLA: But—what's wrong with it?

DR. KIRBY (*easily*): A lot of things. It's worse than my old bike. But you might describe the trouble—

123

K

shortly—as a valvular lesion with inefficient compensation. Oh—I do what I can about it, of course. I don't work as hard as I used to do, though it's not easy to rest here. And I give myself digitalis—and other things. I get along—but——

STELLA: It's serious—then?

DR. KIRBY (*smiling*): No joke at all. In fact—I'm very glad you've come to see us now.

STELLA (*very distressed*): Dad!

DR. KIRBY: Easy, Stella. It seems a shabby trick landing you with this the minute you arrive, but I think you might have noticed something. And I'm telling you quite frankly so that you won't discuss it with Lilian and Wilfred. It's our little secret. Not much of one—but there you are.

STELLA: I shan't say anything.

DR. KIRBY: That's right. They haven't settled down to their lives yet as you have to yours. In fact, I'm sometimes a bit worried about Lilian. I'm not grumbling about myself. I've had a good run. I'd like to live long enough to see this country settling down a bit better.

STELLA: Oh—bother the country, I don't care about that. It's you.

DR. KIRBY: Yes, but this has been a very unsettling, worrying year so far. Two big strikes. Ulster arming for rebellion. Young women being forcibly fed in gaol. This health insurance business. Everybody wanting to rush about at thirty and forty miles an hour, up in the air as well as on the roads. Not much sunset calm

about things.   But in a year or two we may have settled
down again.   I like to think so.

STELLA (*in low voice*): I hope so—for your sake.

DR. KIRBY (*briskly*): Ah well—that's enough about
me.   Dismal stuff.   I've got to hear about all your
triumphs.   Been all over the place, haven't you?

STELLA (*with forced animation*): Yes, all over.   Like a
crazy parcel.

DR. KIRBY: And enjoyed it, eh?   Constant change,
excitement, applause, eh?   But don't let it spoil you.

STELLA (*with little ironic smile*): I'll do my best, Dad.
Unless I'm spoilt already.

DR. KIRBY: No sign of it.   I was against you leaving
home and going on the stage, but chiefly, I think, for
your mother's sake.   I believe it does girls good to go
out into the world.

STELLA: Sometimes.

DR. KIRBY (*lowering voice*): I've never said anything
to her—and of course I've been glad to have her here—
but I've often thought that Lilian's been at home too
long.   She might have done a lot better for herself if
she'd followed your example and found something she
wanted to do away from home.   Don't tell her that.

STELLA: I won't.   But probably she stayed on
simply because I went.   For your sake.

DR. KIRBY (*heartily*): Oh no, I don't think so.   I
never asked her to stay.   She likes being at home.   A
lot of girls do, of course.   Quite natural.   (*Looks at
his watch.*)   Must be nearly supper time.   Where's
Lilian?   (*Goes to door on left.*)

STELLA: I ought to be doing something.

DR. KIRBY: Nonsense. You're a guest. The work here's easy, and we've plenty to do it. Lilian and old Sarah—and a woman from the village comes in every day. (LILIAN *enters*.) Ah, Lilian, I was just wondering about supper. Stella must be hungry.

LILIAN: It'll be ready in about ten minutes.

DR. KIRBY: Good. (*Goes out, closing door behind him,* LILIAN *advancing into the room*.)

LILIAN: Your room's ready now, if you want to go up. And Wilfred's taken your trunk upstairs.

STELLA: Thanks, Lilian. I suppose I ought to go up. I'm probably filthy, but I've been too excited to care.

LILIAN: You look all right.

STELLA: We old travellers know all sorts of dodges. (*Stares at* LILIAN.)

LILIAN: What's the matter?

STELLA: You know—you're different.

LILIAN: Naturally. It's such a long time since you saw me last.

STELLA: Are you happy?

LILIAN (*rather impatiently*): I don't know. Isn't that —rather a silly question?

STELLA: Is it?

LILIAN: I think so. I mean, one isn't always asking oneself about happiness.

STELLA: I am.

LILIAN: Yes, you. You always were.

126

STELLA: And whether you ask or not, after all, you always know whether you're happy or not.

LILIAN: Most of the time one isn't either happy or unhappy.

STELLA: Like you—now?

LILIAN: Like me—now.

STELLA (*going over to her*): But there's something about you I don't understand.

LILIAN: Well, why bother?

STELLA (*taking her hands*): But, my dear, I want to bother.   You talk as if we were strangers.

LILIAN: Aren't we?   We haven't set eyes on one another for years.

STELLA: Yes, but I've been thinking about you all the time.

LILIAN: Even if you have, that's not enough.   I'd only just left school when you went away.   I'm quite different.

STELLA: I see that.

LILIAN (*looking down at* STELLA's *left hand*): We'll get to know one another again—perhaps.   But don't force it.

STELLA (*trying to smile*): And that's not meant for a snub, I hope?

LILIAN (*gravely*): No.   Tell me something.

STELLA (*lightly*): Anything.

LILIAN (*in low voice*): You're married, aren't you?

STELLA (*startled, but in low voice*): Yes.   How did you know?

LILIAN: I saw the mark of the ring. (STELLA *stares at her left hand and rubs the ring finger.*)

STELLA (*troubled*): I'd probably have told you all—later. But please don't say anything—yet.

LILIAN: What happened?

STELLA: I married three years ago—in Australia. He was an actor, in the same company. After the first year it didn't work—very well. We've separated now.

LILIAN: Where is he?

STELLA: A week ago I couldn't have told you. We separated in America. But three days ago I called at my agent's in town—and I saw him there. We have the same agent. It was queer.

LILIAN: What's his name?

STELLA: Charles Appleby. He's not famous or anything. Just a goodish actor. Very nice family. And he can be quite charming—at times. We were very happy together for a little while.

LILIAN: And now you're separated.

STELLA (*with a pitiful smile*): Yes. All bust up. Yet I'm not really Stella Kirby any more, but Mrs. Charles Appleby, not living with her husband.

LILIAN: Is there going to be a divorce?

STELLA: I don't know. (*There is a ring heard through door on left.*) It's all a muddle. Let's stop talking about it. And please, Lilian, don't say anything. We'll talk afterwards, if you like.

> *Voices heard outside door on left.* STELLA *and* LILIAN *look towards it, the latter expectantly.* WILFRED *enters, followed by* GEOFFREY FARRANT *and*

DR. KIRBY. FARRANT *is a fair brown-faced man in his late thirties, dressed in tweeds. There is still something of the regular officer in his appearance. He walks with a slight limp.*

WILFRED: Stella, look who's here. Miss Kirby, this is Captain Farrant.

STELLA (*with animation*): Geoffrey! (*Holding out her hand.*)

FARRANT: Stella! (*Shaking hands.*) This *is* a surprise. (*Turning, offhandedly.*) Hello, Lilian.

STELLA: You've hardly changed at all, Geoffrey. How have you managed it?

FARRANT (*pleased and shy*): Oh—I don't know—quiet life—plenty of exercise, riding—that sort of thing. (*Looking at her, smilingly.*) You've not changed much yourself, you know.

STELLA: Not much! I suppose that really means I'm looking a hag?

FARRANT: Of course it doesn't.   Anything but——. Matter of fact, you're looking prettier than ever. Isn't she, Dr. Kirby?

STELLA: Well, it's terribly nice seeing you again, Geoffrey. And so soon, too. I'd hardly hoped for that. And still living at the old place, too.

FARRANT: Yes, still at the old place.   It's mine now, you know.

STELLA: Do you remember the birthday party you had, just after your leg got better, and we let that enormous pig loose from the farm?

FARRANT (*laughing*): Good lord, yes. Do you remember that?

STELLA: Of course I do. I remember everything. And that time when old Birtley got so drunk when the beagles were meeting at your house?

WILFRED: By jove, I remember that.

FARRANT: I should think you do. So do I. Poor old Birtley. I say, Stella, we *have* got something to talk about. It's going to take us days——

LILIAN (*cutting in*): Supper will be ready in a few minutes. I'll ask Sarah to tell you. (*Moving to door on left*.)

DR. KIRBY: Why, where are *you* going, Lilian?

LILIAN (*shortly*): I'm going to bed. I don't want any supper. I've got a headache. Good-night. (*Goes out quickly*.)

FARRANT (*after a pause*): Oh I say—poor old Lilian.

DR. KIRBY: Didn't know she wasn't feeling well.

WILFRED (*carelessly*): She'll be all right. Just one of her moods. She's very queer sometimes. Best to leave her alone.

FARRANT: Excitement, perhaps. Stella coming back, eh?

WILFRED: I say, Stella, did you see "Gipsy Love" at Daly's? I did. Been trying to play bits ever since. (*Going to piano*.) I've got the music of some of the new musical comedies. (*Holds up sheets*.) You're just the person I wanted. Come and play some of them.

STELLA: What now?

WILFRED: Why not? Just a minute or two.

FARRANT: Go on, Stella. Fine to see you at the piano again. (*With mock air of gallantry, leads her over to the piano.*)

STELLA (*laughing*): All right. (*Sits down.*)
WILFRED: Try this one.

> STELLA *begins playing a popular waltz number, with* WILFRED *standing by the piano and* FARRANT *looking on admiringly, and* DR. KIRBY, *seated, beating time. As she gets into the swing of the waltz she begins singing.* SARAH *opens door on left, and stands in doorway, smiling. Slow curtain as the music goes on.*

END OF ACT ONE

ACT II

Same as ACT I. *Afternoon four days later.*

WILFRED *is discovered. He is very uneasy. He approaches the telephone, hesitates, listens, then goes to door on left, looks to see if anybody is about, closes the door and comes back to telephone, reaches out as if to take off the receiver, and then hesitates again. Finally he comes away from it and picks up a copy of " Punch " that is lying on the table. Then the telephone bell rings. He dashes off to the telephone, obviously in high hopes.*

WILFRED (*at telephone, eagerly*): Yes? Yes? Hello. Yes? (*Is obviously disappointed.*) Oh—Dr. Philips. No, Dad—Dr. Kirby—isn't back yet. Yes, I'll see him, I expect. . . . Yes, in a few minutes. . . . At your house—Monday afternoon, three o'clock. I'll tell him. Good-bye.

> *As he leaves the telephone,* SARAH *enters from right.*

SARAH: It'll be teeming down afore so long.

WILFRED (*gloomily*): Well, let it.

SARAH: Did Miss Stella take her mackintosh?

WILFRED: I don't know. I expect so.

SARAH: She'll want it.

WILFRED: You ought to see it rain in Africa.

SARAH: Does it rain there an' all?

132

WILFRED: Of course it does.

SARAH: Well I remember young Greenhead—the butcher's lad who went out to fight Kruger—telling me it never rained at all. All dry and dusty, he said it was. Never a drop o' water.

WILFRED: That's a different part of Africa. That's South Africa.

SARAH: Where are you then?

WILFRED: West Africa. Two thousand miles away. Quite different. Very hot and wet. Millions of blacks.

SARAH: Eh, fancy! And it only seems a week since you wor a little lad.

WILFRED: It's years since. And anyhow what's that got to do with it, Sarah, you old chump?

SARAH: A lot more nor you think. But then, lads has no sense. And they don't get ower-loaded with it when they stop being lads. You can't stir up in the doctor's room for daft old birds' eggs.

WILFRED (*accusingly*): Sarah, you've broken some more.

SARAH: Only two. You can't move for 'em, and if you so much as look at 'em, they break.

WILFRED: You've gone and broken the only two specimens of the egg of the Great Spotted Gofoozle we have in the country.

SARAH: How do you know? You didn't see 'em.

WILFRED: I shall tell him.

SARAH: Master Wilfred, if you do that—— But you wouldn't, would you? You see, if you say nowt,

133

he never misses 'em, for he's more eggs nor he knows what to do with. So long as he thinks they're all there, he's contented.

WILFRED: You're a wicked old woman.

SARAH: If you start telling on me, I'll tell on you.

WILFRED: Blackmail, that is. Besides, you've nothing to tell.

SARAH: What about them three cigars I saw you take?

WILFRED (*laughs*): Three cigars? Why, that's ages ago. At least seven years. Dad wouldn't care now. (*Listens.*) I think he's here, isn't he?

SARAH: Yes. I heard him. (*Going to door left.*) Nobody can say I'm hard o' hearing. I can still hear a lot better nor some of you. I'll ask him if he wants owt.

    She goes out. WILFRED *settles down with the "Punch."* DR. KIRBY *comes in, wearing an overcoat.*

DR. KIRBY: Hello, Wilfred, any messages for me?

WILFRED: Yes. Dr. Philips of Martinbro just rang up to say that there'd be a meeting at his house next Monday afternoon at three.

DR. KIRBY: Next Monday at three? Well, I've no doubt some of us will be there, if our patients will let us.

WILFRED: What's it about? Health Insurance?

DR. KIRBY: Yes. Where are the girls this afternoon?

WILFRED: Geoffrey Farrant called for Stella, and they've gone out for a walk. And Lilian went out somewhere, I don't know where, about quarter of an hour ago. And I'm here, looking at "Punch."

DR. KIRBY: So I see. Good number?

WILFRED: Not so far. I don't see the point of some of these jokes. (*Turning pages.*) This for instance. (*Reads.*) Candid Friend (to M.F.H.): "I don't think much of your cubhunters, Jack." M.F.H.: "They're very useful horses; you see, we can either ride 'em or eat 'em." What's the point of that?

DR. KIRBY: No idea. I'll have to look at the drawing.

WILFRED (*turning pages*): And here's another. Officer (visiting outpost): "If you saw one of the enemy, what would you do?" Sentry: "I calls 'im to 'alt." Officer: "Suppose he won't halt?" Sentry (with relish): "I takes and 'unts 'im wiv me bayonnit." I don't think that's very funny.

DR. KIRBY: It wouldn't be very funny for the enemy. I saw some photographs of bayonet wounds once.

WILFRED: My hat, no. I shouldn't like anybody after me with a bayonet.

DR. KIRBY: Well, I shouldn't worry. It isn't very likely that anybody will be. The world's got a lot more sense than it's given credit for in the newspapers. And it's got science now to help it.

WILFRED: Dad, are you sorry I didn't go in for something scientific? That I'm not a doctor, for instance?

DR. KIRBY: Not if you're happy as you are.

WILFRED: Well, I don't know that I'm *happy*.

DR. KIRBY (*hastily*): I didn't mean that. Silly word. Reasonably contented, let us say.

WILFRED: Well it's not bad, you know.

DR. KIRBY: After all, you're seeing the world. More than I've ever done.

WILFRED (*hesitantly*): Yes. Only I don't seem to belong anywhere. I don't seem to belong to this place any more, and yet I can't really fit in with West Africa—nobody could.

DR. KIRBY: Well, that shouldn't bother you at your age. And after all, you've plenty of time. Years and years and years.

WILFRED (*hopefully*): Yes, that's true. Do you often wonder what you'll be like in ten years' time?

DR. KIRBY (*drily*): Not often, no.

WILFRED: No, of course, naturally you wouldn't.

DR. KIRBY (*grimly amused*): Oh? Why?

WILFRED: Well, being older—you're completely settled, aren't you? You've always been here and——

DR. KIRBY: And I always will be, eh? You talk as if I wasn't so much perishable human stuff, just like yourself, but the Cow Rock up there on Eden moorside. I suppose that's how I seem. I was here, all complete, when you arrived, and I'll simply go on and on. That's the result of being a parent. You're an institution not a human being.

WILFRED: I wouldn't mind if I was a bit more of an institution, Dad. Everything seems to slide away from me all the time. And I never seem to be in the right place.

DR. KIRBY (*briskly*): Partly liver, and partly boredom. You ought to be having a sharp walk now. (*Moving to door left.*) By the way, now that Stella's here—and looks like stopping a few weeks—I think we might entertain a bit more, don't you?

WILFRED: Good idea. If you can find anybody worth entertaining.

DR. KIRBY: Shouldn't be impossible. Just think of some people—young people, the sort Stella would like —we could have. (SARAH *appears at door on left.*) What is it, Sarah? Do you want me?

SARAH (*handing him note*): That little lad o' Mrs. Hepple's brought it.

DR. KIRBY (*glancing at it*): All right. I'll call. Back in about an hour or so, Wilfred, if anybody wants me.

He goes out, SARAH *standing aside to let him pass. Then* SARAH *comes in, closing door behind her.*

SARAH (*after waiting a moment*): Now I'll tell you what it is——

WILFRED (*picking up " Punch "*): Oh shut up, Sarah. I want to read.

SARAH (*offended*): That's a nice way to talk, isn't it?

WILFRED: No. But I want to be quiet.

SARAH (*moving slowly to door right*): I've seen the time when you'd have got a good slap from me for answering back like that. But now you're a big lad and I'm an old woman. Yes, and I know what you're telling yourself—a silly old woman. Well, old I may be, but I'm not so silly as some folk think——

WILFRED (*deliberately*): I want to read.

SARAH (*a parting shot*): And a lot o' good it'll do you.

She goes out, closing door behind her. WILFRED *looks up, looking at both doors, then gets up. He is rather indecisive. He moves over to the telephone, takes a little book from his pocket rather as if to make doubly*

sure of the telephone number he wants, than to find it for
the first time, then stretches out a hand for the instru-
ment, hesitates and listens, is relieved at hearing nothing,
then puts his hand on the receiver again.   SARAH opens
the door on right.

SARAH (*with malicious triumph*): I thought you wanted
to read.

WILFRED (*withdrawing from receiver, startled and angry,*
shouts): What's it got to do with you what I want to do?

SARAH: That's not reading, playing about with that
thing.

WILFRED (*not so loud*): That's my business.

SARAH: You've been wanting to get at it on the
quiet, half the day. I've seen you. And not for the first
time neither. And if you'd any sense you'd let it alone.

WILFRED: You don't know what you're talking
about.

SARAH: Oh yes—I do. It may be all right for the
doctor—folk being poorly and in a hurry—but no
good'll come to you, talking down that thing. If it's
worth saying, it's worth saying properly, instead o'
gabbling into a daft machine. And if you thought
anything o' the lass——

WILFRED (*sulkily*): How do you know it is a lass—
as you call it?

SARAH: You wouldn't be making such a palaver if
it worn't a lass. And she can't be up to so much when
you've got to keep so quiet about her. Leave her alone,
I say, and that telly-machine with her.

WILFRED: Oh—rats! And there's somebody coming now. You *are* a nuisance, Sarah.

SARAH: It'll be Miss Lilian.

They look towards door left. It is opened by CHARLES APPLEBY, *who comes in, quite at ease. He is a man about forty, probably wearing rather loud Harris tweeds, very much the actor in the country. At this moment he is also wearing a very large ulster, which is spotted with rain. There are signs that he drinks too much. The evidence of breeding and charm is still there, but it is doubtful how much longer it will be there.*

CHARLES (*smiling*): Beginning to rain. What a lot of rain we've had this autumn, haven't we?

WILFRED (*gaping at him*): Yes.

SARAH: Have you come to see Dr. Kirby?

CHARLES (*enjoying himself*): Not particularly. Now I'm not quite sure about you. But (*to* SARAH) I know who you are. You're Sarah.

SARAH: Well, what if I am?

CHARLES: Recognised you at once, you see. Heard a lot about you.

SARAH: Well, I've never set eyes on you before, young man.

CHARLES (*to* WILFRED): Not quite sure about you. Can't place you. But perhaps you're not one of the family here.

WILFRED: Yes I am. I'm Wilfred Kirby.

CHARLES (*smiling*): Of course. Well, I'm one of the family, too.

SARAH: That you're not.

139

L

CHARLES: Sorry, but I am. I'm Charlie Appleby.

SARAH: We're no wiser now.

CHARLES: This won't do. (*Turns and opens door, calling.*) I say—er, Lilian—Lilian—you'd better come and introduce me. They don't know anything about me in here. We're all very embarrassed.

WILFRED: I say, is this a joke?

CHARLES (*coming in from door*): Not much of one, old boy. (*Turning.*) Here's Lilian.

Enter LILIAN.

LILIAN: Wilfred, this is Mr. ——

CHARLES: Whoa, stop! Not Mr. Just Appleby, Charlie Appleby—Charlie.

LILIAN (*rather grimly*): He's our brother-in-law. Stella's husband.

SARAH (*moving forward a step or two*): Never!

CHARLES: Sorry. Know how you feel, Sarah.

WILFRED: But look here—when—when did this happen?

CHARLES: Three years ago. In Australia. Let's complete the ceremony of introduction, shall we? (*Holds out a hand.*) How do you do?

WILFRED (*laughing nervously and shaking hands*): How do you do?

CHARLES (*moving forward and holding out a hand*): Sarah.

SARAH (*moving forward uncertainly*): And you really are Miss Stella's husband?

CHARLES: Mrs. Stella's husband. Yes.

140

SARAH (*bewildered and suspicious*): But she's never said a single word to me about it, not a single word. I can't understand it.

LILIAN (*rather sharply*): Just a minute, Sarah. I want you to help me.

> *She moves to door.* SARAH *follows slowly, with a puzzled and suspicious look at* CHARLES. *The latter notices it, though he is now lighting a cigarette.* LILIAN *and* SARAH *go out.*

CHARLES: The poor old girl is convinced I'm an imposter. And I must say I never felt so much like one before.

WILFRED: But, you see, we didn't know anything about it.

CHARLES (*drily*): No, I've gathered that.

WILFRED: She's been home four days, and never said a word.

CHARLES: Didn't know how to break the news, I expect. Difficult, sometimes. I'm not a good news-breaker myself.

WILFRED: Are you on the stage, too?

CHARLES: Such is fame. Am I on the stage?

WILFRED: I'm sorry—but——

CHARLES: Don't apologise. I expect you lead a quiet life. It looks a quiet life, from the little I've seen of it.

WILFRED: Oh—I'm only home on leave. From Africa.

CHARLES: Soldier?

WILFRED: No, I'm with the British West African trading company.

CHARLES: This family gets about a bit, doesn't it? And why I'm still wearing this damned thing, I don't know. (*Begins taking off his ulster*. WILFRED *gives him a hand with it*.) I've been on the stage twenty years. Ran away from Oxford to go on the stage. Been all over, played nearly everything. Juvenile leads. Character parts now. Soon I'll be doing the heavies. What a life!

WILFRED: Don't you like it?

CHARLES: Never been able to decide. Do you like Africa?

WILFRED: I'm not sure. (*They both laugh*.) I say, are you staying here?

CHARLES: Looks like it, doesn't it?

WILFRED: I hope you are.

CHARLES: Why?

WILFRED: Well, we might go round a bit. Unless you want to be with Stella all the time.

CHARLES (*drily*): No, I don't think I shall want to be with Stella all the time, old boy. Certainly let's go round a bit. I can't imagine where we'll go, from the little I've seen of the neighbourhood, but no doubt you know where the lads of the village—the ber-hoys, the ker-nuts, disport themselves. I don't suppose you come all the way from West Africa simply to watch the rain dripping off the old stone walls—do you?

WILFRED: Rather not.

CHARLES: You must take me round, you must show me the sights, and we'll see if we can't have some fun.

I've never been to a place yet—and I've been to some dam' rum places—where one couldn't have some fun if one tried.

WILFRED: I'll do my best for you.

CHARLES (*yawning*): Matter of fact, you're a find. I'd forgotten about you. I saw myself simply having some grim chats about appendicitis in the surgery with your governor. What's he like, by the way?

WILFRED: Oh—Dad's all right.

CHARLES: To tell you the truth, I wasn't looking forward to meeting him. After all, it's a bit thick suddenly having a son-in-law thrust on you. Actor, too. Greasy hair, dirty collar. No money. Probably a bad lot.

WILFRED (*enthusiastically*): I think it's going to be fun, having you here.

CHARLES: Thank God somebody thinks so. But I'm not in good form at the moment. Feel half dead. Got up too early to catch that train. And what a train! (LILIAN *enters.*) I'm just saying I feel half dead after that train.

LILIAN: I hope you don't mind a camp bed.

CHARLES: Not at all, so long as it isn't the kind that tries to fold itself up again in the middle of the night.

WILFRED: No, it's all right. But, look here, you can have my bed and I'll have the camp bed.

LILIAN: Well, you can settle it between you, because I've put him in your room, Wilfred.

WILFRED: Good. (*Hesitates.*) Though—I say—oughtn't he to be—you know?

LILIAN (*briskly*): That's all right.   I'm running this house.

CHARLES: Running it very well, too, I should think. I'd like to turn in for an hour if nobody's any objection.

LILIAN: No, I expect you're tired.   Are you hungry?

CHARLES: No, thanks.   I'm not hungry.   But I'm devilish thirsty.   Could I have a drink?

LILIAN: Would you like some tea?

CHARLES (*with mock gravity*): Sorry, but it doesn't agree with me.   If there's such a thing as a whisky and soda going——

WILFRED: There's some in the dining-room.

LILIAN (*moving to door left*): Come along.   And I'll show you where your room is.   Then I must go out again.

CHARLES (*following her*): I'll take my drink up to my room and not be in anybody's way.

> *They go out, and* WILFRED *follows them.   The room is darker now.   The rain can be heard.   After a moment* WILFRED *returns, carrying a mackintosh and a cap.   He closes the door after him, carefully, then goes to the telephone nervously.   Once more he looks at his little book.   Then he takes off the receiver.   He is very nervous, and catches his breath as he talks.*

WILFRED (*at telephone*): Hello . . . I want *Denly Two Six*. . . . Hello, is that Denly Two Six? Is that the "White Hart"? . . . Could I speak to Miss Alice Murgatroyd, please? . . . Oh, but you could get her, couldn't you? . . . It's—er—a friend. . . . Yes, it's *important*. . . . Oh, thanks very much. . . . Oh (*gasps*)

is that you, Alice? It's Wilfred . . . (*Louder.*) Wilfred—
you know—Wilfred Kirby . . . (*Disappointed.*) Didn't
you recognise my voice? . . . Oh, I see. . . . Do you
remember the other night? Listen, can I see you to-
day? . . . Oh no, it isn't the same thing at all seeing
you in the bar. . . . But I must see you alone . . .
please, Alice. . . . Oh (*Disappointed.*) . . . But listen,
if you don't go on duty until seven, I could see you
before then. I'd come over at once. . . . But you
can't have so much to do. (*Joyfully.*) Oh, good. I'll
come over at once on my bike. . . . (*Desperately again.*)
No, honestly, it isn't raining much. It's nothing.
Really. And it'll probably be all over by the time I get
there. . . . All right. At the bridge, eh? . . . Oh, but
you must be there. . . . Hello, hello.

> *He puts down the receiver, breathes hard, wipes his
> forehead, and puts on his mackintosh. He hears voices
> through door on left, so after one glance in that direction
> hurries out through door on right. The room now is
> almost dark. The door on left opens and* STELLA *and*
> FARRANT *come in, both wearing wet overcoats or
> mackintoshes.*

STELLA: Nobody in, thank goodness. We can still
go on talking. Will you light the lamps?

FARRANT: Yes. And it won't be the first time I've
done it here, either. (*He strikes a match and lights the
lamps.*) Aren't you awfully wet?

STELLA: Wettish. (*Takes off her coat.*) I think we'd
better put our coats in the nursery to dry. Give me
yours.

FARRANT (*taking off his*): No, I'll take them both in.
Give me yours.

> *He takes the coats into room on right.* STELLA
> *tidies her hair, shakes out her skirt, and so forth. She*
> *is dressed now in country clothes, different from those in*
> *Act One. Then she hums a tune. She is obviously*
> *happy.*

FARRANT (*returning*): Nice in here after the rain outside. Looks—cosy.

STELLA (*laughs*): That's very elderly of you, Geoffrey.

FARRANT: I don't see that. Always like to be cosy
after I've been out. Did when I was a boy. (*They
both sit down.*) This is when a pipe tastes its best, indoors
after the wind and the rain. (*Holds up his pipe.*) Do
you mind?

STELLA: I've told you before. I adore your pipe. I
think I'll smoke, too. Have you a cigarette for me,
please?

FARRANT: Yes, of course. (*Holds out a case. She
takes one.*)

STELLA (*holding up the cigarette, smiling*): Do you mind?

FARRANT: I admit I *have* objected to women smoking,
in my time. But I don't mind when you do it.

STELLA: You mean, it doesn't matter if a tough old
hag like me takes to such bad habits?

FARRANT: Don't talk such rot, Stella. You're prettier
than ever. And there never was anybody less *tough*—as
you call it.

STELLA: You're becoming suspiciously neat at this
sort of thing, Geoffrey, much better than you used to

be.   You've had lots of practice while I've been away.
(*He lights her cigarette, and then lights his pipe.*)   Well, the
walk didn't last long, and there was too much rain—
but I loved it.

FARRANT: That's good.

STELLA: The rain suits this country here.

FARRANT: Good thing it does.   We get plenty of it.

STELLA (*dreamily*): I wonder if you can understand
what it means to come back after being so long away.

FARRANT: Of course I can.   I was away over two
years during the Boer War.   Don't forget that.

STELLA: No, I'm not.   But I've been away much
longer than that.   It seems centuries.   Dirty provincial
towns.   Dozens of 'em.   They may not have all been
dirty, but looking back on them they seem grimy and
dreary.   Horsehair sofas, huge double beds in tiny dark
bedrooms, landings smelling of cabbage and old
blankets.   Stinking little dressing-rooms.   Stage doors
down back streets.

FARRANT: Sounds beastly.   Marvel to me how you
stuck it.

STELLA: Then London.   The real London.   Cheap
digs in Victoria and Paddington.   Meals in tea shops.
Fog for days and days.   No space, no fresh air.

FARRANT: But it was better when you went away
touring?

STELLA: Yes, we saw a lot.   Some of the places were
lovely.   And some—weren't.   But, my dear, there was
nothing like this anywhere.

147

FARRANT: There isn't, you know, if it's your own country.

STELLA (*ecstatically*): The grey stone walls climbing up the moors, Geoffrey. The little streams dashing down. The ling and the bracken. The green, green fields. The huge dark brooding hills. That heathery, salty, fresh smell. Oh—lovely, lovely. I feel like someone who's just been let out of prison. I'm alive again. You don't read poetry, do you, Geoffrey?

FARRANT (*apologetically*): Not much. Kipling, y'know. But can't get on with most of the others.

STELLA: Well, there are two lines of Wordsworth's that give me this country as nothing else does. I've repeated them over and over again—in hot dressing-rooms, in railway carriages when I couldn't sleep, in all kinds of hellish places—and they've always brought me back home here.

FARRANT: Good for them! What are they?

STELLA: They're at the very end of some ridiculous poem about a young shepherd coming into an estate. I remember the two lines that come before, so I'll put them in too. (*Quoting, giving the last two lines with deep feeling.*)

" Love had he found in huts where poor men lie ;
    His daily teachers had been woods and rills;
  The silence that is in the starry sky,
    The sleep that is among the lonely hills."

FARRANT: Say the last bit again.

STELLA:

  "The silence that is in the starry sky,
    The sleep that is among the lonely hills."

148

FARRANT (*thoughtfully*): I get what he's driving at there, y'know. That's Wordsworth, is it? I must tackle him again.

STELLA *laughs*.

FARRANT: What's the joke?

STELLA: I suddenly saw you—in that den of yours at the Manor—*tackling* Wordsworth.

FARRANT (*after short laugh*): You can understand why I stay on at the old place——

STELLA: Heavens, yes.

FARRANT: There isn't really a lot to do, looking after the estate, and sometimes I've told myself I'm a slacker, just hanging on there, doing a bit of hunting and shooting. I'd have been glad to have stayed in the army, of course, but my leg made that impossible. And, somehow, I've never been attracted to anything else. Probably because I don't want to leave the old place.

STELLA: You must never leave it.

FARRANT: Old Bickley, the shoemaker here in Eden End—he's a Socialist—always tells me that sooner or later he and his pals will have me out of the Manor and the estate. And I always tell him that if they do, he'll have to give me a job—cobbling with him. He's not a bad sort, Old Bickley, though he does talk a lot of hot air.

STELLA: I remember him. A nice old thing. I remember when I was a little girl somebody—it may have been Sarah—told me that Mr. Bickley didn't believe in God, and after that I used to look at him with horror. He had a fascination for me. I could see

149

him going to Hell. You know, these last few days, I've been thinking again of my childhood. Things—oh, dozens of things—I'd forgotten have suddenly come back.

FARRANT: Do you like that?

STELLA: Yes. Even though some of the things are unhappy things.

FARRANT: I hope I wasn't one of 'em.

STELLA: No, you come in afterwards, Geoffrey. When I was growing up—or when I thought I was growing up. When I was (*in absurd tone*) a *girl*.

FARRANT: You're still a girl.

STELLA: My dear man, don't be ridiculous. I'm a woman. Very soon—horrors—I shall be an *old girl*.

FARRANT: That puts me well into the decayed class, then, for I'm older then you.

STELLA: It's different for a man. You're merely coming within sight of maturity.

FARRANT: I hope I'm maturing well.

STELLA: You're maturing beautifully, Geoffrey.

FARRANT: Nevertheless, you've changed, and I haven't.

STELLA: How have I changed? (*Hastily.*) If it's something unpleasant, don't tell me. I won't have to-day spoilt.

FARRANT: It isn't unpleasant.

STELLA: Go on, then, and tell me all about it.

FARRANT: When I've thought about you——

STELLA: Oh, have you thought about me?

FARRANT (*gravely*): I've thought about you a lot. Wondered where you were, what you were doing, and so on, and I've always thought that after being on the stage and knocking up and down——

STELLA: I don't know that I want to be one who has knocked up and down.

FARRANT: Well, you know what I mean. I thought that you'd be much harder. Harder, that is, than you used to be.

STELLA: And I was hard enough to you, wasn't I? Poor Geoffrey. I was a nasty, cocky, little beast.

FARRANT: No, you weren't. But you led me an awful dance sometimes, didn't you?

STELLA: I did. And now I apologise for it. Never mind, Geoffrey. I treated you very badly, and you've been well revenged since.

FARRANT: Oh? How? Who by?

STELLA: Don't look so alarmed. I mean by—well—life. I thought I knew everything then. I knew nothing, and when that fact was forced upon me, it hurt. But go on. You thought I'd be harder still.

FARRANT: Yes. And you're not. You're——

STELLA: Softer. (*Laughs.*) Oh—but I don't want to be softer. It sounds horrid.

FARRANT: I didn't mean that. You know I'm no good at this sort of thing.

STELLA (*gently*): You're much better than you think you are. Besides, I've had the misfortune to meet a lot of men who prided themselves on being good at this sort of thing.

FARRANT: All blighters, I'll bet.

STELLA: Yes, Geoffrey.   Mostly blighters.

FARRANT: What I meant to say was, that you're still yourself—Stella—but you're nicer, kinder—dash it, I'll say it—gentler than you used to be.   At least to me you are.

STELLA: I'm glad you think so.   I should like to be. I've learnt a good deal these last eight years.   I've often thought how badly I treated you in the old days here. And—miles away—years away—I've been ashamed. Sometimes, just lately, I've been tempted to write and tell you so.   But I didn't know what had happened to you.   You might easily have forgotten all about me.

FARRANT (*in a low voice*): I've tried hard enough.

STELLA: I can understand that.

FARRANT: I wanted to get on with my own life. You'd got on with yours.   That's reasonable, isn't it?

STELLA: Yes.   And I should think that's what was the matter with it.   Too reasonable.

FARRANT: Yes, too reasonable.   I knew that the moment I came in here, the other night, and saw you again.   I hadn't been doing badly the last year or two.

STELLA: At forgetting me?

FARRANT: Yes.   I'd even been able to come here a good deal—sometimes to see your father, and Wilfred when he was on leave, but chiefly to see Lilian.   I've seen a lot of her, you know.

STELLA: Yes, I gathered that.

FARRANT: Lilian's a fine girl, you know.

STELLA: I'm sure she is. That sounds absurd, doesn't it, when I'm her sister. But the fact is, I don't know her very well now. She's grown-up, and she's changed in the process, I suppose. But I'm sure there's something very strong and fine about her. She always had more courage and strength and honesty than I had. (*As he is about to protest.*) No, I mean that. Do you think I don't know myself now? I'm changeable, I'm weak, and I'm a coward.

FARRANT: You're not.

STELLA: You don't know, my dear. I'm being weak and cowardly at this very moment.

FARRANT: I don't believe you.

STELLA (*almost in tears, but smiling*): I don't want you to believe me. (*Smiling at him.*) Dear Geoffrey.

FARRANT: You may be changeable. I don't know. But I know this. I'm not changeable. (*Goes over and takes her hands.*) I loved you years ago. I love you now, just the same. I see why nobody's ever meant anything all this time. It's because of you. There's only you. I love you, Stella.

> *He looks down at her. She raises her face to him and he kisses her. Then she rests her head against his sleeve, closing her eyes. Nothing is said. Then she makes a little gesture with her hand that releases her.*

FARRANT: I may not be able to read poetry, Stella, but I've imagined that—over and over again.

STELLA (*with a tiny smile*): I've thought of it too—sometimes.

FARRANT: By jove, have you? If I'd known that I'd have come charging all over Australia and the United States looking for you. See what I've missed.

He threatens to kiss her again, but she holds up a hand and shakes her head.

No, probably you're right. Now we've got to talk.

STELLA: Yes, but not the kind of talk you mean, Geoffrey. No plans, no arrangements, no time tables, no—"seeing how we stand." Nothing like that.

FARRANT (*bewildered*): Oh!

STELLA: We can't be always arranging ourselves in the world's eye, like goods in a smart shop window. Not that sort of talk at all. Just idle, foolish talk that gets you nowhere, that means nothing and yet can mean everything. It doesn't matter now who we are or how we stand, or anything like that. Just think of the two of us here, in a cosy little room, lost in the moorland rain. We're lost too. There isn't anybody else. Just us. And time's stopped for us.

FARRANT: I see. At least I think I do.

STELLA (*dreamily*): Or we needn't talk at all, if you like. Just be quiet. Trying to make time stand still for us. It flies at a terrible speed really, Geoffrey.

FARRANT: Oh, I don't know. Things don't change much.

STELLA: They do. Even in ten years time—in Nineteen Twenty-two—what a queer year that sounds, doesn't it——

FARRANT: We shall only be in our forties.

STELLA: I know. And yet everything may be different. You never know. We might look back at this year and see it—oh! a thousand years away. In another world, a lost world.

FARRANT: But things don't change much here.

STELLA: Yes, they do. I haven't been away so long, yet it's all different really. Mother gone. Wilfred and Lilian grown-up—half strangers. Father much older —too old. I sound like Stevenson's Wanderer. Do you remember the verse I used to keep saying over and over again?

> *She repeats the verse beginning "Home was home then, my dear," very softly.*

"Home was home then, my dear, full of kindly faces.
Home was home then, my dear, happy for the child.
Fire and the windows bright glittered on the moorland.
Song, tuneful song, built a palace in the wild."

> *Just before the end the door on left opens quietly and* CHARLES *stands there, looking like a man who has just had a nap.* FARRANT *stares at him in surprise. When* STELLA *sees him she gives a sharp cry and stands with a hand pressed against her heart.*

CHARLES: Sorry if I startled you, Stella, but I didn't want to interrupt the performance.

STELLA (*with an enormous effort*): Charles?

CHARLES (*cheerfully*): Didn't they tell you I was coming? Too bad. Wanted to make a surprise of it, I suppose. Something to pass the long autumn evening.

STELLA: But how did you get here?

CHARLES: Train, my dear. Train from town. Hours and hours and hours of it, and started about dawn. I'm feeling a bit muzzy too. (*Indicating* FARRANT, *who is standing rigid.*) I'm afraid we're embarrassing your friend—this gentleman. Hadn't you better introduce me?

STELLA (*silent a moment, then making a big effort*): Geoffrey, this is Charles Appleby—my husband. Captain Farrant.

CHARLES: How d'you do? An old friend of my wife's, I expect. Think I've heard her mention you. (*Looks shrewdly from one to the other.*) If you'll excuse me one minute, I'll go and get myself a drink. Always get thirsty on trains, most curious thing.

He goes out. FARRANT *stares at* STELLA.

FARRANT: Is this true?

STELLA: Yes.

FARRANT: But why didn't you tell me?

STELLA (*with a miserable smile*): I told you I was weak and cowardly, didn't I?

FARRANT (*contemptuously*): Yes, but I didn't know it was as bad as that.

STELLA: Please, Geoffrey, don't try to hurt me. I'm hurt enough as it is.

FARRANT: What about me? I suppose you think I'm enjoying myself.

STELLA (*in tears*): Please, Geoffrey. It isn't as bad as it seems. We were married three years ago. We've been separated for nearly a year now. I don't know why he's here. I didn't ask him here.

156

FARRANT: I don't think I want to hear any more about it just now. I must go.

STELLA: Only a few minutes ago I was happy. I thought it couldn't last long. It didn't even last as long as I thought.

FARRANT: It didn't deserve to last a second. I'll get my coat.

> *Goes to room on right.* STELLA *makes a great effort to avoid breaking down altogether. As* FARRANT *re-appears with his cap and coat,* CHARLES *appears in the other doorway with a whisky and soda in his hand.*

CHARLES: What? Going?

FARRANT (*curtly*): Yes. Good-bye.

> STELLA *turns away from them.* CHARLES *stands aside to let* FARRANT *pass.* FARRANT *goes out. You hear the outer door bang outside.* STELLA *is still turned away.*

CHARLES (*who has no malice in him, an insensitive, good-humoured chap*): I'm sorry, Stella. Didn't mean to barge in at the wrong moment like that. Always putting my foot in it. No tact. It's just cost me a job. You'll laugh when I tell you about it.

> STELLA *sits down, away from him, and stares straight in front of her. She is not sulking, but is temporarily oblivious of anything at the moment but her own misery.*

Shall I tell you? Perhaps I'd better keep it. No good spoiling the story. But you will laugh when I tell you.

> *He takes a good gulp of his whisky and soda, and looks across at her rather wistfully.*

STELLA (*in a muffled voice*): Why have you come here?

157

CHARLES (*trying to keep it light*): Oh—well—you see, I was resting and a bit fed up with town. Thought the change might do me good. All in order, you know. I had an invitation to come down here. I thought it might have come—indirectly—from you.

STELLA: It didn't.

CHARLES: No, I'm gathering that. Nobody seems to know much about me here. Haven't met your father yet.

STELLA: No—that's not going to be easy.

CHARLES: Why?

STELLA: I can't explain.

CHARLES: I'm beginning to feel like a baby that's turned up at a wedding. A warm welcome was given to Mr. Charles Appleby, always a favourite in the North of England. Good old Charlie, they cried.

STELLA (*wearily*): Oh—don't be funny, Charlie.

CHARLES: Well, I've got to be something. Damn it, look at it from my point of view. I've got feelings as well as you and your old friend, the bronzed, clean-living English gentleman who's just pushed off in a temper. I come here because I'm invited. I imagine you've something to do with it. After all, you're still my wife. I get up at some unearthly hour this morning—in pitch darkness—travel most of the day, and then when I arrive here, I'm treated as if I were a bad dose of small-pox.

STELLA: Oh, I know. It's not your fault.

CHARLES: By the way, what's the telephone number here?

STELLA: I don't know. It's there.

CHARLES (*goes over to telephone, and notes number*): I must send it to the agents. They may want me in a hurry. One or two new tours going out. Somebody said something about *Old Heidelberg* touring again. And *The . Monk and the Woman*. A title like that ought to bring 'em in. You know that Hilda Moore's touring in *Bella Donna*. If she wants to get back to town and they want to keep the tour going, there might be a chance for you there—you've played Hilda Moore parts.

STELLA: I've finished with the theatre.

CHARLES: Don't believe it. I've heard that before. Nobody's finished with the theatre until the theatre's finished with them. You'll be working again in a month.

STELLA (*shaking her head*): I shan't.

CHARLES: I've said that, you know. We all have. Meant it too when we've said it. I remember once—it was about two years before I met you—I was out in *A Message From Mars*—and——

> Enter LILIAN, *carrying account books, etc.*

CHARLES: Hullo! You look business-like.

LILIAN: I have to do Dad's accounts.

STELLA (*with hostility*): Why?

LILIAN: He's so forgetful now.

STELLA: Oh. I haven't noticed it.

LILIAN: You haven't been here long enough to notice it.

CHARLES (*looking from one to the other*): Er . . . no.
I think I'll have a look round. (*He escapes. Nothing is
said for a moment.*)

STELLA: It was you, of course, who asked Charles to
come here.

LILIAN: Yes.

STELLA: How did you find him?

LILIAN: You'd told me his name and you said that
you both had the same agent. When I was helping to
turn out your room, I saw a letter from your agent——

STELLA: I see. Quite simple. These things usually
are if you don't mind going into other people's rooms
and reading their letters.

LILIAN: Perhaps if you'd condescended to do your
own room—instead of going out for a walk with
Geoffrey, I shouldn't have seen the letter.

STELLA: I wasn't asked to help with the housework
here, was told, in fact, not to do anything. On the
other hand, I *was* asked to go for a walk by Geoffrey.
But that has nothing to do with it. You read my letter,
probably read all my letters.

LILIAN: I've not the least desire to read your letters.
That particular one happened to be lying open on your
dressing-table. Your agent's name and address on it
were big enough to be read a yard away.

STELLA: I'm glad he saved your eyesight. Why did
you ask Charles to come here? It was no business of
yours. I'd told you that we had separated. We haven't
lived together for over a year. We haven't spoken to
one another, haven't seen one another—except the

other day at the agent's—for months and months. If
I'd wanted him here, I would have asked him myself.
You'd no right to interfere. And if it had been anybody
else but Charles—who's a fool—he'd never have come
here on such an invitation.

LILIAN: Three years ago, you were sufficiently in
love with him to marry him. Now you can't stand him
in the same house.

STELLA: That's my affair.

LILIAN: By the way, I've put him in Wilfred's room.

STELLA: I suppose I ought to be grateful you haven't
put him into my bed.

LILIAN: You needn't be disgusting.

STELLA: And you needn't be such a beastly little
hypocrite. Why did you send for him?

LILIAN: He was your husband. You weren't happy,
I could see that. I thought you'd like another chance.

STELLA: All lies. You're still talking like a beastly
little hypocrite. You're lying, Lilian, you're lying.
Why did you send for him?

LILIAN: I've told you.

STELLA: You've told me nothing, and you know it.
But I'll make you tell the truth. You made me confess
about my marriage, you've read my letters, you've
interfered in my private affairs—and now you imagine
you can put me off with a few silly lies. (*Going nearer.*)
Do you think I'm a fool?

LILIAN (*contemptuously*): Yes.

   STELLA, *blazing with fury, slaps her face, hard. The
   effect is very marked on each.* LILIAN *stands rigid, filled*

with a cold anger. STELLA *steps back and then turns away, trembling, her anger rapidly vanishing. She sits down.*

STELLA: I oughtn't to have done that. I'm sorry, Lilian.

LILIAN (*contemptuously*): It doesn't make me think you any less of a fool. It's like nearly everything else you do —violent and silly and useless.

STELLA (*roused again*): Is it? Well, I'll tell you now why you sent for Charles. It had nothing to do with me and my marriage. You don't care a rap about that. Do you?

LILIAN (*calmly*): Not much. Why should I?

STELLA: No, you did it because you're in love with Geoffrey Farrant. What's the use of pretending? You know. And I know. You're in love with Geoffrey, and you're terrified of losing him. I knew that the very first night I came back, when you went sulking off to bed, pretending you'd a headache. Even before that, before Geoffrey called, the moment I arrived, I knew there was *something*. You didn't really want me back here. I felt at once there was something resentful about you.

LILIAN (*herself roused now, but still colder and harder than the other*): And why should there be anything else? Why should you expect us all to fall on your neck the minute you condescended to come home again?

STELLA: That's unfair——

LILIAN: It isn't. And if you didn't think about yourself all the time, you'd soon see that. You always had

162

more of everything than Wilfred and I had. Before you went away, you let Geoffrey fall in love with you, made him follow you round, laughed at him—yes, and to us, and even then, I hated you for it——

STELLA: I cared more for Geoffrey then than you think.

LILIAN: I don't believe you know what it is to love anybody properly. You think being sentimental is caring for people. It isn't. Then you insisted on going on the stage, although you knew very well that mother had a horror of theatres. She couldn't help it. That's how she'd been brought up. You went away, without caring how much mother and father were worrying.

STELLA: That's not true. I cared terribly. You can't begin to understand——

LILIAN: That helped to kill mother.

STELLA (*breaking down*): Oh—you're cruel, Lilian. That's not true.

LILIAN: Yes, it is. You said you'd make me tell the truth, and here it is. Mother died. Father was left lonely and miserable. I didn't want to stay here all my life. I had plans of my own. But I had to stay then, to look after the house and father. He needed me.

STELLA (*through her tears*): He didn't. If you'd decided to do something away from home he wouldn't have tried to stop you. He simply thought you wanted to stay at home.

LILIAN: How do you know?

STELLA: He—oh it doesn't matter. The point is, you stayed at home because you wanted to stay at home.

And now you're making a great virtue out of it. You're one of these self-appointed martyrs.

LILIAN: I'm not pretending to be a martyr. I'm simply explaining why I didn't think you were so very wonderful. You went off, not caring about us, to do what you wanted to do. And while you were enjoying yourself, you didn't bother about us. You could even get married without telling us. Then, when you thought you'd had enough of the stage and had made a mess of your marriage, you decided to come home.

STELLA: Yes, and you seem to forget that, after all, it's my home just as much as it's yours.

LILIAN: No, it isn't, and you know very well it isn't. It stopped being your home when you ran away from it, years ago. And it's my home, more than ever, because I've stuck to it and helped to keep it going. We'd made a life here without you, and now you have to come charging back into it, upsetting everyone.

STELLA: Upsetting everyone? You seem to forget that everybody here was glad to see me again—except you.

LILIAN: Yes, and a lot of good it'll do them.

STELLA: All you're thinking about is Geoffrey, only you won't admit it.

LILIAN: I'm not afraid of admitting it. I do love Geoffrey—I have done for years—and I believe I could make him happy. And I know you couldn't, and wouldn't even try very long.

STELLA: So you made up your mind at once that he must see for himself that I have a husband. Oh—yes, they've met already. I'm sorry you weren't here.

LILIAN: It wasn't just that.   You have a life of your own—a life that you've made quite apart from us—you can't run away from it.

STELLA: But you see, I'm away from it now.   And I'm not running back to it.   You've done your best. Charles is here—and he's a nuisance—but he won't stay long.   But I'm staying.   You've played your trick, Lilian—and a very dirty little trick it was—but you haven't won.   Nothing has happened except that now I realise that either you've changed completely or I never really knew you.

LILIAN: I can't see that it matters which it is.

STELLA (*distressed*): What does matter to me is that you and I could have talked to one another as we have done.   I've never even tried to hurt you, and you've deliberately hurt me.   I'd looked forward so much to seeing you again.   We'd shared so many things before. I thought we'd be able to have a wonderful time together.   If you'd been open and friendly from the first, I couldn't have taken anything, anybody, away from you.   I could have been happy just because you were happy.   Oh—Lilian—you wouldn't be so hard if you hadn't been shut up here so long in a safe little corner.   It's because you don't know how much misery there is in the world, how circumstances and time can change and hurt us.

LILIAN: You're not really unhappy now.   In a way you're enjoying it.   You see, I'm not made like that. I can't enjoy my emotions.

CHARLES *appears in doorway on left.*

CHARLES (*to* STELLA): I say, Stella, your father's just come in. He thinks I'm a patient. You'd better come and explain. (*He goes out.*)

STELLA (*in a low voice*): I hope you don't think I'm going to enjoy this.

LILIAN (*scornfully*): You're not afraid of Dad, are you?

STELLA: I'm afraid for him. You can't begin to understand how hateful this is going to be for me. (*She goes to the door and calls, with assumed cheerfulness.*) Dad!

DR. KIRBY (*off*): Yes.

STELLA: Just a minute.

> *She goes off, banging the door to behind her.* LILIAN
> *sits down to her accounts and gradually loses control of*
> *herself. As the curtain falls, she is crying.*

ACT III

SCENE I

As before. Late on Saturday night. When the curtain rises, the room is empty. Lamps are lit, but turned low. There is a good fire. On the table are a tray, holding a thermos flask, small bottle of brandy, a glass and some biscuits, and another tray with whisky decanter and soda syphon and glasses on it. A clock outside in the hall strikes twelve. Before it has finished striking the voices of CHARLES *and* WILFRED *are heard outside.* CHARLES *enters first and begins turning up the lights. He is dressed as in* ACT II. WILFRED *staggers in, with a folded mackintosh slung over one shoulder, and he sticks to this for some time. They are both drunk.* WILFRED *is the worse of the two. It should be quite obvious that they are drunk, but they must not indulge in the usual antics, and though their voices are thick, they must be clearly heard. There must be no hiccupping.*

CHARLES (*looking round the room*): Nice. Very nice. I call this very snug, old boy.

WILFRED: Not bad qua'ers, not bad qua'ers at all. Wish I'd something like this in Bri'sh West.

CHARLES (*solemnly*): In where, old boy?

WILFRED (*solemnly*): Bri'sh West.

167

CHARLES: Never heard of it.

WILFRED (*deliberately*): Bri-tish West—Africa.

CHARLES: Oh—yes. Africa. I've been to Africa—
South Africa. It's all right, Africa is, old boy.

WILFRED (*very seriously*): It's fine. I like Africa,
Charlie.

CHARLES (*wandering round*): Quite right. We pass
Africa. (*Going to table.*) Hello, drinks. But what's
this business?

WILFRED (*peering at the thermos flask*): That's for my
father.

CHARLES: Where is he?

WILFRED (*waving a hand*): Out—working. Somebody
somewhere must be very ill. Having a baby p'r'aps.
Or pegging out.

CHARLES: And your poor old governor's looking
after 'em.

WILFRED: Yes, and that's for when he comes in.
Hot milk. Brandy. Biscuits. And he deserves 'em,
Charlie.

CHARLES: He does, old boy. He's a noble fellow.
As soon as I saw him—yesterday afternoon—I said to
myself: "Stella's father—my father-in-law—he's a
noble old fellow." I think we ought to drink his
health.

WILFRED (*solemnly*): I ag-agree.

    CHARLES *pours out two whiskies and sodas during
the next two speeches.*

CHARLES (*with air of profundity*): If my old man had been a doctor, a lot of things would have been different —very different.   But he wasn't.

WILFRED: What was he—your old man?

CHARLES (*very solemnly*): Nothing, old boy—nothing. Just a bloody English gentleman.   But never mind him. (*Sternly, raising glass.*)   Here's to Dr. Kirby—a noble old fellow.

WILFRED (*raising glass*): Here's to him—good old Dad.

CHARLES (*still solemnly*): Let's sit down.

WILFRED: Yes.

  They sit down. CHARLES *lights a cigarette.*
  WILFRED *looks rather sleepy.*

CHARLES: You know, old boy—we've had a good evening.   I told you yesterday—when we first met—I said then " We can go out—you and I—and have a good evening here."   Didn't I?

WILFRED: You did.

CHARLES: Well, we've had one.   What was the name of the fellow that gave us a lift in the trap?

WILFRED: Harper.

CHARLES: Harper.   A very nice fellow—Harper. But he was badly screwed, y'know, old boy.   He ought to have let me drive.

WILFRED: I met a fellow on the boat coming home called Harper.   He came from Manchester and he had a glass eye.   I hate glass eyes.

CHARLES: And I hate Manchester. If I'd to choose between a glass eye and Manchester, I'd rather have a glass eye. You meant a glass eye, old boy, didn't you—and not an eye glass?

WILFRED: Yes, glass eye. One of our chaps in the Company——

CHARLES: What company? You're not on the stage, you're in Africa.

WILFRED: Yes, I mean the Bri'sh West African Company. He has an eye glass. He says he used to own two racehorses when he was home. Awful nut.

CHARLES: Probably lying, old boy. There's a terrible lot of lying about. When you're my age you'll have found that out. Everybody lies like the devil. Women worse than men.

WILFRED: That's true, Charlie. A girl on the boat told me a lot of lies. (*With sudden energy.*) Absolute lies.

CHARLES: I know, I know. If I'd had a sovereign for every lie that girls on boats have told me, I'd be rich man now. And I'll tell you another thing about women, old boy. Women—and I don't care who they are—all women—can't stand seeing men enjoy themselves *by* themselves. It annoys 'em. It makes 'em furious. They like to think they're indis-indispensable. We've had a good evening, haven't we?

WILFRED: Yes.

CHARLES: All right then. We've had a good evening. No harm in it, no harm in it at all. A few pubs. A few rounds of drinks. A talk with some of the local boys. Social harmony and innocent mirth, as somebody said somewhere. A good evening. But do you think you could get any woman to admit we'd had a good evening? No, old boy. Take it from me. You couldn't. Stella's a nice girl. Would she admit we'd had a good evening? No. Your other sister—Lilian—would she admit it? No. Old boy, they'd turn it down flat. "Where have you been? Look at you."

WILFRED: Well, I don't know. There's a girl I could mention—lives round here—and I don't think she——

CHARLES (*holding up his hand*): She's different. Don't you believe it. They're all different—they don't mind anything—no, not until they've got hold of you. But once they've got you, they won't have this, they won't have that. The thing—the very thing—they told you once they liked you for—that's what they want you to change, old boy. If they liked your little jokes before you were married, then after you're married they ask you why you're always trying to be funny. See what I mean?

WILFRED: Yes, I suppose so. One of our chaps in Africa——

CHARLES: Just a minute. Tell me afterwards. Don't forget. I want to hear about that chap. But what I was going to say was this. It doesn't matter what women do, or who tells you lies, or whether you go to Africa or not, life's a very wonderful thing. Do you realise that, old boy?

WILFRED: By Jove—yes. I was just thinking coming along——

CHARLES: A wonderful thing. You can't get away from that.

WILFRED: You can't get away from it, Charlie.

CHARLES: I've had my troubles. Even you've had your troubles——

WILFRED: I should think I have. Do you know when I first went out to Nigeria——

CHARLES: You had a hell of a time. Yes, and I've had a hell of a time. But in spite of everything, I think —I *know*—life's a wonderful thing.

WILFRED: There's *something* about it, isn't there?

CHARLES: You've hit it. There's *something* about it. Here I am—in—where is it?

WILFRED: Where's what?

CHARLES: Here—this place.

WILFRED: Eden End.

CHARLES: Here I am in Eden End. Never been here before—may not ever come here again——

WILFRED: I hope you will, Charlie.

CHARLES: I hope so, too, old boy. But you never know. That's another thing about life (*very solemnly*)— you never know. A week ago I didn't know I was going to be here—sitting here with you.

WILFRED: And I didn't know you existed.

CHARLES: Didn't you? Dam' shame. But there you are, you see. Here I am. And here you are. Having a drink together. Everything's quiet. Women asleep upstairs—or I hope they are. Your governor out there somewhere—helping some poor devil out of the world—or perhaps helping some other poor devil into the world—and here we are. And you'll go back to Ceylon——

172

WILFRED: Africa.

CHARLES: It's all the same, old boy. This isn't geography. And I'll go back to town. Get a job. Go on tour again perhaps. People will come to see me. They don't know much about me. I don't know anything about them. Never mind. Perhaps I make 'em cry. Perhaps I make 'em laugh. And, mind you, old boy, give me a part with the ghost of a bit of comedy fat in it, and I *can* make 'em laugh. I can make 'em yell. Weedon Grossmith—Weedon Grossmith, mind you—once said to me : "You've got a touch, Appleby, old boy. You've *got* something." And I have. The trouble is—and this is where *luck* comes in—most of the time I've had to make something out of nothing.

WILFRED: I'll bet you're awfully good, Charlie. Do you know what old Stansted—one of the Company's chief men out there—said about me?

CHARLES: No?

WILFRED: He didn't say it *to* me, but he told one of the other fellows. He said that of all the young men who'd come out lately I'd got the best idea of handling the niggers.

CHARLES: I'm not surprised, old boy. It doesn't surprise me at all. That's because you've got sympathy. You're human. You're like me. You've either got it or you haven't got it. We've got it.

WILFRED (*sleepily*): We've got it. I think—you're an awfully fine chap, Charlie. And I'm glad you came to stay with us.

CHARLES: Thanks, old boy. So am I. All the best. (*Drains his glass.*)

WILFRED: All the best. (*Drains his.*)

CHARLES (*getting up*): We'd better be getting upstairs. What was the name of that biggish place at the cross-roads?

WILFRED: That's the " White Hart." My favourite.

CHARLES: Quite right. Best of the lot. We'll concentrate on that one next time. Did you notice the little barmaid there, the little fair one?

WILFRED: Yes. That's Alice.

CHARLES: Alice, is it? Well, she's all right. A promising little tart, that. (*Puts his glass back on the table, humming or singing " Where My Caravan has Rested"*)

WILFRED (*suddenly rigid with attention*):Why do you call her that?

CHARLES (*carelessly*): Didn't you notice her? Something doing there, old boy. Can't miss it. Quite pretty and absolutely asking for it. Didn't you see her giving me enormous glad eyes? Wanted me to come round and see her when it was quieter.

WILFRED (*suddenly shouting*): She didn't. You're a liar.

CHARLES (*good-humouredly*): Here, steady, steady.

WILFRED (*not so loud now, but with intensity*): I tell you she didn't, and you're a dirty liar.

CHARLES: You're screwed, old boy. Take it easy.

WILFRED (*half shouting, half crying*): Tell me it isn't true.

CHARLES: Anything you like so long as you stop making that row. What the devil does it matter whether it's true or not?

WILFRED: It matters to me.

CHARLES: Oh—I see.

WILFRED: It's the only thing that matters to me.

CHARLES: Don't be a damned fool. Of course it isn't.

WILFRED (*vehemently, clutching hold of the other*): She didn't ask you to come round and see her, did she? Tell me she didn't. (*Raising his voice.*)

CHARLES: Not so much noise, you young ass.

WILFRED: Tell me she didn't, Charles.

CHARLES: She didn't, then. It must have been somebody else—one of the others.

WILFRED (*distressed*): Are you sure?

CHARLES: What I am sure of, old boy, is that you're badly screwed and that it's time I got you up to bed.

> LILIAN, *in night things and a dressing-gown, stands in the doorway on left, looking at them.*

LILIAN: You're making a frightful noise. (*She comes into room.*)

CHARLES: Sorry—Lilian. Just been having a little argument, that's all. I'm taking Wilfred up to bed now. He's a bit—tired.

LILIAN (*contemptuously*): You mean he's drunk. You both are.

CHARLES (*indignantly*): Oh—no, no, no, no.

> STELLA, *also in night things and dressing-gown, appears in open doorway.*

STELLA: What's the matter?

WILFRED (*miserably*): I think—I'm going—to be sick.

CHARLES (*putting arm round him*): That's all right, old boy. That's all right. You stick to me. Steady, steady. (*To* STELLA, *who comes in and clears the doorway, and* LILIAN.) I'll look after him. (*To* WILFRED, *who is groaning.*) That's all right, old boy. I've got you. Steady, steady. (*To the* GIRLS.) Don't worry. He's all right.

> *He escorts him through the doorway. He can be heard, repeating his "All right" and "Steady" outside.* STELLA *stands near the doorway, watching them.* LILIAN *stands in the middle of the room, watching* STELLA. *Finally the latter closes the door, and comes in, looking troubled.* LILIAN *picks up* WILFRED'S *glass, which is on the floor, and puts it on the table, then picks up his mackintosh, which is sprawling over a chair, and begins to fold it.*

LILIAN : Thank God, Dad's still out, that's all.

STELLA: That's what I was thinking.

LILIAN: He hates drunkenness. So do I.

STELLA: He needn't know anything about this.

LILIAN: Don't imagine that I shall tell him. But this has never happened before. Wilfred does go into the local pubs sometimes, but he's never had much to drink. As a matter of fact, I believe he thinks he's fallen in love with a barmaid somewhere. But he's never been like this before.

STELLA: No, this comes of going out with Charles —the very first night too.

LILIAN: And—I hope—the last.

STELLA: I didn't ask Charles to come here. He's your guest.

LILIAN: He's your husband.

STELLA: He was.

LILIAN: He still is. (*A pause.*) Why did you marry him, Stella?

STELLA: For the usual reasons. I was in love with him. Queer, no doubt—but true. As a matter of fact, I was very much in love with him.

LILIAN: Were you?

STELLA: Poor Charlie! I suppose it does seem incredible to you. I think I'll have one of Dad's biscuits. (*Takes one.*) You have one. (LILIAN *has one.*)

LILIAN: Has he changed very much?

STELLA: No, he hasn't—really. But it's one thing seeing him here, quite out of his element, not working, rather depressed. And it's quite another thing seeing him—as I did for months when we were touring the East and Australia—as the most amusing and charming person in the company. And to be working and travelling and laughing with him month after month, thousands of miles from home. It's no use, Lilian, you can't begin to understand my life. We were very happy for a time. Poor Charlie.

LILIAN: Why do you say "Poor Charlie"?

STELLA: Because—although he doesn't deserve it—I can't help feeling sorry for him. I suppose I'm still fond of him.

LILIAN: Then why don't you look after him?

STELLA: Why should I?

LILIAN: He belongs to you.

STELLA: I can't think about people like that. I'm not possessive. (*Startled.*) What's that?

It is CHARLES, *looking in at the door. He is soberer than he was, but still ripe—and very sleepy.*

CHARLES: Are you two quarrelling again? You're always quarrelling. Why don't you take it easy? Live and let live.

STELLA (*sharply*): Never mind about us. What about Wilfred?

CHARLES: That's what I came down to say. He's been sick. He's in bed. He's fast asleep.

STELLA: Well, you get to bed now, Charles, and you can both sleep as long as you like in the morning.

CHARLES: It was his own fault, you know. He would mix them. I said to him, right at the first, I said "Now, take my tip, and don't mix 'em." But he wouldn't——

STELLA (*wearily*): Oh—get to bed, Charlie. And don't make a noise. Father may be in any minute.

CHARLES: A noble old fellow. Wouldn't disturb him for the world. Good-night, girls. (*Withdraws.*)

STELLA: Poor Charlie. Nobody knows better than I do how maddening he can be, but there's something rather sweet about him. He's only a great child. There are dozens of them—great children, just like him—in the theatre.

LILIAN: Well, if he's a child, all the more reason why you should look after him.

STELLA: Don't nag at me, Lilian.

LILIAN: And child or no child, he can't be allowed to spend any more evenings like this with Wilfred.

STELLA: Well, if Wilfred is developing a passion for barmaids, he's quite capable of getting drunk by himself.

LILIAN: No, he isn't. Wilfred's only a silly baby yet. Besides, it's Dad I'm really thinking about.

STELLA: Yes, there's Dad.

LILIAN: Well?

STELLA: You're just trying to drive me out, aren't you, Lilian? I can't understand you. I don't mean what you're doing—I understand that. But you—yourself. You seem to have no feeling for me at all, less than a stranger would have. It doesn't seem to matter to you that I've been desperately unhappy these last months and that when I came home it was like beginning a wonderful new life. Doesn't that mean anything to you, Lilian?

LILIAN: Yes. And it would mean a lot more if I really believed in it.

STELLA: You think it's all insincere, made-up stuff, an actress letting herself go—don't you?

LILIAN: I think you encourage your emotions, so that whatever they are—in a way—you enjoy them.

STELLA: We shall never agree, of course. We've grown up to be thousands of miles away from each other. We live in different worlds. I think you're rather like mother.

LILIAN: I think I am.

STELLA: But what hurts me is that, underneath all this difference, there isn't, with you, any affection or friendship. If you'd lived so long among strangers, in places where nobody knew or cared about you at all, you'd understand how this can hurt. You've behaved very badly to me—you've deliberately set yourself against me—and yet to me you're still Lilian, my sister, and I'm longing all the time to talk properly with you, to remember all the silly old things we did, to laugh and cry together. Can't you see?

LILIAN: The trouble is, Stella, you can afford to feel like that. I can't.

STELLA: What do you mean?

LILIAN: It hasn't been fun for me—treating you like this. It's not true that I don't care at all. I do. But I know—and I knew it the moment you came back—that if I gave in, you'd overwhelm me, sweep me away——

STELLA: And why not?

LILIAN: Because you'd knock down everything I've built up here. You'd take Geoffrey again, without really wanting him. You'd unsettle Dad, Wilfred, everybody and everything. And just when they'd all come to depend on you again, you'd run away—as you did before. People like you, Stella, don't want to make other people unhappy——

STELLA: I don't. Never, never. I know too much about it myself.

LILIAN: But, for all that, you *do* make people unhappy. You can't help it, I suppose. But there's no real responsibility in you.

STELLA (*in despair*): But why are you so responsible —so old and wise? You say I make people unhappy. I may do. I don't know. But I can make them happy too. Can you?

180

LILIAN: Yes, in my own way.

STELLA: And a dull and dusty way it seems, too.

LILIAN: No it isn't. What do you know about me?

STELLA: How can I know anything about you when you're all shut up inside yourself and won't come out? Oh—it's no use.

LILIAN: We'll never agree.

STELLA: I don't want us to agree. That doesn't matter. But we could at least be *real* together. Even that's impossible, it seems.

LILIAN: It's years too late. Let's be reasonable.

STELLA (*wearily*): Go on, then, let's be reasonable.

LILIAN: You saw what happened to-night? Wilfred —and your Charles. What are you going to do?

STELLA: I don't know. I want to think.

LILIAN: You'll go sooner or later, you know.

STELLA: Why should you say that? You don't know. You don't know what my life's been like. You don't realise what it's meant—coming back—home.

LILIAN: You'll soon get tired of it.

STELLA (*uncertainly*): No. No. I'm sure I shouldn't.

LILIAN (*mercilessly*): Just as you did before. You'd go on smashing things, other people's lives as well as your own. Dad thinks you've had a wonderful time on the stage, that you're going to be a famous actress, that you're happily married——

STELLA (*in distress*): I know. Please, Lilian. I want to think.

LILIAN (*without malice, but forcefully*): If you wanted to stay, you'd have to tell him that you'd failed in everything. And that's only the beginning. You'd never get back into this life properly. You'd be restless. You'd be a person without a real life anywhere. You'd think yourself a failure.

STELLA (*stopping her*): Oh—stop, stop! I won't listen to any more. (*The front door shuts rather noisily.*)

LILIAN: There's Dad coming in.

STELLA: You go to bed, Lilian. I want to talk to him for a minute.

LILIAN: Don't keep him up. He'll be awfully tired.

STELLA (*wearily*): No, no, I know. But I must talk to him. It may be for the last time.

DR. KIRBY *enters. He looks very tired.*

DR. KIRBY: Mrs. Sugden's been delivered of a man-child so big and so like William Sugden that I felt like offering it a pipe of tobacco. Ah, well—I'm tired.

STELLA: You must be, Dad.

LILIAN: Your hot milk and brandy's here.

DR. KIRBY: Thanks. But what are you two doing up?

STELLA: We both heard a noise. It was Charles, and Wilfred. They went to bed but we stayed on, talking.

LILIAN: But I'm going now. Good-night.

DR. KIRBY and STELLA: Good-night.

LILIAN *goes out. DR. KIRBY pours out the hot milk and puts some brandy in it, sits down and nibbles a biscuit.*

182

DR. KIRBY: I'm getting a bit tired of the human body, Stella. I shall be glad to get back to my birds. I don't know that the behaviour of birds is much better than that of people. They can be as greedy and quarrelsome and vindictive as we can. But they're not so heavy and lumpy. They do things with more style. There's more enchantment about them. They ought to have had the fairy tales, not us.

STELLA: Perhaps they have their own. Was Mrs.— Sugden—difficult ?

DR. KIRBY: Not really. Though it's always a worrying job, especially when you've had to wait overtime. But it's done now. And there's another of us arrived in the village.

STELLA: Poor little chap.

DR. KIRBY: Oh—you needn't be sorry for him. To begin with, he looks a fine healthy specimen—the Sugdens are. And then again, with any luck he'll see a better world than you and I will ever know. That's certainly true of me. I'm not one of these elderly men—and I meet enough of 'em—who think everything's going to the dogs. There's a better world coming, Stella— cleaner, saner, happier. We've only to turn a corner— and it's there. I don't suppose I shall turn it, but you will. And this baby of Sugden's won't know anything else. When he grows up—sometime in the Nineteen Thirties—he simply won't understand the muddle we lived in.

STELLA (*sitting at his feet*): It is a muddle, isn't it?

DR. KIRBY (*sipping his drink*): Yes, and it's mostly our own fault. Yet it isn't either. Have you noticed—

183

or are you too young yet—how one part of us doesn't seem to be responsible for our own character and simply suffers because we have that character? You see yourself *being* yourself, behaving in the old familiar way, and though you may pay and suffer, the real you, the one that watches, doesn't seem to be responsible.

STELLA (*eagerly*): Yes, I was thinking about that only to-night. It's true.

DR. KIRBY (*tenderly*): Queer to see you looking like that again, with your hair down. It makes the last twenty years seem like nothing. You might be a child again. (*He puts a hand on her hair, in an awkward caress. She takes his hand and leans her face against his arm.*)

STELLA (*gently*): Dad, I'm afraid Charles and I must go to-morrow.

DR. KIRBY: That's bad news, my dear. I'd hoped you were staying a long time.

STELLA: So had I. But—well—we've just been offered two very good parts.

DR. KIRBY: And you're right to take them. Though I think you could do with a longer holiday than you've had. But if the English Theatre won't even let go of you for a few weeks, we must put up with it, that's all.

STELLA: I don't want to go.

DR. KIRBY: You mustn't mind us. I'm proud of you. I like to think of you forging ahead in your profession, getting all you can out of life. You know, you're doing it for me, as well as for yourself. As I told you before, I think I made a mistake. Your mother wanted me to settle down here, so I did. Nobody

184

knows but you that I've ever regretted it.   That's our secret.

STELLA (*distressed, deeply affectionate, pressing her face against his arm*): Dad!

DR. KIRBY: You're rectifying that mistake, my dear. And only you.   Lilian's your mother over again.   As long as she's a house of her own—and a man in it— she'll be happy in her own way.   Wilfred's a good lad, but he's a bit weak and easy-going.   He'll never do much.   But you're going on, living as I could have lived.   I'm glad.   I'm proud.   (*Putting a hand gently on her face.*)   So there can't be anything to cry about.

STELLA (*jumping up*): Of course not.   I'm stupid. And it's bedtime.

DR. KIRBY (*briskly*): Sunday to-morrow.   Only one train to London.   The Four Twenty.   And a brute.

STELLA (*going to door*): That's nothing.   We're used to brutal Sunday trains.   They're almost the only kind we know.   (*Turning at door, trying to smile at him.*)   Good-night, Dad.

DR. KIRBY: Good-night, Stella.   (*He finishes his milk and brandy as the curtain falls.*)

Same as before. Sunday afternoon. It is a dark afternoon. The door on the left is open. DR. KIRBY *enters, followed closely by* SARAH, *who is talking volubly and dividing her attention between the window and him. He is trying as best he can to search through the drawers at the table.*

SARAH: If you'd a bit o' sense you wouldn't let her stir out to-day, let alone go to London. Sunday an' all. Travelling o' Sunday in a fog. Nowt good'll come of that. It's as thick as ever it wor. Nay, thicker. It'll be worse afore it's better. What they want to run trains at all for o' Sundays, I don't know. Why can't they let folks have a bit o' peace and quiet for one day in the week? (*Taking advantage of her back being turned*, DR. KIRBY *escapes.* SARAH *does not notice or turn round.*) Stop at home and sit by the fire. London 'ull still be there to-morrow. It'll keep, London will. Unless it goes rotten. Daft, I call it.

WILFRED *pops his head round the corner.*

WILFRED: I say, Sarah. Who do you think you're talking to?

SARAH: Not to you.

WILFRED: Well, you're not talking to anybody else, because there's nobody else here.

SARAH: Then I'm wasting my breath.

WILFRED (*entering*): The car'll be here in another quarter of an hour.

SARAH: Are they having a motor-car to take 'em to the station?

WILFRED: Yes, old Thompson's Arrol-Johnston.

SARAH: I call it tempting providence.

WILFRED: I can't find my records. Have you seen them?

SARAH: Do you mean the things for that talking machine?

WILFRED: Yes. I can't find them anywhere.

SARAH: I'll go and help Miss Stella to finish her packing. (*Moves towards door.*)

WILFRED: I believe you know where they are.

SARAH: You shall have 'em in the morning.

WILFRED: I thought as much. Cheek! Where've you put them?

SARAH: Where you won't find them. We don't want no talking machines on a Sunday. You can play it to-morrow all day if you like.

WILFRED (*shouting*): I don't want to play it all day to-morrow. I want those records now.

SARAH: If I gave 'em you, you wouldn't have time to play 'em. (DR. KIRBY *bustles in. He is in a very fussy mood.* SARAH *darts at him.*) What you're letting Miss Stella go for to-day, Sunday, and wi' this fog and in a motor-car too, I don't know.

DR. KIRBY (*very fussily*): Don't be fussy, Sarah. Don't be fussy. I left a little book somewhere round here this morning. (*Ring at door.* Dr. KIRBY *calls through open door left.*) See who that is, Sarah. (*Almost to himself.*) And I hope to goodness, I'm not going to be called away now.

SARAH (*calling off*): It's Captain Farrant.

DR. KIRBY (*calling to her*): All right then, send him in, send him in. (*To* WILFRED.) It's a little book—about that size—called *Moorland Bird Life.* Have you seen it?

WILFRED: No. And Sarah's hidden my gramophone records away somewhere, because it's Sunday. Damned cheek!

FARRANT *appears in doorway.*

DR. KIRBY: Hello, Geoffrey. Come into the surgery with me, will you? I want to get something for Stella to take away with her.

DR. KIRBY *bustles him out.* WILFRED, *muttering "Too much fuss," lights a cigarette.* CHARLES *enters.*

CHARLES: How's the head now?

WILFRED: Getting better, thanks.

CHARLES: You mixed 'em too much, old boy. (*Comes in and looks out of window.*) God!—what a beast of a day. And I don't feel too crisp.

WILFRED (*not without gloomy satisfaction*): You'll have a rotten journey.

CHARLES: I know we shall. You can't tell me anything about long train journeys on foggy Sundays. If we'd any sense, we'd stay here and sit in front of the fire and talk about West Africa and wild birds and operations and Gaby Deslys and the Bunny-Hug.

WILFRED: Can you do the Bunny-Hug?

CHARLES: No. Nor the Turkey Trot. Nor the Tango. Not my line—thank God! At the moment, I feel that my line is playing old family solicitors, rheumaticy, toothless old scoundrels. (*Imitates one.*) " I have been instructed, Sir Rupert, to acquaint you with the te-r-r-rms of your uncle's will."

WILFRED (*laughs*): Jolly fine, I wish I was an actor.

CHARLES (*gloomily*): And I wish I was in West Africa —the hottest and blackest bit. (*Coming closer, and lowering voice.*) By the way, just let me give you a tip, while I've a chance, old boy. Take it or leave it. But I think if I were you, I should give that pub—you know the one—the "White Hart"—a miss, and give the little girl Alice a miss with it. I don't want to interfere, old boy—and couldn't preach if I tried. But they're no good, those bits. Not to a youngster like you. She'll only lead you up and down the garden. I know. I've had some in my time. Give it a miss, old boy.

WILFRED (*sullen*): Yes—but you don't understand——

CHARLES: Absolutely understand everything. I've been there. I've had some. Just think it over, old boy.

WILFRED (*wearily*): The trouble is—— I'm having a hell of a time.

CHARLES (*patting him on the shoulder*): It'll pass. I know. Try and find another little girl. There must be plenty round here. Squires' daughters with round red cheeks who'll sing the Indian Love Lyrics to you after dinner. (*Sings, in burlesque manner.*) "Ler-hess than the der-hust, Be-neath thy chariot whee-heel."

    STELLA *enters, dressed as in* ACT I. *She carries a small case which she puts on the table.*

STELLA: Oh, Wilfred, Lilian wants you.

WILFRED (*gloomily*): All right. (*Goes off.*)

CHARLES: Haven't you finished packing yet, old girl?

STELLA: Very nearly. All but some needlework and a couple of books. Charles, I want to talk to you.

CHARLES: And I want to talk to you. Haven't had a chance yet to-day. Look here, what's happening? I get up——

STELLA: At lunch time.

CHARLES: Admitted. And not feeling very bright. And I find we're leaving this afternoon. I gather, from what your father said, that we're supposed to have just been offered two wonderful parts.

STELLA (*hastily*): That's what I told him. I hope you didn't——

CHARLES: Now, now. You know me better than that. I murmured something about Tree and His Majesty's Theatre—big new pːoduction. Nearly convinced myself.

STELLA (*relieved*): That's all right, then.

CHARLES: Yes, as far as it goes. But I want to know what's happening.

STELLA (*smiling faintly*): Well, we're both getting on the same train for town and sitting in the same compartment. Once we're out of sight, if you don't want to talk to me, you needn't, Charles.

CHARLES: I see. We're putting on a performance for these people here.

STELLA: Yes. It's probably the only performance we shall put on for some time, so we'd better make the best of it.

CHARLES: Look here, Stella, couldn't we go on with it when we get to town?

STELLA: Do you want to?

CHARLES: I do. You ought to know that. But do you, that's the point?

STELLA (*gravely*): I think I'd like to try again, Charles.

CHARLES (*happily*): That's wonderful of you, it really is, old girl.

STELLA (*half laughing, but sharp*): And you mustn't call me "old girl."

CHARLES: Sorry, I forgot.

STELLA: How much money have you?

CHARLES (*humorously*): Now I know we *have* joined up again. Quite like old times. Yes, I've some money. About seventeen pounds. And then there's a fellow at the club who owes me a tenner——

STELLA: I haven't forgotten him. He still doesn't count. You haven't much, have you? And I've only about twenty left. We shall have to get a job quick, Charles.

CHARLES: We'll walk into one to-morrow, now that we're together again. Might pick up a couple of leads for the road. What about trying for one of God's own countries again, eh?

STELLA: Yes, I wouldn't mind. In fact, I'd like it. If I'm going away, I might as well go a long way.

CHARLES: You're right, y'know, to clear out. You'd never settle here. All right for a break, but that's all. You're doing the right thing.

STELLA (*indulgently*): And am I doing the right thing —taking you back again?

CHARLES: It's a risk, I know—I'm no catch—but I won't let you down. We've had some fun together. We'll have some more yet. What do you say?

STELLA: (*after a pause*): You've got the wrong tie on. Why do you keep wearing that tie?

CHARLES: It's the only one I brought. What's the matter with it?

STELLA: It's awful.

> FARRANT *opens the door.*

FARRANT: Oh—sorry.

CHARLES: That's all right. Come in, old boy. We're just having a chat about ties.

> FARRANT *comes in.*

STELLA: We haven't long now. (*To* CHARLES.) Will you and Wilfred get my trunk down?

CHARLES: All baggage will be stacked in the hall— immediately. (*Goes out, whistling.*)

STELLA: Well—Geoffrey?

FARRANT: You're going.

STELLA: Very soon. Back to town.

FARRANT: I'm going too.

STELLA: You're going? Where? When?

FARRANT: I'm going out to New Zealand for a year or two, perhaps longer. To my cousin.

192

STELLA: But, Geoffrey, you were saying, only the other day, that you were so fond of this place you couldn't bear to leave it.

FARRANT: So I thought. Then I found I was wrong. I wanted to get away.

STELLA: And you've really made your mind up?

FARRANT: Yes. I cabled my cousin yesterday. I shall take the next boat.

STELLA (*involuntarily*): Poor Lilian!

FARRANT: Why do you say that?

STELLA: Don't you realise that Lilian's in love with you, and has been for years?

FARRANT (*embarrassed*): Awful question to ask a chap!

STELLA: Well, she is, you know.

FARRANT (*embarrassed*): I'm sorry. Matter of fact, I'm very fond of Lilian. She's a fine girl. We've seen a lot of one another.

STELLA (*softly*): Then why don't you marry her, Geoffrey?

FARRANT: Because I don't want to, Stella. And I don't understand why you should ask me to. I don't understand women, at all, I'm afraid. I can't make you out—for instance.

STELLA: Then don't try.

FARRANT: I was angry with you when I left the other afternoon.

STELLA: I know you were, my dear.   I'm sorry.

FARRANT: In a way, I'm still angry.   But it's no use.

STELLA: It isn't any use being angry with people—
like that.   I'm beginning to see that.

FARRANT: I don't mean that—quite.   I mean—well,
here I am, you see.   And I didn't know you were going
when I called.   I just couldn't keep away.

STELLA: But you were determined to go yourself—
and a long way, too?

FARRANT: That was your doing, of course.   I knew
you'd be leaving us soon, and I felt you'd just leave me
and the whole place as flat as a pancake.   I couldn't
stand the thought of that.   I had to do something.

STELLA (*distressed*): I'm sorry.   It's all such a muddle,
Geoffrey, and I seem to be muddle-maker in chief.   For
years, while I stayed away, I had the thought of this
place—home—always in my mind, and here, I felt, it
was different—no muddle.   For an hour—no, only
for half an hour—it was all I had thought it was, and
I was so happy.   Then I found it was all mixed up with
the rest of the world.   And now I haven't even got this
to think about.

FARRANT: You talk too much about happiness,
Stella.

STELLA (*with a faint smile*): I think I do, Geoffrey.   I
must be a braver traveller.   We have our lives to get
on with, to live them as best we can.   There's no
running away.   No escape.   No miracles.

*There is a burst of talking, off, as if the kitchen door
had been opened.*

CHARLES (*off*): I'll carry the tray.

FARRANT: I think the others are coming. Good-
bye, Stella.

STELLA (*quickly*): But you're coming to the station?

FARRANT (*very quietly*): Yes, but this is the real good-
bye. And good luck. I—well—I shall always love
you.

STELLA: It's more than I deserve. Good-bye, my
dear.

*She kisses him, lightly, quickly. SARAH enters,
followed by CHARLES carrying a tray on which are cups
of tea. A car can be heard hooting outside. DR. KIRBY
and LILIAN follow CHARLES.*

*WILFRED arrives a moment later. They are all
wearing or carrying overcoats, etc., and are ready for the
journey.*

CHARLES: Enter ye butler!

SARAH: I don't care if all the motor-cars in England
is blowing and puffing and tooting outside, you're all
going to have a good hot cup o' tea afore you go.

STELLA: Of course we are. Lovely tea. Thank you,
Sarah.

WILFRED (*entering*): The car's here. You haven't
much time. (*The tray is on the table and they are now
grouped round it.*)

SARAH (*going off right, grumbling*): Plenty o' time. Let
the thing wait.

195

CHARLES (*trying tea, in low voice*): Strong stuff, isn't it?

DR. KIRBY (*also in low voice*): Far too strong. But she's made it specially. Must try and drink some just to please her.

CHARLES: Rather.

STELLA: Of course. (*In loud ringing tone.*) Lovely tea.

FARRANT: Hello, Lilian!

LILIAN (*smiling charmingly*): Hello, Geoffrey. Isn't it a horrible day?

FARRANT: Beastly.

LILIAN: How's the roan?

FARRANT: Better than I thought. The vet says it's a sprain. (*Moves away negligently.*)

    Enter SARAH *from right, carrying small parcel.*

SARAH: I'd nearly forgotten this, Miss Stella.

STELLA: What is it, darling?

SARAH: Why, your fancy dress I found the other day —very day you came home.

WILFRED: She doesn't want it, Sarah.

STELLA: Of course, I do. I shall hang it up in my dressing-room—always, wherever I am. A lovely present, Sarah. And the tea's so good.

CHARLES: Extraordinary.

DR. KIRBY: Now, Sarah, you must stop in, y'know. No station for you.

STELLA: Good gracious, no! Much too cold and foggy for you. Besides I can say good-bye to you much better here.

SARAH: All right, then. Won't you have a drop more tea, love?

STELLA: No, thank you, darling.

WILFRED: Time we were off.

> *There is a vague stir but no definite move towards the door.*

CHARLES (*idly*): If that telephone rings when we've gone, I'll bet it's to offer me the biggest part I've ever known—and I'll miss it.

WILFRED: More likely to ask me to go shooting rabbits with the Mowbrays.

DR. KIRBY (*heartily*): Don't you worry. I'll be the person who'll be wanted. And I've a good idea who'll be wanting me—poor soul. Well, all ready?

> *They straggle out, first* WILFRED *and* DR. KIRBY, *then* LILIAN *and* FARRANT.

CHARLES (*with* STELLA's *parcel*): Now, Sarah, old girl, you stay here and keep warm. And I'm delighted to have met you. Heard a lot about you from Stella, y'know. Good-bye. (*Holds out his hand.*)

SARAH: Good-bye. (*Shaking hands timidly.*) And— look after her.

CHARLES (*with mock salute of sword*): With my life! Good-bye. (*He goes out.*)

SARAH: He's not a bad sort for an actor chap, though I'll bet he takes a bit o' watching. But you look after him, too, love. He's nowt but a big daft lad—like em all.

STELLA (*whispering*): Oh, Sarah. I don't know what to say. There aren't any words.

SARAH: Nay, love. Nay, little love. (*Fondling her face.*) And don't catch cold when you're coming out o' the theatres. (*Very softly.*) I'm an old woman now, a'most past my time. Happen I shan't see you again.

STELLA (*crying*): Yes, you will. You must.

SARAH: Oh, I'll see you sometime. There's a better place than this, love.

Noise of motor engine starting up outside.

CHARLES (*off, calling*): Come on, Stella.

STELLA (*breaking loose*): I must go. Good-bye, Sarah, darling. (*She takes a last look round.*) Good-bye— everything.

She hurriedly kisses SARAH, *then runs out blindly. The door bangs to behind her. Then the outer door is heard closing with a bang. Noise of car going away. SARAH goes to the window, stares out for a moment, then closes the curtains, so that there is no light but that from the fire. She goes over to the fire and lights a taper. The telephone bell begins ringing. SARAH goes to the telephone with the lighted taper in her hand, holds the light close to it for a second, staring at it in bewilderment, then slowly withdraws into her own room. The telephone ringing is fainter, the firelight fades, until at last there is silence and there is darkness, and we find that the curtain has fallen and the play has ended.*

END OF ACT III

CORNELIUS

A Business Affair in Three Transactions

CHARACTERS
(in order of appearance)

MRS. ROBERTS
LAWRENCE
MISS PORRIN
BIDDLE
CORNELIUS
RUG MAN
ERIC SHEFFORD
PAPER TOWEL MAN
COLEMAN
YOUNG WOMAN WITH SOAP, etc.
EX-OFFICER
JUDY EVISON
DR. SCHWEIG
FLETCHER
ELDERLY MAN (Prophet)
MRS. READE
PRITCHET
MORTIMER
TWO WALKING-ON CREDITORS
ROBERT MURRISON

The action takes place in the general office of
Briggs & Murrison, Birdcage Street, Holborn. The
First Act on Monday morning, the Second on Wednesday afternoon, and the Third on Friday evening two
weeks later.

*Produced at the Theatre Royal, Birmingham, on March
11th, 1935, and at the Duchess Theatre, London, on March
20th, 1935, with the following cast:*

MRS. ROBERTS	MURIEL GEORGE
LAWRENCE	TOM GILL
MISS PORRIN	ANN WILTON
BIDDLE	JAMES HARCOURT
CORNELIUS	RALPH RICHARDSON
RUG MAN	ALBERT WARD
ERIC SHEFFORD	WILLIAM RODWELL
PAPER TOWEL MAN	PAUL SMYTHE
COLEMAN	FELIX IRWIN
YOUNG WOMAN	HAZEL CARNEGIE
EX-OFFICER	RAYMOND HUNTLEY
JUDY EVISON	VICTORIA HOPPER
DR. SCHWEIG	FELIX IRWIN
FLETCHER	RAYMOND HUNTLEY
ELDERLY MAN	ALBERT WARD
MRS. READE	DOROTHY HAMILTON
PRITCHET	VICTOR TANDY
MORTIMER	ROBERT GILBERT
ROBERT MURRISON	HARCOURT WILLIAMS

Play produced by BASIL DEAN.

ACT I

Office of Messrs. Briggs & Murrison, Aluminium Importers, Birdcage Street, Holborn. Monday morning. An ordinary general office room of the more old-fashioned kind, with a recess at the back lit by opaque window in the wall. Window to street on left, main door on left at right angles to window. On right wall door to Private Office. A long high desk in recess at back, and a desk at each side further down, one of them with a typewriter and a telephone. Small table with typewriter (covered at first) and typist's chair in front of window on left. Copying-in corner by recess on right. Ledgers, files, etc., prominent on walls.

When curtain rises, the office is empty. There is a pale wintry sunshine coming through window on left. Then Private Office door opens, and MRS. ROBERTS *backs out, followed by gusts of smoke. She coughs and angrily mutters: "Oh, blast the thing!" then goes back into the room. She is a stoutish Cockney woman in her fifties, with a red face, a hoarse voice, and a ripe character.* LAWRENCE *enters, a rather weedy youth of* 19, *wearing a raincoat that is not very adequate for this cold weather. He comes forward carrying a number of unopened letters—the morning's mail—which he puts down on the nearest table while he blows on his hands. Then he puts his hat and coat away in the cupboard meant for that purpose (probably down stage* R.) *and then sees*

P

Mrs. Roberts *coming out of the Private Office again, followed by smoke.*

Lawrence: Hello, you're late.

Mrs. Roberts: Yes, and you'd be late if you'd that devil of a thing in there to deal with. (*Coughs.*)

Lawrence (*idiotically*): It's smoking again.

Mrs. Roberts (*with immense irony*): Do you know, I believe it is. (*With gusto.*) Smoking! You can't see across that little bit of a room for smoke. If I've told 'em once, I've told 'em fifty times. There's something wrong with that chimney. The place's full of soot. I give it up.

> Lawrence, *who from now on is getting on with his first duties. He puts the letters on various desks. He fills all the inkwells from a large bottle of ink, puts clean sheets of blotting paper on the various desks, takes the covers off the two typewriters, and so forth.*

Lawrence: Well, it doesn't matter.

Mrs. Roberts: It doesn't matter to me if it doesn't matter to them.

Lawrence: Mr. Murrison's still away, and Mr. Cornelius won't mind. He nearly always stays out here, anyhow.

Mrs. Roberts: Good luck to him!

Lawrence: Only we'd better get his table out.

Mrs. Roberts: Come on then. I want to finish up.

> *They go into the private office and return carrying a small working table. The top is covered with newspapers. They put this near the door into the private office, and*

then, while MRS. ROBERTS *is taking off the newspapers and beginning to dust a little,* LAWRENCE *returns to bring out a chair, which he puts behind the table. During the dialogue that follows, while* LAWRENCE *gets on with his ink and blotting paper business,* MRS. ROBERTS *does a little more perfunctory dusting.*

LAWRENCE (*grumbling*): Look at me. Still doing this!

MRS. ROBERTS: Well what about it?

LAWRENCE: This is an office boy's job.

MRS. ROBERTS: What of it? Aren't you the office boy?

LAWRENCE: Yes.

MRS. ROBERTS: Well then?

LAWRENCE: I'm nineteen.

MRS. ROBERTS: Never! (*Then stares at him speculatively.*) No, I dare say you are.

LAWRENCE: There's no *dare say* about it. I know I am. I'm nineteen. I've been here nearly five years, and I'm still the office boy.

MRS. ROBERTS: Fancy!

LAWRENCE: They won't get a kid to do this. They won't promote me. And I'm nineteen. It's absolutely rotten.

MRS. ROBERTS: Why don't you leave then?

LAWRENCE: I would if I could get another job. I keep trying.

MRS. ROBERTS: That's right. You keep on trying. And if at first you don't succeed—suck eggs. (*Gives a sudden roar of laughter.*)

LAWRENCE (*properly ignoring this*): I've written for hundreds of jobs. I'm taking a correspondence course in wireless now.

MRS. ROBERTS: Now that's a good job—wireless. I've a nephew—my sister's oldest—who's in that. Has a shop of his own in Hackney. Wireless and gramophones.

LAWRENCE: I'm making a gramophone. I've nearly finished it.

MRS. ROBERTS: Well I call that clever. I wouldn't know how to start.

LAWRENCE: I've made lots of wireless sets.

MRS. ROBERTS: You're just like my nephew—the one at Hackney. Of course he's older. But I expect you'll be taking the girls to the pictures now—eh? Or don't you bother with 'em?

LAWRENCE (*gloomily*): Not much.

MRS. ROBERTS: Alfred—my nephew—was just the same. He'd rather be doing his wireless and what not. But then one fine day—before you could say Jack Robinson—lo and behold—he goes and gets married, and to as flighty a little piece as ever I saw. One o' these fancy blondes that's always having their hair waved. Goes right from Hackney to Kensington High Street—Pontings and Derry and Toms—to do her shopping. At least, that's what *she* says. I wouldn't trust her a yard. I'd like to have a look at her Derry and Toms. And I think that'll do.

She stops dusting and takes her apron off. MISS PORRIN *enters. A little woman in her early thirties, spectacled, rather dried up, very simple in manner.*

MISS PORRIN: Oh—good morning, Mrs. Roberts.

MRS. ROBERTS: Morning, miss. Quite strangers, aren't we? How are you getting on among it all?

MISS PORRIN: Quite well, thank you. And how are you?

MRS. ROBERTS: Fair—just fair. I'm not getting any thinner and you're not getting any fatter—that's right, isn't it?

MISS PORRIN (*taking off her hat and coat*): It looks like it, doesn't it? Good morning, Lawrence.

LAWRENCE: Good morning.

MRS. ROBERTS: Here—how's Mr. Cornelius these days?

MISS PORRIN: All right, I think.

MRS. ROBERTS: He hasn't got married again, has he?

MISS PORRIN: Oh—dear no.

MRS. ROBERTS: Well he ought to, a big fine man like him. He must have been a widower now—oh—for seven or eight years. I call it too long. You ought to set about him yourself, Miss Porrin.

MISS PORRIN (*brightly*): Such a strange thing happened to me—just now—in the bus. I was carrying my German book—I'm studying German, you know, Mrs. Roberts—I'd been reading it in the bus, but then I'd stopped because it made my eyes ache—and the bus gave a jerk and I dropped my German book, and a gentleman sitting opposite picked it up and handed it to me. And do you know—wasn't it strange?—he was a German himself. He told me so when he saw what the book was. Wasn't it strange?

207

MRS. ROBERTS (*with a wink at* LAWRENCE): When are you meeting him?

MISS PORRIN: Oh no, certainly not. I'm not meeting him anywhere. It wasn't like that at all. He just picked up the book and——

LAWRENCE (*brutally*): And gave it back to you and told you he was a German. We know.

MISS PORRIN: Don't be rude, please, Lawrence. (*Smiling at* MRS. ROBERTS.) But that's all that happened.

MRS. ROBERTS: Good job too, if you ask me. Don't you start taking up with foreigners, Miss Porrin. You don't know where they'll land you.

LAWRENCE (*in melodramatic tone*): White Slave Traffic!

MRS. ROBERTS (*preparing to go*): Well, a girl I used to know married one o' them Germans—a writer he was—and she got White Slave Traffic all right, a basin full, for he kept her at it, washing and scrubbing and cooking, from morning till night. Well, I'll be off. And tell 'em they can't blame me for the soot and mess, not till they got that chimney in there properly done. I can't work miracles. If I could. I wouldn't be here. Ta ta.

> *She goes out, carefully taking with her a large lump of coal wrapped in newspaper.* MISS PORRIN *goes over to her desk and takes some papers out of a drawer, looks at her typewriter, etc.* LAWRENCE *is slowly finishing his little jobs. Telephone rings.*

LAWRENCE (*at telephone*): Hello! This is Briggs and Murrison. No, we're not. Well, I ought to know, oughtn't I? We're Briggs—(*deliberately*) and Murrison.

(*Puts down receiver.*) And that's silly, when you come to think of it.

MISS PORRIN: What is? Wrong number?

LAWRENCE: No. But every day except Sunday for years at that telephone, I've been saying Briggs and Murrison, Briggs and Murrison, and for years and years you've been writing down Briggs and Murrison, Briggs and Murrison, and all the time there hasn't been a Briggs in the firm at all, only Mr. Murrison——

MISS PORRIN: And Mr. Cornelius. He's a partner.

LAWRENCE: Yes, but I call it a waste of time and breath going on year after year, saying Briggs, writing down Briggs, when there isn't a Briggs. And nearly everybody else doing the same thing.

MISS PORRIN: It doesn't matter.

LAWRENCE: It does. I call it silly and clumsy. You couldn't make a gramophone or a wireless set like that.

MISS PORRIN: That's because they're new things, Lawrence. All new things are neat, like that, but old things aren't. And a lot of business is really old.

LAWRENCE: Yes, but why? Why shouldn't all this be neat and new and sensible? Why should it be so old-fashioned? I'll bet it needn't be. I'll bet——

> But MR. BIDDLE *has entered. He is a clerkly elderly man, obviously very neat and methodical. He is well wrapped up and carries a folded newspaper—the "Morning Post." He takes off his overcoat, hat, and muffler during the following speeches.*

BIDDLE: Good morning, Miss Porrin. Good morning, Lawrence.

Miss Porrin: ⎫
Lawrence: ⎬ Good morning.

Biddle: It's still raw, very raw. Very little sign of spring about. (*Sniffs.*) Hello, has that chimney been smoking again?

Lawrence: Yes, Mr. Biddle. Ma Roberts says it's completely blocked up.

Biddle: We must have it attended to before Mr. Murrison comes back. Mr. Cornelius doesn't mind being out here, but Mr. Murrison wouldn't like it. Where's Miss Evison?

Miss Porrin: She hasn't come yet.

Biddle: I shall really have to talk very seriously to Miss Evison. She's late nearly every morning now, and even when she is here, her mind's not on her work.

Miss Porrin: I don't think she's very well, Mr. Biddle.

Biddle: Possibly not, possibly not. But that's no real excuse. Mr. Murrison—in my opinion—isn't very well, hasn't been well for some time, but there he is—in the Midlands—up north—travelling all the time, visiting all our customers, not sparing himself.

Lawrence: I think that's quite different.

Biddle (*banteringly*): Oh—you think that's quite different, do you, Lawrence? And why might it be different?

Lawrence: This is Mr. Murrison's own show. It's his firm.

Biddle: And it's my firm. And it's your firm.

Lawrence (*not too rudely*): No it isn't. This is simply

the place where I come and put out blotting paper and copy letters for twenty-five bob a week.

BIDDLE: Yes and you don't always do that very well. Get me the Day Book and the In Ledger.

LAWRENCE *goes to get the books. The telephone rings and is answered by* MISS PORRIN.

If that's Howlett and Company, I'll speak to them. Is it? Right. (*Takes telephone.*) Yes? Biddle here. Oh— is it Mr. Howlett? Yes, Biddle. . . . Yes, Mr. Howlett, I quite understand. We're all in the same boat nowadays, aren't we? . . . (*Laughs.*) That's very good. I must remember that. Now, listen, Mr. Howlett. Our Mr. Murrison's away. . . . Yes, he's gone himself. . . . Back on Wednesday. No, Mr. Cornelius isn't here yet. . . . Now, now, Mr. Howlett . . . you know us. . . . Oh no, Mr. Howlett. . . . Hello, hello!

It is obvious that MR. HOWLETT *has rung off prematurely, possibly in a temper. As* BIDDLE *puts down the receiver, he looks very worried. His speech that follows, which he gives as he begins looking through the letters, is more for his own benefit than for his listeners'.*

I've been in business for over forty-seven years, and and I can tell you that a day of it now is worse than a month of it in the old days. Upon my word, it's misery trying to do business nowadays. Everybody and everything make it as difficult as possible.

MISS PORRIN (*turning round and holding out letter*): I know, Mr. Biddle, I'm so sorry. What about this Excelsior Transport Company's claim? You asked me to remind you.

BIDDLE (*taking letter*): I should think so. Disgraceful,

I call it. Ask that young fellow—what's his name?—
Shefford—to come round at once. Mr. Cornelius had
better take it up with him. He'll deal with that lot.
He'll give them something to be going on with.

 Takes this letter, along with some others, over to
 CORNELIUS'S *table, then returns to his own desk to open*
 some more letters. MISS PORRIN *begins ringing up, but*
 is not heard. CORNELIUS *enters, immediately dominating*
 the scene. He is a well-set-up fellow between forty-five
 and fifty, outwardly an office man, though not too sedentary
 in appearance, but with a certain eager, humorous,
 imaginative way with him that suggests that the youth in
 him is by no means dead. He wears a heavy overcoat,
 with several newspapers stuck in the pockets, and a soft
 felt hat which he removes as he enters. He can be
 smoking a pipe. He arrives with great gusto.

CORNELIUS: Good morning. Good morning.

BIDDLE:
MISS PORRIN: } Good morning, Mr. Cornelius.
LAWRENCE:

CORNELIUS (*immediately going over to the letters on his*
table): Anything from Mr. Murrison?

BIDDLE: I'm afraid not, Mr. Cornelius.

CORNELIUS (*muttering*): Damned nuisance!

BIDDLE: I'm afraid there's no order come through
from Chale's either.

CORNELIUS (*gloomily*): I'm not surprised. As soon as I
saw young Chale's face, I knew there wasn't an order in
it. There was *No* all over it. All permanently screwed
down and hermetically sealed. Marvel to me how he

ever gives himself any food and drink. Why is my table
out here again?

LAWRENCE: It's smoky in there again, Mr. Cornelius.

BIDDLE: We shall have to complain to the landlord
about that chimney.

CORNELIUS: That's not so easy. We owe him some
money. (*As he takes off his overcoat.*) Miss Evison.

BIDDLE: She's not here yet.

CORNELIUS (*gives his hat and coat to* LAWRENCE): Then
she ought to be.

BIDDLE: She's getting very slack, I'm afraid—very
slack.

CORNELIUS (*sitting at his table*): Not ill, by any chance,
is she?

MISS PORRIN: I think she is, Mr. Cornelius.

    As CORNELIUS *begins to look through letters and
papers on his table,* BIDDLE *comes across and stands
attentively behind the table.*

CORNELIUS (*as he goes through letters, etc.*): Hm.
Solicitor's letter. Cattermole, MacIvor and Pritchet—
all very grand, eh?—authorised by something-or-other
Française—to represent French clients—settlement of
claims immediately on best possible terms—that's a
nasty one, Biddle.

BIDDLE: It's no use, sir. We shall have to meet them.

CORNELIUS: Looks like it. Small cheque from Shaw
and Johnston. Not much, but better than nothing.
(*Hands it over.*) Pay it in this morning, and make it look
a lot. That'll keep the bank amused until lunch time.

BIDDLE (*doubtfully*): Shall I take it round myself?

CORNELIUS: Better not. They'll never let you go until we've agreed to see them all on Wednesday. Send Lawrence round with it.

> BIDDLE *takes the cheque to his desk, endorses it, etc., all very carefully.*

What's this? Excelsior Transport Company? Here, I want to talk to these scoundrels. What have you done, Miss Porrin?

MISS PORRIN: I've rung them up and asked that young man who came here first—you remember him, Mr. Cornelius?

CORNELIUS: Yes, of course I do. Soapy young twister! What's his name?

MISS PORRIN: Shefford—Eric Shefford. I've asked him to come round at once and see you.

CORNELIUS: Quite right. (*Goes through more letters.*)

BIDDLE (*giving envelope*): Take this round to the bank, Lawrence.

> LAWRENCE *takes hat and goes.*

CORNELIUS: Another grim letter from Czecho-Slovakia—Hecht and Drapok. Why don't they use a typewriter? And why the devil isn't Miss Evison here? And if she can't come, why doesn't she let us know? (*Puzzling over letter.*) Something about their Dr. Schweig. Oh, what a letter! These people ought to be in the secret service. (*Puzzles over it.*)

> *There enters breezily a fellow with a red face and a hoarse voice and a confidential but loud manner. He is carrying two rugs over his arm.*

RUG MAN: Now I'm a sailor, gentlemen, just landed

yesterday at Tilbury Dock, and while I was away I picked up a few things that I think would interest you gentlemen——

CORNELIUS (*looking up*): Go away. You're not a sailor. And we don't want any rugs this morning.

RUG MAN: That's right, sir, it's a few rugs I'm selling. Now just cast your eyes over this one—

CORNELIUS (*ferociously*): If that flea-bitten rug isn't out of here in two seconds, I'll throw it out of the window.

RUG MAN (*folding up rug, pugnaciously*): All right, all right.

CORNELIUS (*getting up, dangerously quiet in manner*): It isn't all right.

> *As he steps round the table, the* RUG MAN *suddenly bolts.* CORNELIUS *laughs and sits down again. The telephone bell rings.* MISS PORRIN *answers it.*

MISS PORRIN: It's the bank. The manager would like you or Mr. Biddle to call and see him, this morning.

> CORNELIUS *and* BIDDLE *look at one another, rather ominously.*

CORNELIUS: You'd better go, Biddle. I couldn't get Murrison back before Wednesday afternoon—if they insist upon a meeting as early as possible. And say there's no point in our creditors meeting before Murrison does come back, simply because we're hoping his trip will have saved the situation.

> BIDDLE *nods and begins getting his coat on.*

Tell them Mr. Biddle's coming round at once. (*Returns*

215

to examining letters and papers.) Good God!—what's this. North London Crematorium?

BIDDLE: Oh—I'm sorry, Mr. Cornelius. Those two letters are mine.

CORNELIUS: Is there another one? Oh—yes. Valley of Rest Crematorium. Here you are. (*Handing them over.*) But why?

BIDDLE (*as he takes letters, carefully folds them, etc.*): I made up my mind some time ago that I'd like to be cremated, and so I've been getting estimates. There's a difference of about thirty-seven shillings between the two.

CORNELIUS: But perhaps the more expensive people make a better job of it?

BIDDLE (*seriously*): No, I don't think so. Both of them follow the same routine, I believe.

CORNELIUS: Don't tell me what it is. Tell them at the bank.

> BIDDLE *goes to the door, goes out, but immediately returns.*

BIDDLE: The young man from the Excelsior Transport Company's here—Shefford.

CORNELIUS (*grimly*): Tell him to walk straight in.

> BIDDLE *withdraws and* SHEFFORD *enters. He is a rather weedy, vaguely handsome young man, smartly dressed. He is not feeling very comfortable.*

SHEFFORD: Oh—good morning. Excelsior Transport Company. You wanted to see me, I think.

CORNELIUS (*taking up paper and moving towards him*): I did. I do. We've got a claim here from your Company for eight shillings a ton more than we agreed to pay you.

SHEFFORD: No, that's a mistake, I'm afraid.

CORNELIUS: Oh—you mean your people aren't going to claim the extra eight shillings a ton?

SHEFFORD: No, that's the usual rate. I mean, you must have misunderstood my quotation. What I gave you was the actual freight, without clearing and cartage charges, and—er—as you must have seen—it's on all our memo forms—there's an extra twelve and a half per cent for clearing and cartage charges—which works out at an extra eight shillings a ton. It's—er—all perfectly straightforward.

CORNELIUS: It's about as straightforward as a cork-screw. You knew very well when we accepted your quotation that we knew nothing about that extra eight shillings a ton, that we were in a hurry to get the metal delivered, and that you were getting the business under false pretences.

SHEFFORD: No, I didn't. How should I know——

CORNELIUS: Because you made a great point of the fact that your quotation was lower than anybody else's, whereas with this extra twelve and a half per cent, it isn't. And if you want to know what I think you are, I'll tell you. You're a young twister. You wanted the business and you didn't care a damn how you got it. Look—(*tears up the paper and tosses the pieces into* SHEFFORD'S *hat*) that's what we think about you and the Excelsior Transport Company. Now go back and tell them so.

SHEFFORD: All right. I will.

CORNELIUS *turns his back on* SHEFFORD, *who picks*

*the pieces out of his hat and stuffs them in his pocket,
shrugs his shoulders and goes out.*

CORNELIUS: Lot of young men like that about, Miss
Porrin. Twisters. If you have it out with some of them,
they tell you it's not their fault, it's the system. God
knows I don't admire the system. If there is one, it's
getting me down. But they'd still be twisting under any
system. They couldn't go straight on a desert island.

MISS PORRIN: I'm afraid that's true. I'm so sorry,
Mr. Cornelius.

CORNELIUS (*with rough good-humour*): Well, nobody's
blaming it on you, Miss Porrin.

*A little man has just sidled quietly in, holding a large
bag.*

Hello, how did you get in?

LITTLE MAN (*with insinuating voice*): Good morning,
sir, I won't keep you one minute. Now you people have
to wash here. You have to provide yourself with
towels. Those towels have to be sent to the laundry.
They have to be renewed.

CORNELIUS (*back at his table now*): Nothing this
morning, thank you.

LITTLE MAN: Sometimes people use the wrong
towels. It's all very dangerous and very expensive.
Now I have here a selection of paper towels—as used by
some of the biggest firms in the City. They're perfectly
efficient, hygienic, and inexpensive——

CORNELIUS (*firmly*): Not this morning.

LITTLE MAN: Just take a look at some of these——

CORNELIUS: Will you go away?

LITTLE MAN (*with a certain pathetic dignity*): I'm sorry.
Good morning.

*He goes out, as quietly as he came, drooping a little
under the weight of his bag.*

CORNELIUS (*irritably*): Where's Lawrence? Why isn't
he here to keep those fellows out? Either they're
blustering and then they make you angry, or they're
pathetic—like that poor little devil—and then they
make you feel miserable. And all the time there are a
thousand things to be thinking about. And what on
earth's become of Miss Evison? Is she on the telephone
at home?

MISS PORRIN: No, I don't think so, Mr. Cornelius.
And I do agree with you about those men who come
round with things. There seem to be more and more of
them.

CORNELIUS: There are. We'll all be doing it soon.
All calling on one another with rugs and paper towels
and shaving soap.

LAWRENCE *enters.*

Lawrence, go and shut the outer door. Then open that
Enquiries window of yours, ask 'em what they want,
and don't let 'em in unless they've got some proper
business here.

LAWRENCE *proceeds with this. Meanwhile, telephone
rings.* MISS PORRIN *answers it.*

If you don't want to have to get rid of a corpse about
lunch time, Lawrence, then don't let any more of these
fellows in.

MISS PORRIN: It's Brandings, of Birmingham. They
want to speak to you or Mr. Murrison.

219

Q

CORNELIUS (*happily*): That's more like it. (*Goes to telephone. At telephone.*) Hello! Brandings? Cornelius speaking. . . . Oh yes—is that Mr. Flockton? Thought I recognised your voice. . . . Yes, of course. Much as you like. That's what we're here for, as the parson said to. . . . Yes, exactly same quality as before. Our people over there are very dependable. . . . How much? My dear fellow, you're joking. We couldn't buy it at anything like that figure, not with the pound only worth twelve and sixpence over there. . . . No, but we can't help it either. Now be reasonable, Mr. Flockton. We can quote you—hello, hello. (*He lets the receiver droop.*)

MISS PORRIN: Shall I get them again?

CORNELIUS (*bitterly*): No, he meant to go. They don't even wait to say good-bye now. They just ring off. They've no use for you. You're out. It must be taking Murrison all his time to collect a few more orders. I don't know how he's doing it—if he is doing it. (*Goes slowly back to his table.*)

LAWRENCE (*through little window*): What name, please? Have you an appointment? (*To* CORNELIUS.) Mr. Coleman. He says it's important.

CORNELIUS (*getting up*): Yes, yes, of course. I want to see him.

LAWRENCE *admits* COLEMAN, *a middle-aged business man with a sharp jerky manner.*

Morning, Mr. Coleman.

COLEMAN: Morning, Mr. Cornelius.

CORNELIUS: How's copper wire these days?

COLEMAN (*grimly*): You know. (*Produces piece of paper, confidentially.*) Heard anything from Canada lately?

CORNELIUS: Not for a fortnight. Have you?

COLEMAN: Yes. And I was passing, so thought I'd slip in and tell you.

CORNELIUS: Very good of you, my dear chap.

COLEMAN: We had a night letter cable from our man Blake in Ottawa. Just came this morning. Here. (*They look at it.*) You see? Embargo's certain now on everything but low-grade sheet metal.

CORNELIUS: Yes. (*Grimly.*) I like that last bit. All the best and he's just going fishing. What do we reply to that? All the worst and we're just going to cut our throats, eh?

COLEMAN: Make a difference to you people too, won't it?

CORNELIUS: Yes. We haven't been buying much from Canada lately, or it would make a lot of difference. As it is, it takes the last crumb of cheese and leaves us in the mouse trap.

COLEMAN: It's a great life, isn't it?

CORNELIUS (*solemnly*): "And we are glad to report that business conditions everywhere are improving." Loud cheers from everybody *present*, all living on gilt-edged securities.

COLEMAN (*with slight laugh*): Well, thought you'd like to have the news.

CORNELIUS: Much obliged to you, Mr. Coleman.

They shake hands. BIDDLE *enters, looking rather miserable.*

COLEMAN (*going*): Not at all. Morning. (*Goes.*)

CORNELIUS: We're cut off from Canada now, Biddle. Shan't be able to buy a pound of decent metal there. I notice you don't look very cheerful.

BIDDLE (*with small forced smile*): Don't I, sir? I'm sorry. I'm afraid I wasn't feeling very cheerful. (*Begins taking things off.*)

CORNELIUS: What happened?

BIDDLE: Well, as you know, Mr. Cornelius, I've been going round to the Middlesex and Central Bank a good long time now. I knew most of the old lot very well. I used to like going round there, sir. I regarded it as one of the pleasantest parts of my duty. We used to have a good deal of quiet fun——

CORNELIUS (*pleasantly sardonic*): It must have been very quiet.

BIDDLE: Well, you know. Mr. Cornelius—we'd chaff one another, have our little jokes.

CORNELIUS: And there aren't any more little jokes, eh?

BIDDLE: Well, it's a bit of a shock to go in as I did this morning—the manager was quite pleasant, but——

CORNELIUS (*lowering voice*): What happened?

BIDDLE (*coming nearer, confidentially*): They're pressing very hard. They say it's head office.

CORNELIUS: You told them about Murrison making a big drive for orders?

BIDDLE: I made a great deal of it, said you staked everything on it.

CORNELIUS: I do. I know Bob Murrison. *He can do it.*

BIDDLE: I had to promise we'd make a definite statement to them and the other creditors here on Wednesday afternoon.

CORNELIUS: I thought you'd have to. Well, I'll wire Mr. Murrison at once. And you'd better let all these people know—these solicitors—Cattermole, MacIvor and the rest of it. And the Central Forwarding Company. And—Miss Porrin—you'd better wire Hecht and Drapok—I don't know where their Dr. Schweig is—telling 'em we're having a meeting of creditors—an *informal* meeting of creditors—here on Wednesday afternoon, about three.

MISS PORRIN: Yes, Mr. Cornelius. Hecht and Drapok.

CORNELIUS: Those are your men, Biddle. (*Hands him some letters.*) And cheer up. A lot of things can happen on Wednesday.

> CORNELIUS *begins writing furiously.* BIDDLE *looks thoughtfully at the letters in his hand, then walks slowly up to his desk with them.* MISS PORRIN *is listening at the telephone. She puts it down in disgust.*

MISS PORRIN: Can I send Lawrence down to the Post Office with this telegram to Hecht and Drapok? I can't get through to foreign telegrams on the telephone.

CORNELIUS (*still writing quickly*): Yes, and he can take this one to Mr. Murrison with him too.

> *Finishes letter, puts it in envelope, hastily addresses envelope.* LAWRENCE *takes completed letter from him,*

> *then goes to* MISS PORRIN *who gives him telegraph form
> and some money from small cash box.* LAWRENCE
> *hurries out.* CORNELIUS *relaxes and lights his pipe.*

By the way, there's the landlord. He ought to be told
about Wednesday. That old boy's treated us very
decently, hasn't he?

BIDDLE: Very decently indeed, sir. We can't complain at all in that direction.

MISS PORRIN: May I say something, Mr. Cornelius?

CORNELIUS: Why not?

MISS PORRIN (*with timid resolution*): Well, I think—
when you take everything into consideration—that a lot
of people are very *good*. (*Gives quick nervous laugh and
returns to work.*)

CORNELIUS: Perhaps. But you've got to take a devil
of a lot into consideration though. It seems to me
sometimes——

> *He stops and stares because a young woman, cheaply
> but fairly smartly dressed, and with a very assured
> manner, has just entered the office. She is carrying a small
> case.*

YOUNG WOMAN (*brightly*): Good morning.

CORNELIUS (*rising*): Good morning.

YOUNG WOMAN: I'm sure you gentlemen are needing
some shaving soap, tooth paste, talcum powder,
brilliantine——

CORNELIUS: I'm not. Are you, Biddle?

BIDDLE (*looking round hastily*): Oh—no, certainly not.

YOUNG WOMAN (*opening case and descending upon* COR-
NELIUS *with terrific smile*): Now I'm sure I can tempt *you*.

CORNELIUS: I'm sure you can too.

YOUNG WOMAN: Well then? All good new lines. Cheaper than the shops. What about some shaving soap then?

MISS PORRIN (*suddenly and surprisingly coming forward*): Please—go away. Go away at once. Nobody wants anything here. And you know very well they don't.

YOUNG WOMAN (*surprised*): Here, wait a minute. I wasn't talking to you.

MISS PORRIN (*indignantly*): I know. But I don't care. It's disgraceful—taking advantage—just because you're a woman. You're much worse than the men.

> *Telephone rings.*

CORNELIUS (*rather drily*): Telephone, Miss Porrin.
> MISS PORRIN *with a final glare at the intruder, turns to answer the telephone. The* YOUNG WOMAN *turns her batteries on* CORNELIUS *again.*

(*Mumbling.*) All right. I'll have a tube of shaving cream. That'll do. How much?

YOUNG WOMAN: Two shillings, please.

CORNELIUS (*producing money*): Cheaper than the shops, eh? I wonder what shops. Here you are. (*Takes shaving cream and hands over money.*)

YOUNG WOMAN: Nothing else? Thank you, good morning. (*To* MISS PORRIN.) Good morning.
> *Goes out.*

MISS PORRIN (*rather severely*): It's Mr. Howlett, wishing to speak to you, Mr. Cornelius.

CORNELIUS: Tell him I'm out, Biddle, but that I'm writing to him.

BIDDLE *goes to telephone and repeats this message while* MISS PORRIN *is talking as below.* MISS PORRIN *comes forward with a letter.*

MISS PORRIN: What about this account, Mr. Cornelius? (*Hands it to him.*)

CORNELIUS (*looking at it*): Eighty-seven pounds! I didn't know it was as much as that.

MISS PORRIN: It's been owing several months, and there was the typewriter and the table and chair, as well as the usual things.

CORNELIUS: Well, we can't pay it, that's all. Are they pressing us hard?

MISS PORRIN: I'm afraid they are.

CORNELIUS: I could talk to them—but it doesn't look very good when——

MISS PORRIN: If you like, I think I could go and talk to them. They know *me* because I've always ordered the things there. I could tell them you're both away and that one of you has to pass the account before we can settle it.

CORNELIUS: Yes, all right. Try that. Go round now. (*Hands her the account back.*) I say, you were very severe with that young woman who came in just now, weren't you?

MISS PORRIN (*hesitates then gathers courage*): Well— Mr. Cornelius—you don't mind my saying this, do you? But I do think it's such a shame—you're so firm with all those poor men who come round worrying us, and then, just because this is a girl and she comes in so impudently—oh, they're so much worse than the men.

I'm sorry for most of the men, but these women—
they're horrible. (*Goes for her hat and coat.*)

CORNELIUS (*ruefully*): I dare say you're right.

MISS PORRIN: I—I know I am. They're just vulgar—
vulgar—shameless——

CORNELIUS (*humorously*): Steady. Steady now.

MISS PORRIN (*rather triumphantly*): Sirens!

And she makes quite a triumphant exit.

CORNELIUS: And that's that, Biddle.

BIDDLE (*thoughtfully*): I've noticed before, sir—and
you must have done too—the female sex hasn't a lot of
sympathy for itself.

CORNELIUS: I have noticed it. And how the quiet
little shy ones hate the big bouncing ones.

*Takes a small account book and begins making little
calculations on paper from it. He looks thoughtfully
across at BIDDLE, who is now dealing with a ledger.*

Biddle, suppose we can't *carry on*. What's going to
happen to you?

BIDDLE (*slowly*): Well, it might be worse, sir. It
might be a lot worse, sir. I've a married daughter
living in South Devon. They've a little business, and
they'd like us to join them. We've got something saved
up. We've been careful——

CORNELIUS (*dryly*): You must have been.

BIDDLE: Yes, we've been very careful, and so we've
got something saved up. And that would come in
useful down in South Devon. And it's very *nice* down
there—very *nice* indeed.

CORNELIUS: That's *good*. But don't you ever feel—doesn't it ever come over you quite suddenly—that you've been wasting your time?

BIDDLE (*seriously*): But I don't waste my time, Mr. Cornelius.

CORNELIUS: I don't mean that. I mean, that you've wasted your life, just as if you'd taken it and poured it down a drain.

BIDDLE: No, I never think that for a minute. I've led an honest and useful life, Mr. Cornelius, and I'm not ashamed of it and I don't regret any of it.

CORNELIUS: Well, that's something to be thankful for. It would be horrible, at your age, if you felt anything else. It's bad enough at my age. You're a lucky man, Biddle.

BIDDLE: Yes, Mr. Cornelius, in some ways I am. I've always been able to work, and I've always enjoyed my work. The fact is, Mr. Cornelius, there's always been something very attractive to me about *figures*, numbers. In a sort of way, they're alive. For instance, seven has got quite a different character from eight. And five is one sort of person and six is quite a different sort of person. Like all of us.

CORNELIUS (*amused*): So all the time, while you were pretending to work, you've been having the most astonishing adventures in that corner?

BIDDLE: In a way—yes, I have.

CORNELIUS: I tell you—you're a lucky man, Biddle. *You've* never felt you were worrying the hair off your head, the sight out of your eyes, for what was nothing better than a piece of damned futility. I have—some-

times. Only sometimes. If I hadn't been working here
with Bob Murrison——

> *Stares at nothing for a moment, then turns back to his
> accounts. A man in his early thirties enters, carrying a
> sample case. He still holds himself well, but he looks
> pale, thin, nervous. He wears a short moustache and has
> the rather clipped speech of the ex-officer.*

Ex-Officer (*not very confidently*): Good-morning,
gentlemen. I'd like to show you some samples of the
stationery and other office supplies my firm is offering.

Cornelius (*shortly*): No thanks. 'Morning.

Ex-Officer: Any kind of stationery, carbons,
typewriter ribbons——

Cornelius (*decisively*): No.

Ex-Officer (*sticking it*): I'm sure you will find we
can quote you office supplies at a very cheap rate. And
they're all—er—of first-class quality. My firm—

Cornelius: We don't want anything, and I don't
want to hear about your firm.

Ex-Officer (*desperately*): Can't I possibly interest
you, sir, in our office stationery, carbons, ribbons—

Cornelius (*jumping up and flinging open cupboard on
right*): You're just being a nuisance, wasting our time as
well as your own. There's a cupboard full of stationery,
carbons—(*in his impatience he takes the young man by the
shoulder and swings him towards the cupboard*) ribbons,
paper fasteners, rubbers, and God knows what. More
than we can use up this year. Stacks of it, stacks of it.
Look here, what's the matter?

> *For the* Young Man *is in danger of collapsing.*

229

Steady man. (*Supporting him.*) What's the matter? Here, sit down, sit down.

> *The* YOUNG MAN *does, closing his eyes, for a moment, then, with an effort, opening them, with* CORNELIUS *standing almost over him and* BIDDLE, *rising, also watching him.*

EX-OFFICER (*with an effort*): Sorry. Suddenly felt giddy. Did a stupid thing—this morning. Only had a cup of coffee before coming out. Not enough perhaps on a cold morning.

CORNELIUS (*staring hard at his face*): No, not enough. And you hadn't enough yesterday or the day before either. In fact, you're half-starved, aren't you? That's why you nearly collapsed.

EX-OFFICER (*rather confusedly*): Have been a bit on short rations lately. But—anyhow—feeling rather— cheap.

CORNELIUS (*irritably*): You can't come in here starving like that, trying to sell us things we don't want. What are we to do?

EX-OFFICER: All right. I'm going.

CORNELIUS: No you're not, not for a minute or two. But why do you do it? Why don't you get something else to do?

EX-OFFICER (*grimly*): What?

CORNELIUS: Well, what were you originally?

EX-OFFICER: Air Force.

CORNELIUS: Officer?

EX-OFFICER: Yes. Had a bad break-down. North West Frontier. Then I was broke.

CORNELIUS: But surely you could have done something better than trying to sell that stuff? I know jobs are hard to get. But why stick to England at all? Why didn't you go to one of the colonies or to South America?

EX-OFFICER: No money. I tried. They don't want you any more in those places unless you've got capital. They don't want you anywhere. My God—you don't think I didn't try everything before doing this?

CORNELIUS (*incredulous, not contradicting*): I can't believe the world's all shut up like that—with a *Keep Out* sign everywhere.

EX-OFFICER: That's what it looked like to me. You haven't—a cigarette, by any chance?

CORNELIUS *gives him one.*

Thanks. (*Lights it.*) I take it—you wouldn't like any stationery or ribbons or anything? Sorry to be offensive, but a chap's got to live. Or at least I suppose so. No carbons? No account books?

CORNELIUS: Look here, if I spent another penny on that stuff, when we're jammed up with it, I'd be acting dishonestly towards my partner. But I can't see you go out in that condition. You won't be able to carry that case of yours soon. Take this (*holds out note*) and for God's sake treat yourself to a good square meal before you do anything else.

EX-OFFICER: Nice of you—but——

CORNELIUS: Oh—take it—(*forces it on him*) we want to get on with our work.

EX-OFFICER (*rising*): Sorry. No use telling you I'll

231

pay you back some time, I suppose. I will though, if I can sell any of this stuff. And I might be able to once I've got some hot food and a drink inside me.

CORNELIUS: I doubt it. For the love of Mike, try to sell something else.

EX-OFFICER: Yes, but what?

CORNELIUS: Well, anything but that. We get scores of fellows with that stuff. Be original. Strike out for yourself. Come round with fresh lobsters or pipe cleaners or dirty postcards. Think of some new way of earning a living. There must be dozens that nobody's ever tried.

EX-OFFICER: No doubt. But don't you see, if I was capable of inventing a new kind of job, I should never have been in this fix at all. I'm not clever enough. Don't pretend to be. What gets me down is that I'm not allowed to earn my living in any of the old ways. And thanks again for this (*indicating note*). I'll pay you back some day. So long. (*Moves to door.*)

CORNELIUS: Good luck! (*Watches him go, then turns to* BIDDLE.) D'you think that's true, Biddle—that here's a fellow, willing to work, fairly intelligent, who not only can't get anything to do here—I can understand that— but who finds the whole world closed to him, bolted and barred?

BIDDLE: I'm afraid it might be.

CORNELIUS (*with some agitation*): I can't believe it. If you're willing to work hard, willing to take risks, ready to be scorched or frozen, drowned or sent half-mad with thirst, there must be openings for you somewhere in the world. They can't have closed everything up, so

232

that we're all like bees in a glass case. It's unthinkable, Biddle. I've always had at the back of my mind a little open door, with plantations and jungles and pampas and quartz mountains just outside it—with the sun on 'em. Don't tell me that all the time that little door's not been open, has been locked from the outside, screwed fast.

BIDDLE: The Coventry people are worrying about that consignment of circles we sent off last week.

CORNELIUS (*back at his table now*): They've no need to grumble. We're out of pocket now on that deal, thanks to the nice kind French people: sharks with beards and attaché cases.

Telephone rings. BIDDLE *answers it.*

BIDDLE (*at telephone*): Briggs and Murrison. . . . Who? . . . Oh . . . I'll see. Just a minute. (*To* CORNELIUS.) It's the Income Tax people—the inspector —wants to speak to you.

CORNELIUS: Oh. New idea, telephoning, isn't it? But I believe I ought to have seen that chap this morning.

BIDDLE: What shall I say?

CORNELIUS: I'll talk to him. (*Goes to telephone.*) Hello. . . . Yes, this is Cornelius. . . . Oh, yes. Sorry I didn't turn up. . . . Yes, I dare say it is important, but so is this business—to us, and you seem to have an interest in it too. What was it? . . . Well I'm here at the end of the telephone. What's the matter with that? You don't want to *look* at me, do you, my dear chap. . . . A legacy? Yes, I had. A small one. . . . What did I *do* with it? I spent it. . . . Yes, I spent it. . . . What *on*? My dear sir, you take a most flatteringly deep interest in my affairs, don't you? . . . Well,

233

the government then. . . . All right, tell the government I spent it recklessly and luxuriously and with the most devilish abandon. . . . Yes, beautiful mad women. Processions with elephants and brass bands through oriental cities. A private guard of swordsmen and detectives with machine guns. Great glittering white yachts. Fountains of wine. Yes, and tell the government I've no further interest in the country. I've dissolved the partnership. They can keep what they've already had out of me, but they won't get any more. I'm on my own now. . . . All right then, my dear sir. Send me the pink or buff form and I'll deal with it. Good morning. (*Puts down telephone and returns to table.*)

BIDDLE (*chuckling*): I wonder what he's thinking.

CORNELIUS: He's thinking I'm off my head, and he's probably right. This famous legacy he's worrying about—wanting to know what I did with it, mind you— came to me from an old aunt of mine at Waltham Cross, and amounted to exactly eighty-seven pounds and ten shillings. What did I do with it? Tut-t-t-t. (*Tries to work, but sound of voices outside.*) Now what's this?

LAWRENCE *enters.*

What is it?

LAWRENCE: It's Miss Evison.

CORNELIUS: Well, if it's Miss Evison, why doesn't she come in? We've been waiting for her half the morning. What's the matter?

LAWRENCE: It's not our Miss Evison, sir. It's her sister.

CORNELIUS: Oh. Well, bring her in then. She must have a message for us.

LAWRENCE *holds the door open and* JUDY EVISON *enters. She is a girl about twenty, small, pretty, with an engaging childlike quality that makes her markedly different from anybody else who has appeared on the scene. She is oddly composed in manner. She is cheaply, but quite charmingly dressed.*

JUDY (*entering, then stopping*): Good morning.

CORNELIUS (*getting up*): Good morning.

JUDY: Are you Mr. Cornelius?

CORNELIUS: Yes.

JUDY (*not impudently*): You're rather different from what I expected.

CORNELIUS (*good-humouredly*): Well, I don't know that I care much about that. What's happened to your sister?

JUDY: I came to tell you. Her husband's been suddenly taken ill in Newcastle.

CORNELIUS: Her husband! I never knew she had a husband. Did you know that Miss Evison had a husband, Biddle?

BIDDLE: Not the least idea of it, sir.

JUDY: Well, she has. She was married about six months ago.

CORNELIUS: But why didn't she tell us? I call it very unfriendly of her, getting married and never saying a word about it. Not only unfriendly, but also underhand, deceitful.

JUDY (*smiling*): Not really. I can explain.

CORNELIUS: All right then, explain. But see you make

235

R

a good job of it, because we're resentful—aren't we, Biddle?

JUDY *begins laughing.*

What are you giggling about? There's nothing to giggle about.

JUDY (*still laughing a little*): I'm sorry. But—I think you're funny. My sister—used to talk about you, and I always thought you sounded funny.

CORNELIUS (*humorously exasperated*): But my dear young woman, you can't come here—calmly announcing that your sister's married, then giggling, then telling me to my face that I'm funny.

LAWRENCE *suddenly explodes with laughter.*

That'll do, Lawrence. Outside.

LAWRENCE (*recovering*): But where to, sir?

CORNELIUS: Anywhere. Haven't you something for him to do, Biddle?

BIDDLE: Take this round to the Central Forwarding people, Lawrence.

LAWRENCE *takes letter from* BIDDLE, *picks up his hat, then looks at* JUDY *and* CORNELIUS *as he gets to door, goes out and is heard exploding again.*

JUDY (*calmly*): I'm sorry. I didn't realise that boy was so silly.

CORNELIUS: You seem to me a very extraordinary young woman. Now tell us about your sister.

JUDY: They hadn't much money when they married. Her husband's a traveller—for a firm of chemists—but he's only just begun. And Ann thought that if she told you she was married, she might lose her job here, and they couldn't afford that, and it didn't matter about her working because Alec was away so much. And now he's ill—pneumonia—in Newcastle, and she's rushed up there to be with him. And I think she ought to go, don't you?

CORNELIUS: Yes. But I wish she'd told us she had a husband who at any moment might suddenly get pneumonia in Newcastle.

BIDDLE: It's very inconvenient indeed.

JUDY: Yes, I know. But you see—that's why I'm here.

CORNELIUS: Oh?

JUDY: I'm a shorthand-typist too, and I can do her work quite easily.

CORNELIUS: But why haven't you got a job of your own?

JUDY: I left mine last week.

CORNELIUS: Why? I thought nobody left their jobs nowadays.

JUDY: I do. You see I was working for a Spaniard— he was a fat yellow sort of man with a black beard—and he'd come to England because he had a theory about pigs——

CORNELIUS: Pigs?

JUDY: Yes, pigs. And he used to be out all day and I had to stay in a very dirty little room in Victoria with nothing to do, and then he'd come in about five o'clock and begin dictating long, long letters—in the queerest English—all about pigs, and then I had to stay there hours and type them. I hated it. He was a very smelly sort of man too.

CORNELIUS: Perhaps it was the pigs.

JUDY (*seriously*): No, I think it was something he ate. Anyhow, I loathed it. So I left.

CORNELIUS: And now you'd like to come here.

JUDY: Yes, I wouldn't mind it here. And I'm quite a good shorthand-typist. Better than Ann, as a matter of fact.

CORNELIUS: I dare say, but you see we're used to her and it might take us a long time to get used to you.

JUDY: But she may be away for weeks.

CORNELIUS: That's true. But we could easily get somebody. You seem such a formidable young woman.

JUDY (*demurely*): I'm not. I'm very quiet.

She smiles at him and finally he grins back.

CORNELIUS: All right. That's your place over there. (*Indicates table by window.*) You'd better start now—er— Miss Evison.

JUDY: My name's Judy.

Takes her hat and coat off calmly.

CORNELIUS: You already know my name. And this is Mr. Biddle, the cashier.

MISS PORRIN *enters.*

Oh—and this is Miss Porrin, who'll show you what to do, if necessary.

To MISS PORRIN, *who is regarding* JUDY *with surprise and some disfavour.*

Miss Porrin, this is Miss Judy Evison, who's come to take her sister's place. (*Turns away.*)

MISS PORRIN: You're—very young, aren't you?

JUDY (*brightly*): Yes, aren't I? But I've had a very good training.

> *Sits down at her table and examines her machine, etc. There is a sharp rap on the door. MISS PORRIN goes to it and brings back a telegram which she gives to CORNELIUS, who rises and moves forward to read it. He is plainly puzzled by it.*

CORNELIUS: I say, Biddle. (*As BIDDLE comes forward.*) I've a wire here from Mr. Murrison. Read it. (*As BIDDLE reads it.*) I think it must be one of his jokes.

BIDDLE: Funny time this for joking, sir.

CORNELIUS: Yes, but you know what he is. Besides, it's the only explanation. Why should I know anything about two men following him? It's some old joke of his that he's reviving and that I've forgotten. You see what that means, Biddle?

BIDDLE: No.

CORNELIUS: It means he's in good spirits. Probably got a bagful of new orders that he's keeping as a surprise for us.

BIDDLE (*dubiously*): Well, I hope so, Mr. Cornelius. (*Handing back telegram.*)

CORNELIUS (*indicating telegram*): And this is just like him. Now then, Miss Evison the Second, just bring a notebook and pencil over here, please.

> *He sits down, and JUDY crosses with notebook, taking up a position just behind him, standing.*

CORNELIUS (*handing her a letter*): Those people. Dear Sirs, In reply to your letter of the 11th instant, we regret to inform you that no further supplies of the French

239

metal your number A73—are—er—avilable at anything
like the price you mention, owing to present foreign
exchanges. We—er—should like to draw your attention
—however—to our Canadian sheet metal—too fast?

JUDY: Much.

CORNELIUS: Which-will-not-be-available—er—long-
at-present-prices—owing——

> *A voice is heard outside saying. "Briggs and Murri-
> son? 'Morning." in the brisk manner of postmen, and
> now* LAWRENCE *enters with two letters and a parcel.
> He hands one letter to* BIDDLE *and the other letter and
> parcel to* CORNELIUS.

(*To* JUDY.) Just a minute.

> *Opens letter, which he tosses aside, then he opens
> parcel, which contains a large octavo modern book. At
> this moment the telephone rings.* MISS PORRIN *answers
> it and after a moment can be heard saying "Mr. Corne-
> lius? Yes, I'll ask him." There is now a sharp rapping
> at the Enquiries Window, which* LAWRENCE *opens. He
> can now be heard saying to the invisible caller "Mr.
> Cornelius? What name, please?" Meanwhile,* CORNE-
> LIUS, *after looking at the title and title page of his book,
> is now glancing at the first page.*

CORNELIUS (*to* JUDY): I ordered this book from a
second-hand catalogue. Don't often do that. It's about
the Andes.

MISS PORRIN: Mr. Cornelius, you're wanted on the
telephone.

LAWRENCE: Mr. Cornelius, there's somebody called
Frensham wants to see you.

JUDY: Mr. Cornelius, what about this letter? (*These three speeches can overlap.*)

CORNELIUS (*still staring at book*): I like the look of this. Listen. "After a week in the Indian village, we decided to take the track into the clouds, to find among those heights *the lost city* of the Incas . . ."

> *As the curtain descends, we hear them saying again, more urgently, "Mr. Cornelius, Mr. Cornelius." But he has not looked up yet from staring at the Andes.*

END OF ACT ONE

ACT II

Office, as before. Wednesday afternoon.

JUDY *is working down left, typing letters.* MISS PORRIN *is carefully copying out some figures at her desk at the back. Then* MISS PORRIN *obviously comes to the end of the task, for she closes the office books she has been glancing at, rises with two sheets of paper in her hand.* JUDY *keeps on typing. As* MISS PORRIN *moves towards the door of the private office, it opens and* CORNELIUS *comes out a step or two. He is holding a half-finished glass of stout in one hand and a half-eaten ham sandwich in the other. He is chewing the sandwich as he comes out.*

MISS PORRIN (*eagerly*): Oh—Mr. Cornelius——

CORNELIUS (*his mouth rather full*): Yes?

MISS PORRIN (*showing papers*): I've got those figures out for you—if you should want them at the meeting this afternoon.

CORNELIUS (*looking at them as she holds the papers out*): Yes, might be very useful—very useful indeed. They're for the last three years, of course?

MISS PORRIN: Yes, they cover everything for the last three years. And you'll find them quite accurate.

CORNELIUS: I'm sure I shall. Thanks very much, Miss Porrin. You ought to be going off and getting some lunch now. You're very late.

MISS PORRIN: Oh—it doesn't matter. I—I never eat much lunch.

CORNELIUS (*thoughtfully*): No, I don't suppose I do—really. I like a better lunch than this though, only to-day I hadn't time to go out and get it. You know, Miss Porrin—(*he stops and takes a thoughtful bite of sandwich.*)

MISS PORRIN (*hopefully*): Yes. Mr. Cornelius?

CORNELIUS: There's something queer about the ham in this sandwich. I told Lawrence to get it at the pub below. I hope he did. As a rule, a pub makes you a good sandwich—a good, hearty, honest sandwich. But this ham tastes—put those figures down there, please, Miss Porrin—it tastes—there's a sort of cheesy flavour. Now why should it taste like that?

JUDY (*calmly calling across*): Because it's bad, I expect.

MISS PORRIN (*too sweetly*): Shall I help you to finish those letters, Miss Evison?

JUDY: No thanks, I'm just doing the last.

> CORNELIUS *has now put the last of his sandwich in his mouth, and has taken up the papers* MISS PORRIN *put down and given them another glance.*

MISS PORRIN (*eagerly*): Oh—Mr. Cornelius——

CORNELIUS (*negligently*): Yes?

MISS PORRIN: I do hope everything—everything—you know—goes on all right this afternoon at the meeting.

CORNELIUS: Yes, of course we all do.

MISS PORRIN: Oh—I don't mean just for the firm and for myself—but for your sake, Mr. Cornelius. I know

you've worked so hard and been so worried and yet
been so cheerful—and—and bright—and kind to us all
—and you do *deserve* everything to be all right.

CORNELIUS (*rather astonished*): Well—yes, I suppose
so. I don't know.

MISS PORRIN (*eagerly*): And I appreciate it. I *do*
appreciate it, Mr. Cornelius. And if there's anything
more I can do, just to help you—I'd love to do it, I
really would.

> *She looks beseechingly up at him. He stares at her,
> rather embarrassed.*

CORNELIUS: No thank you, Miss Porrin. There's
absolutely nothing else you can do, and you've been
very very helpful. Now go and get some lunch. And
don't worry about this meeting. Mr. Murrison will be
back and then we'll surprise some of these creditors.

MISS PORRIN (*timidly laying a finger on his arm, then
hastily withdrawing it, then smiling and blinking*): Oh—I do
hope so. (*She goes quickly for her hat and coat and puts them
on.*)

CORNELIUS: And don't forget you needn't come back
until about five. That'll give us time to get the meeting
over. You needn't come back at all this afternoon——

MISS PORRIN (*with a false brightness*): Yes, of course I
will. There may be lots and lots to do.

> *As she hurries out,* CORNELIUS *takes a last drink of
> his stout and* JUDY *takes her last letter out of the
> machine and begins reading it over.*

CORNELIUS (*almost to himself*): There's something
very queer about Miss Porrin these days——

JUDY (*calmly*): She's in love with you.

CORNELIUS (*humorously exaggerating a real note of protest*): Miss Judy Evison. You can't come into this office—this place of business, this commercial establishment—saying things like that.

JUDY: Why not?

CORNELIUS: Because it won't do. It's all wrong. We don't talk like that here. It's not the sort of thing that's going on here.

JUDY: But it's true. I saw it at once. I could have told you on Monday.

CORNELIUS: Well, I'm very glad you didn't tell me on Monday. And I'm sorry you've told me now.

JUDY: So am I if you feel like that about it. But you wanted to know why she's queer. That's why she's queer. (*Laughs.*) She thinks you're absolutely marvellous.

CORNELIUS (*with rather hastily assumed dignity*): Miss Porrin has been working with me here for some years now——

JUDY (*demurely*): I've finished the letters you gave me, Mr. Cornelius. Will you sign them please? (*Bringing them over.*)

CORNELIUS: You'd better clear the things off your desk before you go. We shall have to get the place ready for the meeting.

> *He goes into the private office with the letters, leaving the door open slightly.* JUDY *tidies up her desk and begins singing. He returns with the signed letters. She stops singing, naturally—not suddenly breaking off.*

CORNELIUS: Here you are. (*Handing her the letters.*)
You know, you've got a very pretty voice there, a very
pretty voice. Done much singing?

JUDY (*putting the letters into their envelopes*): I had a few
lessons once.

CORNELIUS: You ought to keep on with it. (*Takes
out his pipe and looks at it.*) Wonder if I ought to smoke?

JUDY: Why not?

CORNELIUS: I'm thinking about these creditors. We
don't want them coming in here—sniffing—and saying
to themselves "Place reeks of tobacco. These people
come here to smoke, not to do business." But then—
why should they? I've been a creditor myself in my
time, and I never talked like that. (*Lights his pipe, then
laughs.*)

JUDY (*who has just finished her envelopes*): What's the
matter?

CORNELIUS: I was just thinking it's a pity we can't
give these creditors a good entertainment this afternoon
instead of a meeting.

JUDY (*amused*): That would be grand.

CORNELIUS: You could sing—you sing very nicely,
y'know—a very pretty voice there—and I'd—er——

JUDY: Yes, what would you do?

CORNELIUS: I do a very good card trick. The four
Jacks represent four commercial travellers. Do you
know it? I must show it to you some time. But you'd
better get away to lunch now. What do you eat for
lunch?

JUDY (*amused*): Oh—all sorts of things. Poached eggs

246

on toast. Or fish cakes. Or tongue and salad. You know.

CORNELIUS (*looking at her appreciatively*): Yes. Funny. Somehow I can't imagine you eating at all.

JUDY (*laughing*): I eat a lot.

CORNELIUS: Can't imagine it. Now your sister—though she's not a big girl—I could imagine her tucking into enormous steak and kidney puddings and then having two helpings of treacle tart—but you? No. You must let me see you eat some time, will you?

JUDY: Well, I don't think you'd find it very amusing. But you can if you like. (*Prepares to go.*) Oh—do you want me to come back again—after you've finished the meeting?

CORNELIUS: Well—what do you think?

JUDY (*with obvious reluctance*): I will—if you really want me to. Only——

CORNELIUS: No, no, that's all right. Don't bother.

JUDY (*smiling at him*): Thank you. Good-bye.

She goes. CORNELIUS *crosses slowly to her desk, still smiling at his thought of her. She has left a glove behind on the desk. He picks it up, smooths it out, then contrasts it with his own hand, smiling at the two of them together. While he is doing this,* JUDY *hurries in, rather breathless.*

I left a glove. Oh—you've got it.

CORNELIUS (*rather confused*): Yes—I was just wondering whether I could give you a shout down the stairs—and——

JUDY (*smiling*): Here I am. (*Taking glove.*) Thank you.

247

She hurries out. CORNELIUS *frowns now, as if dismissing the trivialities of life, and rather importantly surveys the office, obviously trying to decide where to seat the creditors. Having got them seated, he takes up a position and begins rehearsing a speech to himself, then changes his position. Then he warms to his work of speechifying, finally saying out loud:* "Gentlemen, I put it to you. You are men of business. So are we." *In the middle of this,* BIDDLE *enters and looks at* CORNELIUS *in mild astonishment.*

CORNELIUS (*catching sight of him and breaking rather confusedly*): Oh—hello, Biddle. Where's Lawrence?

BIDDLE: Isn't he back yet, sir? He ought to be. (*Begins taking off coat.*)

CORNELIUS: Of course he ought. Most important afternoon in the whole history of the firm, and we can't get the office boy back in time. Typical—typical of the whole—er—of everything nowadays. We must get this place ready for the meeting, Biddle. I was just wondering where to put them.

BIDDLE (*going to hang things up*): I don't suppose they mind where we put 'em sir, as long as we can promise 'em some money.

CORNELIUS: That's all very well, but there's an art in these things. Put them in one place and they'll all be bad-tempered. Put them in another, and they'll be on our side all the time. Now I think—over there. (*Pointing.*) Let's see, how many of them will there be?

BIDDLE: Not more than eight, I should say.

CORNELIUS: Eight would go there nicely. I can see

248

them sitting there, thoroughly pleased with themselves. Now what about chairs?

BIDDLE: This will do for one. (*Takes* JUDY's *chair and puts it in place.*)

CORNELIUS: And this for another. (*Taking another chair down.*)

BIDDLE (*stopping as he goes for another chair*): You know, Mr. Cornelius, I don't like that chap the Bank's sending round this afternoon.

CORNELIUS: Who's that? What's-his-name?

BIDDLE: Yes, Mortimer. Don't like him. Very hard, he is.

CORNELIUS: Yes. Got a face like a rat-trap. Probably that's why they send him on these jobs. They know he can make his face like a rat-trap. And yet, you know, Biddle, at home and among his pals, he's probably a very nice fellow. Digs his garden, helps the girls with their homework, plays a good game of bowls, toddles along with his missis to the pictures and pretends to be in love with Greta Garbo—eh? Just an ordinary very nice fellow. Yet he comes along here with a face like a rat-trap. As if owing a bit of money to the Middlesex and Central Bank, when they've got more money than they know what to do with, was a crime so terrible— like murdering children! D'you know what I think sometimes, Biddle?

BIDDLE: No, sir.

CORNELIUS (*very quietly*): Sometimes I think it's all bloody nonsense.

BIDDLE (*rather shocked*): No, Mr. Cornelius. Don't

you go thinking that. Whatever you may say, business
—well, it's business. You can't change that.

CORNELIUS: I don't know whether I can change it, or
whether you can change it, but somebody's always
changing it. I've been in business, of one kind and
another, for nearly thirty years, and business has never
been the same for ten years together. You know that
yourself, with your experience.

BIDDLE: Ah—but after all—two and two have still
got to make four.

CORNELIUS: They haven't. You ask the Middlesex
and Central Bank. Now, two and two have got to make
five. And if they had to make four, we couldn't do it,
because we haven't got two and two, we've only got
two and one. These fellows who are coming here this
afternoon, Biddle, they don't want chaps like you as
cashiers. They want Einstein.

BIDDLE (*chuckling*): There's something in that.

CORNELIUS: Yes, Einstein as cashier, and Mussolini
and Hitler and the storm troops as salesmen.

BIDDLE: Well I must say I'm very glad to see you in
such good spirits, Mr. Cornelius. I've been very
worried myself about this afternoon.

CORNELIUS: Have you?—so have I.

BIDDLE (*confidentially*): Tell me, sir, what do you
think our chances are?

CORNELIUS (*confidentially*): If they'd had to depend
on me, Biddle, I'd tell you now our chances were nil.
We'd be finished. You know how things stand here.

BIDDLE (*sadly*): Only too well, sir.

CORNELIUS: But they don't depend on me. They depend on Murrison. He's coming back this afternoon, he's going to talk to these fellows, and he's visited every good customer we've ever had. He's not said much in his letters, but I know Bob Murrison, and I know he's coming back with something good up his sleeve.

BIDDLE (*dubiously*): I hope so.

CORNELIUS: When the head of a decent firm like this goes himself—and when he's Bob Murrison, who knows the business inside out, who's got drive, who's got—well—charm, if you like, who they all know to be an absolutely first-class fellow—I tell you—something happens. You'll see.

BIDDLE (*still dubiously*): Yes—I've no doubt you're quite right.

CORNELIUS (*sharply, like a man compelled to face things he wishes to suppress and ignore*): Well then—what are you talking—looking—like that for? What's the matter with you, Biddle?

BIDDLE (*stammering*): Oh—nothing at all—I'm sure you're quite right, Mr. Cornelius. It was just that Mr. Murrison didn't seem very well when he left us——

CORNELIUS (*impatiently*): That's a month ago. He was on edge a bit. He was worried. I'm worried. We're all worried. We're all on edge. That's nothing.

BIDDLE: And then—being away so long—and writing so little——

CORNELIUS: You're making something out of nothing. I know him. He wouldn't bother writing much.

After all, this is his business, he's no need to explain everything he does to us. He's not like some piffling little salesman out on the road. Besides, Bob Murrison's going to surprise us. I know what he's up to. It won't be the first time. I'll bet he's absolutely hypnotised those miserable devils in the north. He's got them eating aluminium out of his hand.

Enter LAWRENCE.

Where have you been all this time?

LAWRENCE (*sulkily*): You told me to go to the Excelsior Transport Company before I came back. (*Hangs hat and coat up.*)

CORNELIUS (*irritably*): Well, you've been long enough about it. Bring some chairs in from the private office. And don't look so sulky. I'm tired of seeing you look sulky. Too many miserable, sulky looking people about.

LAWRENCE *gives a very audible grunt.*

Now what does that mean?

LAWRENCE *stands silent.*

Well?

LAWRENCE (*flaring up*): It means I'm sick of it.

CORNELIUS (*astonished*): Sick of what?

LAWRENCE: Sick of this place, sick of filling inkwells and copying letters and running silly little errands. I've done it nearly five years now. I'm not a kid any longer. I'm nineteen. Lots of my pals have got proper jobs now, and here I am still doing kid's work. Well, I don't care if the firm does go bankrupt. I've had enough of it.

He goes into the private office for chairs, leaving

252

CORNELIUS *to exchange a glance of astonishment with* BIDDLE, *who also shakes his head. When* LAWRENCE *returns with two chairs,* CORNELIUS *looks fixedly at him.*

CORNELIUS (*quietly*): Just a minute, Lawrence.

LAWRENCE *looks at him and as if almost drawn against his will comes nearer, then stands near.*

LAWRENCE (*mumbling*): I'm sorry I said that—that last bit, Mr. Cornelius.

CORNELIUS: All right. And I'm sorry we've never had a better job to offer you. If you can find one, go and get it. What do you want to do?

LAWRENCE: Something to do with wireless and gramophones. I'm really interested in them.

CORNELIUS: And so is everybody else of your age, as far as I can see. Wireless and gramophones and motor-cars and aeroplanes. Making a noise and rushing off somewhere. And how everybody's going to make a living out of that, beats me. But if you know of anything, go and get it. Go now—if you like.

LAWRENCE: What about the tea?

CORNELIUS: Oh—yes, we shall want that tray of teas.

LAWRENCE: How many?

CORNELIUS: Oh—about eight or nine. Good teas, too. Might make a difference—you never know. About four o'clock. Now you can go, and you needn't come back until you bring the teas.

LAWRENCE *takes his hat and coat and goes.*

BIDDLE (*who has been in the background*): Do you want me to stay—or not, Mr. Cornelius?

CORNELIUS: Well, I think you'd better not. You can come back later.

BIDDLE: Of course. I'm anxious to see Mr. Murrison. Now is this about how you'll want it? (*Referring to chairs.*)

CORNELIUS (*thoughtfully surveying them*): Might just have these two here—(*moves them.*) Like that.

BIDDLE: It's a funny thing, Mr. Cornelius, but to-day's the fifteenth of the month.

CORNELIUS (*still staring at the chairs*): Don't see anything funny about that.

BIDDLE (*laughs*): No, of course. Nothing funny in its being the fifteenth. There has to be a fifteenth. But what's funny is that this is—or may be—an important day in the life of the firm and so an important day in my life. *And* it's the fifteenth. The fifteenth's always been my day. My birthday's on the fifteenth. I was married on the fifteenth. We live at Number 15.

CORNELIUS: Oh, you took that house because it was Number 15. That doesn't count.

BIDDLE: I assure you, we didn't. Just chance, you might say. That is, if there is such a thing as chance, which I doubt. And then, after being a member of our chess club for fifteen years, I took office as president three months ago—on the fifteenth. Now I've spent a lot of my life dealing with figures and numbers, and I believe there's more in 'em than meets the eye. I do, Mr. Cornelius. Take nine, for instance——

A sharp knock on the door. BIDDLE *goes to open it, and admits a youngish foreigner, very sedately dressed, and carrying a black attaché or brief case.* BIDDLE *steps back a pace or two, and the visitor steps inside the room, bows and produces a card.*

FOREIGNER (*with very marked foreign accent*): Messrs. Briggs and Murrizon? I am Doc-tor Schweig—coming here for the houz of Hecht and Drapok——

CORNELIUS (*going forward*): Yes, of course. How d'you do, Doctor—er—Schweig?

FOREIGNER: You are Mis-ter Murrizon?—Schweig.

CORNELIUS: No, my name's Cornelius. I'm Mr. Murrison's partner. He'll be back in time for the meeting. We're expecting him any time now. Sit down, won't you?

SCHWEIG (*gravely*): T'ank you. (*Sits down rather ceremoniously on the nearest of the arranged chairs, keeping his hat and case on his knee.*)

CORNELIUS: Yes—er—(*nothing comes of this.*)

SCHWEIG: It is co-old, eh?

CORNELIUS (*eagerly*): Yes, it is cold, isn't it?

BIDDLE: Very cold.

CORNELIUS: We were saying that. Very cold.

SCHWEIG: But no fog.

CORNELIUS: No, no fog.

SCHWEIG: Alvays, I am thankful when I am in London to see no fog.

CORNELIUS: Yes, I can understand that. Quite right. I say, Biddle, I think we ought to have a table of some sort here. We forgot that. Let's bring that one over.

They take over a small table, facing the chairs. They

*have just got this into position when a brisk ratty type of
Cockney pops his head in.*

BRISK MAN: This is it, isn't it? Thought so. (*He
comes in.*) Mr. Cornelius, isn't it? Central Forwarding
Company—Fletcher. Sit here, I suppose. (*Sits down,
turns to* SCHWEIG.) Bit early, are we? Must be.

SCHWEIG (*consulting watch*): I vas told to com' at
fifteen minutes past three o'clock. Now it is seventeen
minutes past three o'clock.

FLETCHER: Oh, you're making a stop-watch job of it.

SCHWEIG (*puzzled*): Pleass?

FLETCHER: Never mind. Well, Mr. Cornelius, how's
everything looking?

CORNELIUS: Fine.

FLETCHER: That's right. Never say die.

> BIDDLE, *who has now put on his hat and coat,
reaches the door and opens it to find an elderly man
standing outside. This elderly man has an untidy grey
beard and is shabbily dressed in an old-fashioned style.
He is carrying a number of leaflets.* BIDDLE *steps back
to let him in and he comes just inside the door and stands
there beaming rather foolishly.*

ELDERLY MAN: Good afternoon, friends.

BIDDLE: Are you here for the meeting?

ELDERLY MAN: I don't know.

BIDDLE: Do you represent any of the creditors?

ELDERLY MAN: Certainly I do, sir. Certainly I do.

CORNELIUS (*rather irritably*): Well, come and sit down,

my dear sir. Don't stand in the doorway. All right, Biddle, don't wait.

> BIDDLE *goes, after a puzzled backward glance at the elderly man, who now takes another short step or two forward and continues to beam on the company.*

ELDERLY MAN (*very quietly*): I represent the biggest creditor of all, everybody's creditor—God.

> CORNELIUS *stares at him.* FLETCHER *gives a guffaw.*

FLETCHER: Thought I'd seen him before. He's one o' these sort of apostles you see about, that's what he is.

CORNELIUS: My dear chap, you can't come in here talking to us about God. We're busy. We have an important meeting on. This is business.

ELDERLY MAN: Whose business? Is it God's business? He's here, you know.

FLETCHER: Well, if he's here, we shan't need you. (*Guffaws.*)

ELDERLY MAN (*offering* CORNELIUS *some pamphlets*): Read these at your leisure, friend.

CORNELIUS (*taking them*): All right, thanks, I will. But you'll have to go now—

ELDERLY MAN (*quietly at first*): I am going. But I wish I could lend you my vision of you, friends, if only for a moment. I see you in a little place—like a very small fragile raft—in mid air—and Heaven is bright above you, bright with your guardian angels—and (*his voice takes on a rather sing-song dramatic tone*) below you— gaping and roaring—is hell and eternal damnation.

FLETCHER: Oh—gertcha!

CORNELIUS (*as if about to push him out*): My dear chap, we simply can't have you here talking——

ELDERLY MAN (*who has reached the door and opened it*): Friends, I leave behind with you the thought of our Father in Heaven.

> MRS. READE, *a fussily dressed woman of about* 40, *is seen behind him. He too sees her.*

And with you too, sister.

MRS. READE: Me what?

ELDERLY MAN: The thought of our Father in Heaven.

> *He brushes past her. She looks after him for a second, flustered and indignant, then comes a step or so into the room.*

MRS. READE: Oh—he gave me quite a turn with his Father in Heaven. They oughtn't to let old men go about talking like that.

SCHWEIG (*rising, gravely*): Quite so, madame. In my country he would be shut up as a madman.

CORNELIUS: Oh—no. You can't do that.

SCHWEIG: But he is mad.

CORNELIUS: A bit mad. But most of us are a bit mad here. Where you come from, it's probably different.

MRS. READE (*with social manner*): I ought to have introduced myself. This is where you're having the creditors' meeting, isn't it?

CORNELIUS (*staring at her*): Yes. But——

MRS. READE: Well, I'm Mrs. Reade.

CORNELIUS: Oh!

MRS. READE: I don't suppose that means much to

you, does it? But my uncle, Mr. Samuel Rigby—I keep
house for him—he owns this property. You're his
tenants, you see. And he couldn't come himself—he's
got a bit of sciatica to-day—he told me about this
meeting this morning. And so I said: "Well, uncle, let
me go. I've never been to such a thing before and I can
tell you what happens and it'll be a bit of a change."
And he said I could if I wanted to. So I did. I can sit
anywhere, I suppose?

CORNELIUS (*rather wearily*): Yes, anywhere.

MRS. READE: I think I'll try this.

> *Sits down, looks about her, and smiles at* SCHWEIG
> *and* FLETCHER. CORNELIUS *looks impatiently at his
> watch, then goes into the private office, leaving the door
> ajar behind him.*

(*After clearing her throat.*) Well, we're having a nice day
for it, aren't we? I mean, taking it all round. It's cold—
but it's what I should call a healthy cold.

FLETCHER (*indifferently*): It's what I should call it too.

> *He pulls a bit of paper out of his inner pocket and
> begins examining some figures written on it.*

MRS. READE (*mainly to* SCHWEIG): I expect you gentlemen are used to this sort of thing, but it's quite new
to me. A brand-new experience, you might call it.

SCHWEIG (*not taking it in*): Pleass?

MRS. READE (*brightly*): Yes, you're foreign, aren't
you? I guessed you were.

> *The telephone bell rings.*

There, that's the telephone. Always at it. Ring, ring,
ring.

259

CORNELIUS *comes out hastily from the Private Office, as the telephone has not been switched through.*

CORNELIUS (*eagerly, at telephone*): That you, Bob? (*Disappointed.*) Oh! No, we're not interested. (*Puts receiver down.*)

Here, if it is convenient to have one or two nondescript creditors—youngish or middle-aged men—they should enter, and quietly take their seats. They are followed by PRITCHET *and* MORTIMER. PRITCHET *is a middle-aged solicitor, with one of those curiously hollow booming voices that some legal men have.* MORTIMER *is the bank man with the face like a rat-trap. He should have a worrying ratty manner. Both carry small cases.*

PRITCHET (*booming*): Ah—good afternoon. Sorry if we're a little late. I'm Pritchet of Cattermole, MacIvor and Pritchet. (*Going nearer to* CORNELIUS *and producing slip of paper.*) We represent several foreign clients who are—er—interested in these proceedings. You'll find their names there—eh?

CORNELIUS (*glancing at paper*): Yes. Old friends of ours. Good afternoon, Mr. Mortimer.

MORTIMER: Good afternoon, Mr. Cornelius.

CORNELIUS: Sit down, gentlemen.

As they do, MRS. READE'S *voice can be heard.*

MRS. READE: Do you think we're all here now?

CORNELIUS: That's what I was wondering, madam. I think I can take it that we are. (*He goes to door, looks out, then closes the door and carefully and rather importantly takes up a position facing the creditors.*) Gentlemen—I beg your pardon, madam——

MRS. READE (*flattered by this notice*): It's quite all right, thank you.

CORNELIUS (*grandly*): Gentlemen and you, madam—I propose first to outline our position to you. Three years ago——

PRITCHET (*booming unpleasantly*): One moment, please.

CORNELIUS: What's the matter?

PRITCHET: This is not quite in order.

CORNELIUS (*taken aback*): Oh!

PRITCHET: No. This is a meeting of your creditors, my dear sir. You are not one of your own creditors. Therefore you can't take charge of the meeting in this manner.

FLETCHER: That's right.

PRITCHET: I propose that Mr. Mortimer of the Middle-sex and Central Bank should take the chair.

FLETCHER: And I beg to second that.

PRITCHET: All in agreement?

A few hands go up.

Carried, I think. Mr. Mortimer, will you please take charge of the meeting?

> MORTIMER, *silent, goes forward and occupies the chair near where* CORNELIUS *is standing, putting it away a little first, so that* CORNELIUS *is left, so to speak, in the air.*

CORNELIUS (*not without irony*): What do I do now? Leave the room?

MRS. READE (*whispering loudly*): I hope not. I like him.

MORTIMER: I don't think that will be necessary just now. Do you, Mr. Pritchet?

PRITCHET: No, not yet.

MORTIMER: Is your partner, Mr. Murrison, here, Mr. Cornelius?

CORNELIUS: No.

MORTIMER: But I understood——

CORNELIUS (*impatiently*): Mr. Murrison will be here any moment now.

PRITCHET: This seems to me all very irregular——

CORNELIUS (*bitterly*): That's how it seems to me too, very irregular. Everything's irregular. That's why we're all here to-day.

FLETCHER: Only we're not all here. Your partner isn't, for one—— (*Laughs.*)

CORNELIUS: My partner has been travelling the country for the last few weeks. He's been visiting all our customers, chiefly in the Midlands and the North. He's coming straight back from seeing the last of them to this meeting this afternoon.

SCHWEIG: He hopes to get more orders for your houz, eh?

CORNELIUS: Yes. He knows all there is to know about the aluminium trade.

MRS. READE: The what?

CORNELIUS: The aluminium trade, madam. This firm imports aluminium from abroad and sells it to hardware manufacturers.

MRS. READE: Just fancy!

MORTIMER: But don't you employ a traveller?

PRITCHET: Just what I was about to ask, Mr. Mortimer.

CORNELIUS: We had a traveller, but about two months ago we dismissed him.

FLETCHER: What for?

MORTIMER: Was he inefficient?

CORNELIUS: He wasn't at first——

PRITCHET: But he was afterwards, eh?

CORNELIUS: I don't know.

PRITCHET: But, my dear sir, surely it's not difficult to discover whether an employee of this kind is efficient or not?

FLETCHER: 'Ear, 'ear!

CORNELIUS: At ordinary times I suppose it isn't, but in our business these aren't ordinary times. This fellow was a traveller, not a magician.

FLETCHER: And what about your partner, Murrison, then? Is he a magician?

CORNELIUS: *Mister* Murrison is a first-class business man and a wonderful fellow. And this little firm means everything to him. If it hadn't, he wouldn't have gone on this trip. He wasn't very well when he went. We'd had an anxious time here——

MORTIMER (*impatiently*): Yes, yes, Mr. Cornelius, we've all had anxious times. But meanwhile, we're busy men.

PRITCHET: Quite so.

CORNELIUS: Just a minute! (*Listens.*) All right. Sorry!

PRITCHET: I must say if I'd known that your senior partner was absent——

CORNELIUS: He knows about this. He'll be here any minute now.

FLETCHER (*sceptically*): With luck.

CORNELIUS: What do you mean?

FLETCHER: You 'eard me.

CORNELIUS: I resent that remark, particularly from you.

FLETCHER (*pugnaciously*): Oh—and why from me?

CORNELIUS: You wouldn't understand if I told you.

MORTIMER: Gentlemen, this is a business meeting We don't want that sort of talk.

PRITCHET: I should think not indeed. How long is this Mr. Murrison going to be?

FLETCHER: God knows.

MORTIMER: I'm not prepared to wait more than ten minutes at the outside——

PRITCHET: Nor I.

CORNELIUS: I tell you he'll be here any minute now.

SCHWEIG (*standing up*): Mister—er—Gornelius wass going to gif us a stademendt—some figures—of the position of the houz. I think he might gif us that stademendt—pleass. (*Sits down.*)

CORNELIUS (*eagerly*): Yes, of course.

MORTIMER: All right, Mr. Cornelius.

    Moves his chair so that CORNELIUS, *who is still*

standing, now holds the floor. CORNELIUS *produces paper given to him by* MISS PORRIN.

CORNELIUS: Well gentlemen—and you, madam—up to three years ago, our annual gross turnover, averaged over the previous five years, was eighty-five thousand pounds——

SCHWEIG (*who is writing it down*): Pleass? Eighty-five t'ousand pounds?

CORNELIUS: Eighty-five thousand pounds, with an annual net profit ranging from eleven thousand pounds at the beginning of the period to about eight thousand at the end—— (*Pauses.*)

SCHWEIG (*murmuring as he writes*): Eleven t'ousand pounds to eight t'ousand pounds.

CORNELIUS (*reminiscently*): We were doing very well. We were very fine people. It was a good life. You were always delighted to see us at the Middlesex and Central Bank, Mr. Mortimer. Those French clients of yours, Mr. Pritchet, used to send us little presents. Mr. Fletcher here and his Forwarding Company couldn't do enough for us. You all respected us. And really, gentlemen, now I come to think of it, I don't know why you should all have been so affable and respectful then. It was all very easy. We bought the metal, turned it over to our customers, made a nice profit. All very easy, very simple, nothing to boast about at all. (*He looks round, smiling, and catches* MRS. READE'S *eye.*)

MRS. READE (*brightly*): No, I see.

CORNELIUS (*impressively*): Thank you, madam. And then it all changed. My God—how it changed! A sort of nightmare. Every country seemed to be announcing that it must sell more goods than it would buy.

MORTIMER: Isn't this all rather beside the point?

PRITCHET: Hear, hear!

CORNELIUS (*with increasing animation*): It may be beside the point in the Middlesex and Central Bank or near the Law Courts, but it isn't beside the point here. Look what happened. The pound sterling was worth twenty shillings here and only twelve shillings somewhere else. Some countries you couldn't get money into. Some countries you couldn't get money out of. You could send goods in a ship with a blue flag but not in a ship with a red flag. It wasn't business any more. It was a game of snakes and ladders—but without the ladders.

PRITCHET: I really don't see——

CORNELIUS: All right, don't see. But you've got to understand what was happening to us. I've never got much fun out of selling aluminium. And whether Briggs and Murrison of Birdcage Street, Holborn, ever sold any aluminium to anybody couldn't be of any real importance to the world. But—by God!—if we'd been trying to take a lifeboat out to a wreck, we couldn't have tried harder, couldn't have worried and argued and schemed and pleaded more than we did in this office. And what's it all about? If we've to live by private trade, then let it be private trade. Why have they made it like a lunatics' obstacle race? Why are we condemned to scheme and scratch, in these cubby holes? I tell you, a blind monkey could find a better life to live than we've lately had here . . .

MORTIMER (*sharply*): Mr. Cornelius.

266

PRITCHET (*sharply*): I thought you were going to give us a statement.

CORNELIUS: I am. (*Deliberately.*) Unless my partner's been working miracles—and I don't say he hasn't, because he's a desperate man and a wonder—but unless he's worked a few miracles, this firm's broke, bankrupt, bust. And now you can pass a few resolutions on that.

> *He holds it a moment, during which his audience, aghast, can only gape at him. Then he turns away.*

MRS. READE *breaks the spell.*

MRS. READE: Well, I enjoyed that, I must say.

FLETCHER: I can't see what that stuff's got to do with us——

PRITCHET: I really must protest very strongly against this most un-businesslike proceeding——

MORTIMER: Mr. Cornelius, you haven't made any attempt to give us a statement——

CORNELIUS (*holding up his hand, forcefully*): Just a minute, just a minute——

> *He listens in the quiet that follows, then hurries to the door. The creditors watch him and a low buzz of talk breaks out amongst them.* CORNELIUS *opens the door and discovers* MURRISON *at the other side.* MURRISON *is a man about fifty, who is looking very worn. He is wearing a big overcoat and carrying his hat in his hand. His manner from the first should be quick, nervous, jerky, strange.*

(*With affectionate warmth.*) Hello, Bob old boy! Fine! We're all ready for you.

T

MURRISON (*now inside the room, with a quick glance at the creditors, sharply*): What? What'd you mean?

CORNELIUS: The meeting, y'know. Did you come straight from the station, Bob?

MURRISON: Yes. Straight from the station. The taximan's bringing my bags up. (*Whispering.*) You see him out there, Jim, and pay him for me. I don't like the look of him.

CORNELIUS (*hastily concealing his surprise and some misgivings*): Of course I will, old boy.

> CORNELIUS *goes out, and is heard off calling to the taximan:* "Put them down just in here, will you? That's right. How much? Here you are." *Meanwhile,* MURRISON *has very carefully crossed to the Private Office door, ignoring the* "Good afternoon, Mr. Murrison" *of* MR. MORTIMER. MURRISON *goes into the Private Office, so that for a moment or two, the creditors are left to themselves.* MORTIMER *is seen exchanging a puzzled glance with* PRITCHET. CORNELIUS *returns, looks for* MURRISON, *then goes over to the Private Office. There should be an atmosphere of suspense and tension evoked in this little scene.*

CORNELIUS (*looking into Private Office*): Ready, Bob?

> CORNELIUS *should go to the alcove at the back and bring down the only remaining chair, putting it behind the small table.* MURRISON *slowly opens the door and enters hesitatingly. He has taken overcoat off.*

Here you are, sit here, Bob.

MURRISON (*in a loud harsh voice that is startling*): Why are you sitting like this? We want the lights on. Pull that blind down, Jim. I'll put the lights on.

> CORNELIUS, *after a brief surprised look at* MURRI-
> SON, *hastily goes to the window and pulls down the blind.*
> MURRISON *goes to the switch and puts on the lights.*

(*Irritably.*) There's another light somewhere.

MORTIMER: Come, come, Mr. Murrison, we've got
plenty of light in here now.

MURRISON (*irritably*): I want that other light on.

> *Goes and switches it on. There is now the maximum
> of light on the stage and it is almost an uncomfortable
> glare, the lights being very white. Coming back from
> switching on the last light,* MURRISON *stops and looks
> searchingly at* MRS. READE.

What's that woman doing here?

CORNELIUS: That's all right, old man. She's only
the landlord's niece——

MRS. READE (*who is suddenly alarmed and has risen*):
You needn't bother telling him who I am. Because I'm
going. (*As she threads her way towards the door, agitatedly.*)
And you might as well all go, if you'll take my advice.
It's no good staying here—with that man.

> *Indicating* MURRISON. *She is now at the door. Her
> voice rises and trembles as she points at* MURRISON,
> *who is still looking at her.*

You've only got to look at him to see——

> *She goes hastily, the door banging to. Some of the
> creditors, who have half-risen, remain like that for a
> moment.*

CORNELIUS (*reassuringly*): That's all right. She's better
out of the way. We can get on now.

MORTIMER (*who has been bewildered*): I hope so.

(*Looking at his watch.*) Really, gentlemen, I must ask you——

CORNELIUS (*cutting in, to* MURRISON): Bob, you'd better tell them at once what you've been able to do.

> MURRISON *is now sitting behind the small table, facing the meeting.* CORNELIUS *is standing a little behind, to one side.*

MURRISON (*in a low uncertain tone*): It's very difficult. (*He covers his face with his hands for a moment.*) There were two men following me all the time. No, not all the time. Not at first. But nearly all the time.

CORNELIUS (*bewildered*): Following you!

MURRISON (*rather louder now*): Everywhere I went. When I went up to Scotland, one of them tried to get into my railway carriage. But I knew him. (*He looks round suspiciously.*) How did they always know where I was going?

MORTIMER (*firmly*): Well, never mind about that for the time being, Mr. Murrison. We understand that you've been visiting all your customers. And naturally before we reach any conclusion here, we want to hear the result of those visits.

CORNELIUS: Yes. How did you get on, old man? Tell us.

MURRISON (*with passion*): I am telling you. I'm telling you that everywhere I went, I was followed by two men. And there were—other things. (*His voice dropping.*) Worse than that. They tried to poison my food.

CORNELIUS (*expostulating*): Bob!

MURRISON (*excitedly*): They knew where I was going all the time. They sent somebody in advance to all the people who'd been buying from us. Some of our oldest customers wouldn't see me. Why? Because they'd been told filthy lies about us by this fellow who'd been sent ahead of me. I tell you—it's been hell.

FLETCHER (*disgustedly*): Here, come off it!

SCHWEIG (*standing up*): I think, pleass——

MURRISON (*quickly*): Who's that?

SCHWEIG *sits down.*

Some sort of foreigner, isn't he? Why should he come here?

CORNELIUS (*patting him on the shoulder*): Bob, old man you're tired. Take it easy.

MURRISON: You'd be tired. Followed, watched, spied on, day after day. Trying to get at you. There was something about it in the paper yesterday. I expect you'll be reading a lot about it in the papers soon. They'll try to get at me here. They won't leave me alone—— (*Beginning to break down.*) Oh God!—why can't they leave me alone?

CORNELIUS (*bending over him*): It's all right, old man, now. You've nothing to worry about. (*He looks up, and makes a waving gesture to the creditors for them to go, then looks down again.*) You're only a bit done up. You'll be all right after a rest. (*To the creditors, in a low, rather tense tone.*) I'm sorry, gentlemen, but I must ask you to go.

Some of the creditors get up, but nobody makes for the door. They are all staring at MURRISON, *who is sitting with his head between his hands.*

271

MURRISON (*not raising his head*): It's no use, Jim. I'm finished. They're torturing me. (*Breaks down again.*)

CORNELIUS (*very gently, bending over him*): No, no, no. That's all right, Bob, old man. (*Looks up and sees the creditors watching them. Then, with tremendous passion.*) For Christ's sake—get out, can't you?

> *As if completely dominated by his will and passion, they begin to move towards the door at once. As soon as he sees that they are all on the move, he turns away from them and bends over* MURRISON, *who is still sitting with bowed head. Nothing is said until they are alone.*

MURRISON (*raising his head and suddenly giving a short harsh laugh*): They've all gone, you see. (*Laughs again.*) I got rid of them, Jim. It wasn't hard. But it took me to do it, eh? (*Laughs.*)

CORNELIUS (*standing back and staring*): What, are you all right, Bob?

MURRISON (*irritably*): Of course I am. Why shouldn't I be?

CORNELIUS (*relieved*): My dear chap, I don't know what the devil you were playing at with those fellows. And I don't care so long as you're all right. (*Claps him heartily on the shoulder.*)

MURRISON (*sharply*): Don't do that.

CORNELIUS: Sorry, old man. I expect you're tired.

MURRISON (*slowly*): No, but—nearly all the time—I have a pain here. (*Puts his hand to top of his head.*)

CORNELIUS (*heartily*): Really? How did you get that?

MURRISON (*solemnly, emphatically*): Some sort of poison, Jim. Didn't I tell you?

CORNELIUS: No. But tell me now how you got on? Have we got a chance?

MURRISON (*shakes head, irritably*): I've already told you. They sent somebody in advance—to warn all the customers——

CORNELIUS: But who did?

MURRISON: I told you. I was followed all the time. There were two men——

CORNELIUS (*taking him by the shoulders, earnestly*): How! How! For God's sake, Bob, stop talking like that. You're talking to me now—Jim Cornelius. There couldn't have been two men following you all the time. You imagined it.

MURRISON (*withdrawing himself, sharply*): That's a lie. You know it's a lie.

CORNELIUS (*on whom the horrible truth is dawning again*): No, I don't.

MURRISON: Are you going to begin lying to me now, Jim? Won't anybody tell me the truth. (*Confusedly.*) There was a waiter in the hotel last night—he looked a decent sort of chap—but when I asked him if anybody had been trying to tamper with my drink—he wouldn't tell me the truth. And I knew all the time. He ought to have seen that. (*Laughs.*) I knew.

CORNELIUS (*agonised, under his breath*): Oh—God! (*Approaching* MURRISON *again.*) Don't talk like that, old man. Please. Just for my sake.

LAWRENCE *enters, rather proudly, carrying a large tray, on which are about nine cups of tea and a plate of cut cake and biscuits. He is out of breath.*

273

MURRISON (*suspiciously, sharply*): What's this? I don't want any tea.

CORNELIUS (*impatiently*): Take it away.

LAWRENCE (*gasping*): But—where—to?

CORNELIUS: Anywhere—anywhere—back to the teashop.

LAWRENCE: They'll—want—paying for it.

CORNELIUS: Oh—all right—take this——

> *Goes over and throws half a crown on to the tray. After a curious stare at* MURRISON, LAWRENCE *goes out.* CORNELIUS *returns to* MURRISON.

Bob, will you listen to me—quietly—for a minute?

MURRISON (*sullenly*): What is it?

CORNELIUS: It doesn't matter just what's going to happen to us here. Never mind about that. You're tired. You're not well. This journey's upset you. Go home now—never mind about business—and just see your doctor, old man. Tell him about this pain in your head.

MURRISON (*slowly shaking his head*): No. No. He wouldn't believe me.

CORNELIUS: Why not?

MURRISON (*with sinister air of secrecy*): I've never liked that doctor of ours, Jim. Once or twice, when he thought I wasn't noticing, I've caught him looking very strangely at me. I couldn't trust him.

CORNELIUS (*now deeply distressed*): But you can trust me, can't you, Bob? We've been partners, we've been pals, for a good long time now. You know there isn't anything I wouldn't do for you, old man. And I don't

274

like to see you ill—like this. We need you down here, Bob. We can't get on without you. So if you really don't like this doctor of yours, see another one—there are plenty about, good ones too——

MURRISON: It's no use, Jim. It's no use.

CORNELIUS (*with deep affection*): Of course it is. Think of the good times we've had together—even here, in this office. And we'll have some more, won't we? If we can't keep this business going, we'll get out of it and start another—something quite different. What do you say? (*A noise outside.*)

MURRISON (*startled*): What's that?

BIDDLE *enters*.

BIDDLE: Hello, Mr. Murrison. I nearly fell over your bags out there.

CORNELIUS, *behind* MURRISON, *puts his hand to his mouth as a sign to* BIDDLE *to keep quiet.*

CORNELIUS: You'll do that, won't you, Bob?

MURRISON: All right. (*Gets up and fumbles in his pockets, finally producing some keys.*) There's something I want, first. (*Goes slowly into Private Office.*)

CORNELIUS *immediately crosses to* BIDDLE.

BIDDLE (*anxiously*): Is anything wrong, sir?

CORNELIUS (*quickly and softly*): Yes, but there's no time to explain. Go out and get a taxi for Mr. Murrison, and then telephone at once—from that box at the corner—to his house, tell them he's coming home and ask them to get a good doctor in to see him, as he's not very well. That clear?

BIDDLE (*softly*): Yes. Taxi, then telephone.

MURRISON *has come out of the Private Office, carrying a rather bright revolver in his hand. He holds it just long enough to be seen, then slips it into his pocket.*

And he'll want the bags in, of course.

MURRISON (*as* BIDDLE *moves off*): What are you two muttering about there?

CORNELIUS (*with forced cheerfulness*): Nothing, old man. I was just asking Biddle to get you a taxi.

MURRISON (*sitting down heavily, wearily*): No use, Jim, no use. (*Puts his hand to his head, then shakes it.*) Talk to me—about something different. Tell me something about yourself, Jim. Anything. Just talk.

CORNELIUS (*trying to hide his distress*): All right, Bob. You know, I'm reading a book about South America— Peru and the Andes. It's making me feel restless, making me wonder a lot, about what I've missed. You know the feeling, old man. Right on the first page, there was a sentence . . . I keep remembering it, Bob —you know how you remember some things for no reason at all . . . It said——

Now MURRISON *is leaning forward staring tragically into vacancy, while* CORNELIUS *has an affectionate hand on his shoulder.*

"After a week in the Indian village, we decided to take the track into the clouds, to find among those heights the lost city of the Incas . . ."

Curtain

END OF ACT TWO

ACT III

Office as before. Friday evening, a fortnight later. The office is partly dismantled. Files and ledgers taken down from shelves, stacked in corners, some tied in bundles. The staff are obviously at work clearing things up for the last time. The door into the Private Office is open and a light is on in there. LAWRENCE is bringing files, etc., from the Private Office. MISS PORRIN can be looking through files. BIDDLE is having a last go at the ledgers. JUDY is at her table typing hard. Nothing is said for a few moments.

LAWRENCE (*stopping and yawning*): What time is it? (*There is no reply.*) Miss Porrin, what time is it?

MISS PORRIN: Twenty to eight.

LAWRENCE: I've had enough of this.

MISS PORRIN (*indignantly*): You ought to be ashamed of yourself, Lawrence.

LAWRENCE (*astonished*): What for?

MISS PORRIN: On an evening like this—when everything's finishing—and you talk as if it didn't matter a bit——

LAWRENCE: Well, it doesn't to me.

MISS PORRIN: I think you're absolutely inhuman.

LAWRENCE (*muttering*): And I think you're potty.

277

MISS PORRIN: Don't be so rude and stupid. You ought to realise that even if you don't care about—about—all this, the rest of us do because it means a lot to us and——

BIDDLE (*turning*): What's all this about?

MISS PORRIN: I'm sorry, Mr. Biddle. But it's Lawrence—being so rude and stupid. He ought to know I can't help feeling upset, because this is really our last night here——

VOICE OF CORNELIUS (*from Private Office, quietly*): Not so much noise in there, please.

> LAWRENCE *grins at* MISS PORRIN, *who returns to work.*

CORNELIUS' VOICE: Lawrence!

> LAWRENCE *goes in and returns with a mass of papers which he dumps in a corner. Then he yawns noisily.*

JUDY (*with calm malice*): Is it the little boy's bed time?

LAWRENCE: Don't be silly. I'm yawning because I need fresh air. I can't help it.

JUDY: Put your head out of the window.

MISS PORRIN: Oh—do please stop it.

LAWRENCE: Well, I didn't start it, did I?

> *The telephone rings.* MISS PORRIN *answers it.*

MISS PORRIN: Yes, Briggs and Murrison. . . . All right. Wait a minute, please. Miss Everson, it's for for you.

JUDY (*at telephone*): Yes, this is Judy . . . I know, Eric, I'm awfully sorry, but I can't help it . . . No, I shan't be long. If you come round here, you probably

278

won't have to wait more than a few minutes . . . Of course I will darling. (*Puts down receiver.*)

LAWRENCE (*muttering contemptuously*): Darling!

JUDY (*going up to him*): What did you say?

LAWRENCE (*quailing*): Nothing.

    JUDY *returns to her table.*

BIDDLE (*looking up thoughtfully from his account books*): Some very queer things in these old accounts. In December 1922 we spent fifteen shillings and threepence on cheese.

JUDY: Cheese? (*Laughs.*)

BIDDLE: Yes, cheese. (*To* MISS PORRIN.) How did we come to do that? Why should we buy cheese? And fifteen shillings and threepence worth. You could get a lot of cheese for that. Do you remember, Miss Porrin?

MISS PORRIN: No, I wasn't here then.

BIDDLE (*thoughtfully*): Of course not. I must ask my wife. I expect I told her at the time. It'll worry me if I can't remember. Cheese. 1922. Lot of queer things here.

MISS PORRIN: Here too. I never knew before that Mr. Shuttleworth—you know, of the Central Forwarding Company—was called Michael. He's not a bit like a Michael, is he?

BIDDLE: Isn't he? I don't know what a Michael should be like.

JUDY (*without looking up*): Tall, dark, and very romantic.

BIDDLE: That doesn't sound like Mr. Shuttleworth.

A pause. Then CORNELIUS *appears in doorway of Private Office, with a cigar-box in his hand. He is wearing a dark suit and a black tie, and shows signs of having had a bad time. He speaks very quietly.*

CORNELIUS: Look at these, Biddle. Nearly a full box of those big Zarranagas. Must have been at the bottom of that drawer years and years. Isn't it a shame?

BIDDLE (*going over and taking out big but ragged cigar, gravely*): It is a shame, Mr. Cornelius. These must have been expensive cigars.

CORNELIUS: Cost about half a crown each.

BIDDLE (*impressed*): Half a crown! (*Peering into box.*)

CORNELIUS: Take them, Biddle, if you think you can do anything with 'em. They look hopeless to me.

BIDDLE (*taking them*): Oh—thank you. I think if they're trimmed up a bit, they'll make a very good smoke, a very good smoke.

CORNELIUS: Then your commercial career, Biddle, ends in smoke, but in very good smoke. Lawrence, you'd better clear up some of that mess in there. Then you can go. Look, start on the table first.

They go in together.

BIDDLE (*quietly as he returns to his desk with cigars*): Mr. Murrison bought these. He liked a good cigar.

There is a tiny knock on the door, then it opens to admit the head and shoulders of MRS. READE.

MRS. READE: Oh—good evening. May I come in a minute?

Enters, but not far.

BIDDLE: Oh—good evening.

MRS. READE: I'm Mrs. Reade, y'know. The landlord, Mr. Samuel Rigby's my uncle. I've just been up to the top floor—there's a proper private flat there, y'know, we let it out—and I saw a light here and I thought I'd just—(*staring about her*) You look as if you're going for good.

BIDDLE: We are. The landlord knows.

MRS. READE: Yes, I expect so, but he never tells me anything, even if I do keep house for him. But what I really called for—is the tall gentleman here I saw the other day at the meeting? Oh, I think he's in there, isn't he? (*Calling.*) Good evening.

CORNELIUS (*coming out of Private Office with some things belonging to Murrison—flask, personal diary, etc.*): Good evening. (*Puzzled a moment.*) Oh—yes—you're——

MRS. READE: Mrs. Reade, that's right. I was at the meeting here, you remember. We've been away since—my uncle had a bit of sciatica—and I've been wondering what happened after that meeting. You know, I couldn't have stayed another minute, not if you'd paid me a thousand pounds. You remember? I left, all of a sudden.

CORNELIUS (*tonelessly*): Yes, I remember.

MRS. READE: That friend of yours—he frightened me.

CORNELIUS: I'm sorry.

MRS. READE (*confidentially*): Wasn't he—a bit mad?

CORNELIUS: Yes.

MRS. READE: I knew it. Did they—put him away?

CORNELIUS: No.

Mrs. Reade: Oh—what happened then?

Cornelius (*very gently*): He shot himself.

Mrs. Reade: Shot himself?

Cornelius: Yes. (*Showing revolver, which he is carrying with other things.*) With this.

Mrs. Reade (*recoiling slightly*): Oh—how awful! You must have been very upset.

Cornelius: He was my partner and my best friend.

Mrs. Reade (*curious and consolatory*): I don't suppose he knew what he was doing——

Cornelius: I think he did.

Mrs. Reade: When did this happen?

Cornelius: Ten days ago.

Mrs. Reade: Not—here?

Cornelius: No.

Mrs. Reade: Was he——?

Judy (*jumping up with startling effect*): Oh—do stop! How can you stand there asking these idiotic questions?

Mrs. Reade (*indignantly*): What do you mean?

Judy: I mean that there's been quite enough of it already. Can't you see you're hurting him—and making us all want to scream?

Cornelius: Judy!

Judy: I'm sorry—but you ought to have seen it for yourself. (*Begins putting her typed sheets together, trying to calm herself.*)

Cornelius (*to* Mrs. Reade, *courteously*): Good night, madam.

MRS. READE (*after a final glare at* JUDY): Oh—good night!

> *Goes out, leaving the others rigid and silent. Then* CORNELIUS *puts down the things he has been carrying, and then puts away the revolver in a drawer, which must be prominently placed. The silence can be broken here by a dull sort of suppressed sob from* MISS PORRIN.

CORNELIUS (*looking into Private Office*): I don't know you can really do much good there, Lawrence. It's beginning to look like a dustman's job. You'd better clear off, I think. Biddle, you don't want Lawrence for anything, do you?

BIDDLE: Aren't there some letters going out, Mr. Cornelius? He'd better copy them.

CORNELIUS (*with some irony*): There are some letters going out, but I don't think we need copy them.

BIDDLE (*surprised*): No copies?

CORNELIUS: No copies. For once, we'll risk it. We don't know what we've said. Just gone—like that. It doesn't matter. They're good letters but they're not meant to be answered. Perhaps the best letters are never meant to be answered. They're certainly never meant to be copied.

> LAWRENCE *comes out.*

Well, Lawrence, at last you'll be able to make a fresh start in life, eh?

LAWRENCE (*shyly*): Yes, sir.

CORNELIUS (*seriously*): I'm sorry we've wasted your time. But you know we've wasted a lot of our own time too. And we haven't as much to spare as you have. What's it to be?

LAWRENCE (*with a rush of confidence*): I might have a chance of getting into a wireless shop just near us at home. My father knows the man, and he's thinking it over.

CORNELIUS: Good. You've got your reference from us?

LAWRENCE: Yes, sir. And thank you very much.

CORNELIUS: And good luck with the wireless.

LAWRENCE: Thank you, sir. I—I hope you'll be all right, sir.

CORNELIUS (*gravely*): Thank you, Lawrence. I think I shall be all right. Good-bye.

LAWRENCE (*shakily*): Good-bye, sir.

> CORNELIUS *shakes hands with him, then goes into the other room.* LAWRENCE *hastily gets into his overcoat and hat.* BIDDLE *and* MISS PORRIN *leave their work and come forward.*

BIDDLE: I hope I'll see you again some time, Lawrence.

LAWRENCE: I hope so too, Mr. Biddle.

BIDDLE: And just remember—that attention to work is the secret of progress.

LAWRENCE (*earnestly*): I shan't forget—not if the work's anything to do with wireless.

MISS PORRIN: Good-bye, Lawrence. We *have* been good friends, haven't we, even though we *have* had our little quarrels?

LAWRENCE (*in bluff manly tone*): Yes, Miss Porrin, of course we have. (*Shakes hands.*) Good-bye.

MISS PORRIN: And *very* good luck.

LAWRENCE: Good-bye, Miss Evison.

JUDY (*standing up and smiling at him*): Good-bye, Lawrence.

LAWRENCE (*after looking at her an embarrassed second*): And—and I do think—you're awfully pretty.

> *Hastily wrings hand she extends, then rushes out.*

JUDY (*amused*): Sweet!

> *She covers her typewriter, gathers up her letters and envelopes and goes into Private Office.* MISS PORRIN *looks up alertly and watches* JUDY, *then picking up an account book and a few papers, obviously as an excuse to follow her, goes out after her. Meanwhile* BIDDLE *closes his books and tidies up wearily, yawning, etc. Then when the girls are gone, he carefully puts on his overcoat, puts down his hat by the cigar box he is taking home, then brings out his pipe, already charged, and lights it.*

CORNELIUS (*coming out from Private Office and letting the door close behind him*): Biddle—oh, are you going?

BIDDLE: Well, I was feeling a bit tired, Mr. Cornelius. But if there's anything else you want me to do to-night, I'll stay.

CORNELIUS: No, no, my dear chap, not necessary at all.

BIDDLE: I'll come down in the morning and just finish clearing up.

CORNELIUS (*sharply*): No, don't do that.

BIDDLE (*rather surprised*): Oh—all right, Mr. Cornelius. Monday then.

CORNELIUS: No, not Monday. Make it Tuesday.

BIDDLE: Tuesday?

CORNELIUS: Yes. Go away for the week-end, Biddle.

BIDDLE: But I never go away for the week-end——

CORNELIUS: Go down and see that daughter of yours in South Devon. Then you can begin making your arrangements. What sort of business are they in?

BIDDLE: It's her husband's business. Men's outfitting—you know, socks and shirts and collars, all that kind of thing. He's got a nice little business there—the only shop of that kind in the town—and he wants to expand—buy the shop next door.

CORNELIUS: And then you'll help him to sell his socks and shirts and collars, eh?

BIDDLE: I shall have a try.

CORNELIUS: You'll have to learn how to reach up—in one swift continuous flowing movement, Biddle—for all those green and yellow shiny cardboard boxes they have, and then spread them along the counter. "Something in this style, perhaps, sir," you'll say, "we're selling a lot of these this summer." And there they'll be—shiny cardboard boxes—socks and shirts and collars—all in a row. And you'll enjoy it. You'll enjoy every bit of it. Smoking your pipe over the plan for next season's campaign. Spending your weekly half-day holiday looking for the early primroses and violets. You'll be a chief among the elders in that part of South Devon. And you'll play such a devilish game of chess that they'll have to bring a Presbyterian minister specially from Cornwall to beat you. I've told you before, Biddle—and I'll tell you again now, for the last time—you're a lucky fellow, a very lucky fellow.

BIDDLE (*laughing*): Sounds like it, Mr. Cornelius, when you put it that way. I'll look in on Tuesday then. Will you be here, sir?

CORNELIUS (*quietly*): No, I shan't be here.

BIDDLE (*rather taken aback*): Oh!

CORNELIUS: There's nothing more for me to do, is there?

BIDDLE: No—only I didn't—I mean, are you going away?

CORNELIUS: Yes, I'm going away.

BIDDLE (*gently*): I expect you want to get away from here, Mr. Cornelius?

CORNELIUS: Yes.

BIDDLE: I know it's been a big strain—Mr. Murrison —and everything——

CORNELIUS: Yes.

BIDDLE (*quickly*): But he didn't know what he was doing, Mr. Cornelius. You mustn't think about it. He was—he was mad—and he just picked up the revolver.

CORNELIUS: No, you're wrong, Biddle. You heard what I said to that woman a few minutes ago. He knew what he was doing. He was sane then. That was the real Bob Murrison.

BIDDLE (*gravely*): I don't like to think that.

CORNELIUS: Why? He saw a chance of slipping out—quickly, decently—and he took it. That poor gibbering fool we saw wasn't Bob Murrison. But it was Bob himself who destroyed him. Came back from—from somewhere—to do it.

BIDDLE *shakes his head.*

Biddle, I've been thinking a lot about this lately. One thing puzzles me. I've never believed in this going on and on. I've always thought that when you were dead, that was the end of you. But this—suicide business—somehow doesn't fit in with that. Something inside you, we'll say, compels you to pick up a revolver, pull the trigger——

BIDDLE (*distressed*): Mr. Cornelius—please—don't go on. Leave it alone. Don't think about it.

CORNELIUS (*calmer now*): No, that's all right, my dear fellow. Listen. Something inside you—your will, or whatever it is—compels you to pick up a revolver, pull the trigger, and destroy yourself. But how can you destroy the whole of yourself, Biddle? That's what puzzles me.

BIDDLE: You can't.

CORNELIUS: I can understand that you could destroy a part of yourself, just as you could cut off a finger or a leg. But that something inside you that says "I've had enough of this. I'm going," *that* can't be destroyed. It must go on existing somewhere, mustn't it?

BIDDLE: Yes, Mr. Cornelius. I've been taught that all my life. That's why I say that suicide's terribly wrong——

CORNELIUS (*sharply*): No, I won't have that.

BIDDLE (*impressively*): Terribly wrong.

CORNELIUS: I tell you, that's all eye wash. We like to pretend that suicides are cowards when all the time we know damned well they're not. We condemn them because they walk out while we still stay fiddling and frigging behind. They annoy us because they call our bluff.

BIDDLE (*sharply*): No.

CORNELIUS: Yes. They won't have life on any terms. We will—like those people who because they've paid for a meal will eat any muck. We linger on and on in the bit of light that's left—calling it *sticking it*—when all the time we're simply frightened of the jump into the dark.

BIDDLE: No, Mr. Cornelius. You're a cleverer man than I am. But you're all wrong about this. You're not thinking straight.

CORNELIUS: I'm trying to, Biddle.

BIDDLE: If you'll excuse me saying so, you're talking like a man who's tired and a bit sick. After all, who are we to say what life is and what it's worth?

CORNELIUS: We know what it's offered us.

BIDDLE: We know the bit we've taken, that's all. *You* ought to realise that, Mr. Cornelius.

CORNELIUS: Why *me* specially, Biddle?

BIDDLE: Well, sir, you've always seemed to me to be interested in all kinds of things——

CORNELIUS (*ruefully*): At a distance.

BIDDLE: Is it good-bye for the present then, Mr. Cornelius?

CORNELIUS: I think it is.

> MISS PORRIN *comes in from the Private Office and shuts the door behind her. She stands just inside quietly. The other two ignore her.*

You're a lucky fellow, but you deserve to be. Good-bye, Biddle. (*Shaking hands.*)

BIDDLE: Good-bye, Mr. Cornelius. Good night, Miss Porrin.

> *He goes.* CORNELIUS re*mains silent for a moment, still looking at the door.* MISS PORRIN *approaches.*

CORNELIUS: Now then, Miss Porrin, time you were off, isn't it?

MISS PORRIN (*timidly*): Mr. Cornelius—I should like to tell you how—how happy I've been here working with you.

CORNELIUS (*rather surprised, but gently*): Have you?

MISS PORRIN (*eagerly*): Oh yes. The two offices I worked in before this, I didn't like at all, but I've been really happy here—with you.

CORNELIUS: That's fine, Miss Porrin.

MISS PORRIN: And I know I'll never feel like this about any other place——

CORNELIUS (*rather brusquely*): Of course you will. Feel much better. Enormous offices, all glass and metal and light, open at ten and closing at four. That's what you'll have soon, Miss Porrin. Much better than this. Can't compare them.

MISS PORRIN: No. It'll never be the same. And if

290

you're going to stay here I'd like to stay on too—to help you.

CORNELIUS: Very good of you, but really, there's nothing you can do. I've practically finished now.

She looks at him beseechingly and timidly puts a finger on his arm.

MISS PORRIN: If you have finished—if you are going now—I wondered—if you'd like to talk to me.

CORNELIUS (*bewildered*): Talk to you?

MISS PORRIN (*eagerly*): Yes, couldn't we go somewhere —to eat and drink and talk—I mean, I feel you're so lonely now, and I am too—and we'd have so much to talk about—wouldn't we?—having been here together so long. And I'm so sorry about everything. Please, couldn't we? (*As he gently releases himself and shakes his head.*) Or, if you didn't want to talk, we could just sit quietly somewhere. I wouldn't mind. I'd like it. Couldn't we?

CORNELIUS (*gently*): I'm afraid we couldn't, though it's nice of you to suggest it, very nice. But——

MISS PORRIN (*trying to hide her distress*): No, it doesn't matter. You needn't try to explain.

CORNELIUS: I was only going to say that I've still some things to do here. Some of them are rather— important. I'm sorry.

MISS PORRIN (*going towards telephone*): It doesn't matter.

CORNELIUS: Good-bye, Miss Porrin.

MISS PORRIN (*her back to him, muffled*): Good-bye.

He looks at her a moment. She is now dialling a

*number and trying to control herself. He goes into the
Private Office, closing door behind him. She is now
quietly crying.*

MISS PORRIN (*quietly, trying to control her voice, into
telephone*): Is that you, Rose? Miss Porrin. Just—just
tell them I shan't be staying out—after all. No, it's
nothing. I've got—I've got a headache. No, nothing
to eat, just some tea——

> JUDY *comes out, closing door behind her and goes
> across to her table.*

I'll be going straight to bed. (*Puts down receiver, dabs
at her face and is not able to stifle a choking sob.*)

> JUDY *looks at her curiously as* MISS PORRIN *slowly
> goes to put her things on.*

JUDY (*quietly*): What's the matter?

MISS PORRIN (*putting on things*): Nothing.

> JUDY *gets her own things out and puts her coat on,
> but places her hat and gloves, etc., on the table.* MISS
> PORRIN *comes nearer and stares at her fixedly.*

JUDY (*smiling, but not unkindly*): Well?

MISS PORRIN (*in low tense voice*): I wish I didn't hate
you so much. I've never hated anybody like this before.

JUDY: And you've no right to hate me. What have
I done?

MISS PORRIN: Lots of things.

JUDY: What things?

MISS PORRIN: That isn't it.

JUDY: Please tell me why. I don't hate you. I don't
hate anybody. As a matter of fact, I don't even dislike

you, although you've been unfriendly to me ever since I came here. I've been—rather sorry for you.

MISS PORRIN: Why should you be sorry for me? You're only a child yet, a silly child. You don't really know anything.

JUDY: That's stupid you know, Miss Porrin. I may be years younger than you, but I'm not a child. I believe I'm more a grown-up person than you are.

MISS PORRIN (*wildly*): Because you're young and pretty now—you think it's going to be always like this. It isn't—(*breaking down*)—it isn't, it isn't.

JUDY (*distressed, trying to console her*): Miss Porrin, don't—don't please.

MISS PORRIN (*clutching, urgently*): Listen, forget what I said. That doesn't matter now. Only one thing does matter. He mustn't be so quiet, so unhappy. I'm frightened. He oughtn't to be like that. Stay with him if he wants you to. You see, I ask you to, I don't care what I say now. I'm thinking about him. He's a man. He's different. Please——

The Private Office door opens and CORNELIUS *is seen standing there.* MISS PORRIN *gives him one look, then hurries out.* JUDY *and* CORNELIUS *stand perfectly still until there is heard the sound of a distant door slamming. Then* CORNELIUS *turns back to switch off the Private Office light, after which he comes in and closes the door quietly behind him. Meanwhile* JUDY *has hastily gone to the window, pulled away the blind and tried to look down into the street. She comes away and looks at* CORNELIUS *as he approaches.*

293

CORNELIUS (*awkwardly*): I suppose you ought to go now.

JUDY: Yes. (*A pause.*)

CORNELIUS: How old are you?

JUDY (*smiling*): Must you know?

CORNELIUS (*hastily*): No, no. What does it matter? Whatever it is, I'm twice it. You think of a number and I double it.

JUDY (*smiling*): And then I shall take away the number I first thought of—and myself with it.

CORNELIUS: What do you do when you're at home?

JUDY: Oh!—read—sew a bit, not much—listen to the wireless. The usual things. Quite commonplace.

CORNELIUS (*staring at her, musingly*): Perhaps you are quite commonplace—really.

JUDY (*promptly*): No, I'm not. I'm *really* rather special.

CORNELIUS (*absently*): Yes?

JUDY (*indecisively*): I think I ought to go.

CORNELIUS: No, please don't go. You've plenty of time. You've no idea how much time you have—years and years and years.

JUDY (*laughing*): Not to-night, I haven't. Somebody's waiting for me. (*She leans against her table.*)

CORNELIUS (*making conversation*): Have you liked it here?

JUDY: Parts of it.

CORNELIUS: Biddle's a nice fellow, isn't he?

JUDY: Yes. I like Mr. Biddle.

CORNELIUS (*lamely*): Very good chap.

JUDY (*with mock official manner*): And—is that all, Mr. Cornelius?

CORNELIUS: No, it isn't all. It isn't any. It's nothing. I haven't begun to talk yet. I don't know how to begin. Something happened that very first morning you came here. It's not long ago——

JUDY: A fortnight last Monday, to be exact.

CORNELIUS: Not much happened then, perhaps. But afterwards—only a day or two—just before we had the meeting here—and I came in and you were singing.

JUDY: I remember. You were very nice about that.

CORNELIUS (*almost to himself*): It's as if it's been dark here ever since then—and you carried a little light with you. When you came in, it wasn't so dark. There was a light round your head. And the song has never stopped. It's a long time since I felt like this, a long long time. That's why I can't tell you properly. It's—it's a good record but the gramophone's old and rusty. I'm sorry.

JUDY (*putting out a hand*): I'm sorry too.

CORNELIUS (*eagerly*): Are you? How small and clear you are—like the flame of a candle! (*Pauses, then laughs shortly and harshly.*)

JUDY: What does that mean?

CORNELIUS: I was thinking—here's the good old situation they're so fond of in the magazine stories and the comic papers. The business man keeps the typist in the office after hours to make love to her.

JUDY (*sharply*): No. I know it's not like that at all.

295

CORNELIUS (*harshly*): But it is. I'm a business man—
or I was. You're a typist. This is an office. And it's
late. And I'm making love to you.

JUDY: You're not. Not in that way.

CORNELIUS: Yes, I am. In that way, in every way.

JUDY: Oh—why do you say that? Can't you see
you're spoiling everything?

CORNELIUS (*wonderingly*): Am I?

JUDY: Yes. Please stop. You're only hurting
yourself.

CORNELIUS: That's nothing. Tell me what a fool I
am—now, after all this time—to fall in love again, like
a boy. Yes, like a boy.

JUDY: You can't expect me to tell you that.

CORNELIUS (*eagerly*): Can't I? (*Catches her hands as
she smiles and shakes her head.*) Why Judy then—little
Judy—is this real?

> *He tries to kiss her but deliberately she turns her
> face away so that his kiss falls lamely on her cheek. He
> withdraws, bewildered and disappointed.*

Oh!

JUDY (*distressed*): I'm sorry. I ought to have told
you. It isn't that I don't like you. I do. But—you
see—I'm in love with somebody too.

CORNELIUS: I see.

JUDY: He's outside now—waiting for me. That's
why—I couldn't, you see.

CORNELIUS: And you're in love with him?

JUDY: Yes. I know I ought to have told you at once.
It wasn't fair to you.

To her astonishment, he suddenly laughs, not without bitterness, but still—a genuine laugh.

CORNELIUS: *It wasn't fair to me!* I said I was behaving like a boy, and now that very phrase takes me back thirty years. Technical College boys and High School girls, parties and sets of lancers, and somebody saying "It wasn't fair of you, Alice, not to tell Tom you were going with Frank." My God, I've asked for it, I've got it. (*Laughs again.*)

JUDY (*annoyed*): I think I'd better go. I stayed—and listened—because I liked you and I was sorry.

CORNELIUS (*not unkindly*): No other reason?

JUDY: Yes. Because I'm a girl, and I knew what you were feeling, and I wanted to hear what you'd say to me. Any girl would.

CORNELIUS: That's honest of you.

JUDY: I am honest. More honest than you are.

CORNELIUS: Oh?

JUDY (*with force*): Yes. If you meant what you said to me a few minutes ago, you shouldn't pretend now— because it's all no use—that you weren't serious. That's cowardly and hateful.

CORNELIUS (*gravely*): My dear, it isn't so simple as that. I've been as honest as possible with you all the time. It's too late for anything else. And if I offended you a moment ago, I'm sorry, Judy.

JUDY (*smiling at him*): All right. And I'm sorry too.

CORNELIUS: There's one thing I'd like you to do for me. If this young man of yours is waiting outside, I wish you'd call him in for a moment.

297

JUDY (*rather puzzled*): You'd like to see him?

CORNELIUS: Yes. After all, that's not much to ask, is it?

JUDY (*hesitating*): No—only—all right, I'll see if he's out there.

> *She pulls the blind away, goes behind it, and can be heard giving a singing call down into the street below. Then she cries "Eric, come up here," waits a moment, then returns to* CORNELIUS.

CORNELIUS: And you're in love with him?

JUDY: Yes.

CORNELIUS: He's a very lucky young man. And he's in love with you?

JUDY: Yes. We adore one another. We want to get married as soon as he's settled down in his present job. I'm longing to be married. I'd hate to go on years and years, working in offices—like poor Miss Porrin.

CORNELIUS: I'm afraid Miss Porrin didn't like you.

JUDY: Of course not. She was jealous—poor thing.

CORNELIUS: And now it's my turn—poor thing.

JUDY: You don't sound very jealous.

CORNELIUS: I don't think I am. Rather sad perhaps. And very curious.

JUDY: I don't like that.

CORNELIUS: I shall never see you again. You must let me spend a minute or two guessing what the rest of your life's going to be like. And I think I hear it coming.

> *They both turn to the door, expectantly. There is a*

tap, then ERIC SHEFFORD *enters. He is wearing an overcoat and a spotted silk muffler, and carries his hat. He stops when he sees* CORNELIUS.

JUDY: Hello, Eric. Come in. Mr. Cornelius wanted to meet you. This is Eric Shefford.

CORNELIUS (*almost involuntarily*): My God, it's the twister.

JUDY: The what?

ERIC (*sulkily*): All right. I didn't come here to be insulted.

CORNELIUS: We know that. Nobody goes anywhere to be insulted.

JUDY: But do you know one another?

CORNELIUS (*dryly*): Only slightly. A business acquaintance.

JUDY: But why didn't you tell me, Eric?

ERIC: It wasn't of any importance. I'd only called here twice.

CORNELIUS: That's all. We did a little business together, and then somehow I quarrelled with his company, the Excelsior Transport, whose banner has a strange device.

ERIC: I didn't know you were here, else I wouldn't have come in.

JUDY: I want to know what happened?

CORNELIUS: It doesn't matter. He'll tell you some time.

JUDY: What did you call him?

ERIC: He called me a Twister, if you must know, Judy.

299

W

JUDY (*from one to the other*): Why?

CORNELIUS: Never mind now. That's all over.

JUDY (*to* ERIC): Why?

ERIC (*quickly, rather desperately*): He thinks I deliberately misled him about some rates I quoted, and got the business under false pretences.

JUDY: And did you?

ERIC *is silent.*

Eric!

ERIC: Yes, I suppose I did. Though I didn't do anything illegal. But I'd got to get some business, to keep the job. You know what it was like, I told you, Judy. I was desperate. I'm sorry, Mr. Cornelius, but you don't understand what it's like trying to keep a job like that. The competition's terrible. I know I was wrong——

CORNELIUS: All right, all right. It's done with now.

JUDY: Is it?

ERIC: But Judy, you can't blame me. I was doing it for your sake. And you know what a time I'd had before.

JUDY: Yes, I know, Eric.

ERIC: I'm sorry I didn't tell you before. Are you coming along now?

JUDY (*hesitating*): Just a minute, Eric, please.

ERIC: Oh—all right—but I've been hanging about down there—

JUDY: I know. I'm sorry. But please wait outside, I shan't be two minutes.

He goes. They wait a moment. JUDY *faces*
CORNELIUS.

Now tell me what you're thinking.

He shakes his head.

I'm not afraid. You can say what you like. It won't
make any difference to me. I know him. You don't—
really.

CORNELIUS: No, of course I don't, my dear.

JUDY: I know he can be very stupid, very weak,
sometimes. I know we may have all kinds of trouble.

CORNELIUS (*gravely*): I think you may.

JUDY: But it can't be helped. You see, I love him.

CORNELIUS: Yes, I see.

JUDY: You think I'm very young and silly now, don't
you? But I'm not. I know my life with Eric isn't going
to be easy, I know it far better than you do. But it's my
life. I wouldn't run away from it. Even though you're
a girl—and a girl in love—you need courage, a special
sort of courage, if you're going to live properly. My
sister Ann has it. I have it too.

CORNELIUS: Yes, you have. I'll wish you luck. And
do it properly. (*Picking up* MURRISON'S *flask.*) See. I'll
drink your health. His too, if you like.

JUDY: I don't understand you.

CORNELIUS: That's as it should be. Otherwise I'd
have lived these extra five-and-twenty years of mine for
nothing. A solemn toast. (*In manner of toastmaster.*)
My lords, ladies and gentlemen, see that your glasses
are charged, and pray silence for your chairman, the
Wrong Dishonourable James Frederick Cornelius,

Knight of the Ancient Order of Near Bankrupts.

> JUDY *laughs. Then his manner suddenly changes.*

May you always be brave and happy, Judy, always be as clear and beautiful as the flame of a candle.

> *He drinks. Then he sits down at the table, and she stands facing him and the window, very clearly seen.*

No, don't move. Don't speak.

JUDY (*softly, uncertainly*): I wouldn't find it easy—if I wanted to.

> *She stands motionless, he sits with his head in his hands looking at her for a moment.*

CORNELIUS (*very quietly, without raising his head*): Thank you, Judy. Good-bye.

JUDY: Good-bye.

> *Then very swiftly she moves to the table, flings her arms about his neck, kisses him, rests her cheek against his for a second, then as he automatically goes back in surprise, snatches up her hat and gloves and hurries out, with a small choked cry. Very slowly after staring at the door he rises. He gives a glance at the window, then moves like a man in a dream. He holds up the flask so that he can see a reflection of himself in the silver base of it.*

CORNELIUS (*quietly to his reflection*): You silly old fool!

> *Then he goes to a drawer, takes some paper, sits down and begins writing. Then the door is opened, and MRS. ROBERTS enters. She is rather breathless.*

CORNELIUS: What is it?

MRS. ROBERTS: I just called to see if Mr. Biddle had left me my week's money in my envelope, and to pick up one or two of my bits o' cleaning things. (*She goes over to* BIDDLE's *desk for the envelope, and afterwards collects cleaning things, in a black cloth bag from the cupboard.*) All packing up, eh?

CORNELIUS: Yes, finished.

MRS. ROBERTS: What happened to you then? Did you go bankrupt, or what?

CORNELIUS: We came to a private agreement with our creditors.

MRS. ROBERTS: Well, I wish to God I could come to one with mine. Are you going away?

CORNELIUS: Yes.

MRS. ROBERTS: I wish I could get away.

CORNELIUS: Where would you go to?

MRS. ROBERTS: I've always had a fancy for East bourne.

CORNELIUS: I don't think you'd like it.

MRS. ROBERTS: If I could only have my feet up most o' the morning and afternoon and no cleaning and have a nice tea on a fancy tray, then go out and see a bit o' life in the evening, anywhere would do me.

CORNELIUS (*reflectively*): I suppose women are really tougher than men.

MRS. ROBERTS: I should think they are! If women was as soft as men, when a bit o' trouble came—there'd be nothing here but a graveyard soon.

CORNELIUS: It isn't much else here now. Millions of people and none of them real and those that are real are mostly in graveyards.

MRS. ROBERTS: Come, come, Mr. Cornelius, I'm not worrying and I can give you a year or two.

CORNELIUS: You can't. That's the trouble. Nobody can. And I want a few. I've wasted so many.

MRS. ROBERTS: Where?

CORNELIUS: Here, among other places.

MRS. ROBERTS (*indignantly*): Why, you're not going to start grumbling now—are you?—just because you've spent a few years sitting here in a nice office, with other people waiting on you, and three good meals a day and anything else you liked? Gertcha—you don't know you're born.

CORNELIUS: But I do. That's the point. I think a lot of people don't, and it's a bit of luck for them. I know I'm born—when it's too late.

MRS. ROBERTS: Well, my motto is, it's never too late. You look after yourself, Mr. Cornelius. (*Moves towards door.*) Good night.

CORNELIUS: Good night.

She looks at him for a moment, troubled, then goes out. CORNELIUS *gets up, takes the revolver from the drawer. He goes to the main door, locks it and throws the key away, switches off the light and goes over to the windows and idly opens it. Through the window come street noises, then gradually the sound of a banjo being played in the pub below. His face lights up as he listens. Suddenly he becomes decisive, and says loudly and clearly "No." He flings away the revolver.*

CORNELIUS: After a week in the Indian village—

*He picks up a big ledger, speaking—though jerkily—
all the time, and with gathering force.*

we dec·ded to take the track into the clouds—to find—
among those heights—

*He hurls the ledger with such force that the door is
smashed clean open, so that he can walk through, repeating
triumphantly*

—the lost city of the Incas.

CURTAIN

END OF PLAY